DATE DUE

Printed in USA

A HISTORY OF THE PACIFIC ISLANDS

COLLEGE LIBRARY

A History of the Pacific Islands

I. C. CAMPBELL

UNIVERSITY OF CALIFORNIA PRESS
Berkeley and Los Angeles

Also by I. C. Campbell
Island Kingdom: Tonga Ancient and Modern

UNIVERSITY OF CALIFORNIA PRESS
Berkeley and Los Angeles, California
in association with
CANTERBURY UNIVERSITY PRESS
Private Bag 4800
Christchurch, New Zealand

First published in 1989
Reprinted with revisions 1996
Copyright © 1989, 1992, 1996 I. C. Campbell
Copyright © 1989, 1992, 1996 Canterbury University Press

This book is copyright. Except for the purposes of fair review, no part may by stored or transmitted in any form or by any means, electronic or mechanical, including storage in any information-retrieval system, without permission in writing from the publisher. No reproduction may be made, whether by photocopying or by any other means, unless a license has been obtained from the publisher or its agent.

Cataloging-in-Publication data
is on file with the Library of Congress

ISBN 0-520-06901-3

Printed by Kyodo, Singapore

CONTENTS

MAPS

TABLES

A NOTE ON ORTHOGRAPHY AND PRONUNCIATION

Vowels

In the writing of all Pacific island languages, each vowel is pronounced separately, and each has only one sound, unlike in English where a single vowel either by itself or in combination has a variety of possible sounds. There are, however, diphthongs which most English-speakers find difficult to reproduce exactly. These are the approximate equivalents:

a = ah	ai = long i
e = eh	ae = long i
i = ee	ei = long a
o = aw	oe = oy
u = oo	ou = long o
au = ow (as in cow)	

Consonants

All consonants are as in English although g is always hard. Fijian and Samoan have some spelling peculiarities: in Samoan g is always pronounced as ng, and in Fijian the following substitutions need to be made by the reader:

b = mb	q = ngg (finger)
d = nd	c = th
g = ng	

The glottal stop (as in ali'i) is an unvoiced consonant made by a momentary stopping of the breath in the throat.

Map 1 The Pacific Ocean and its Islands

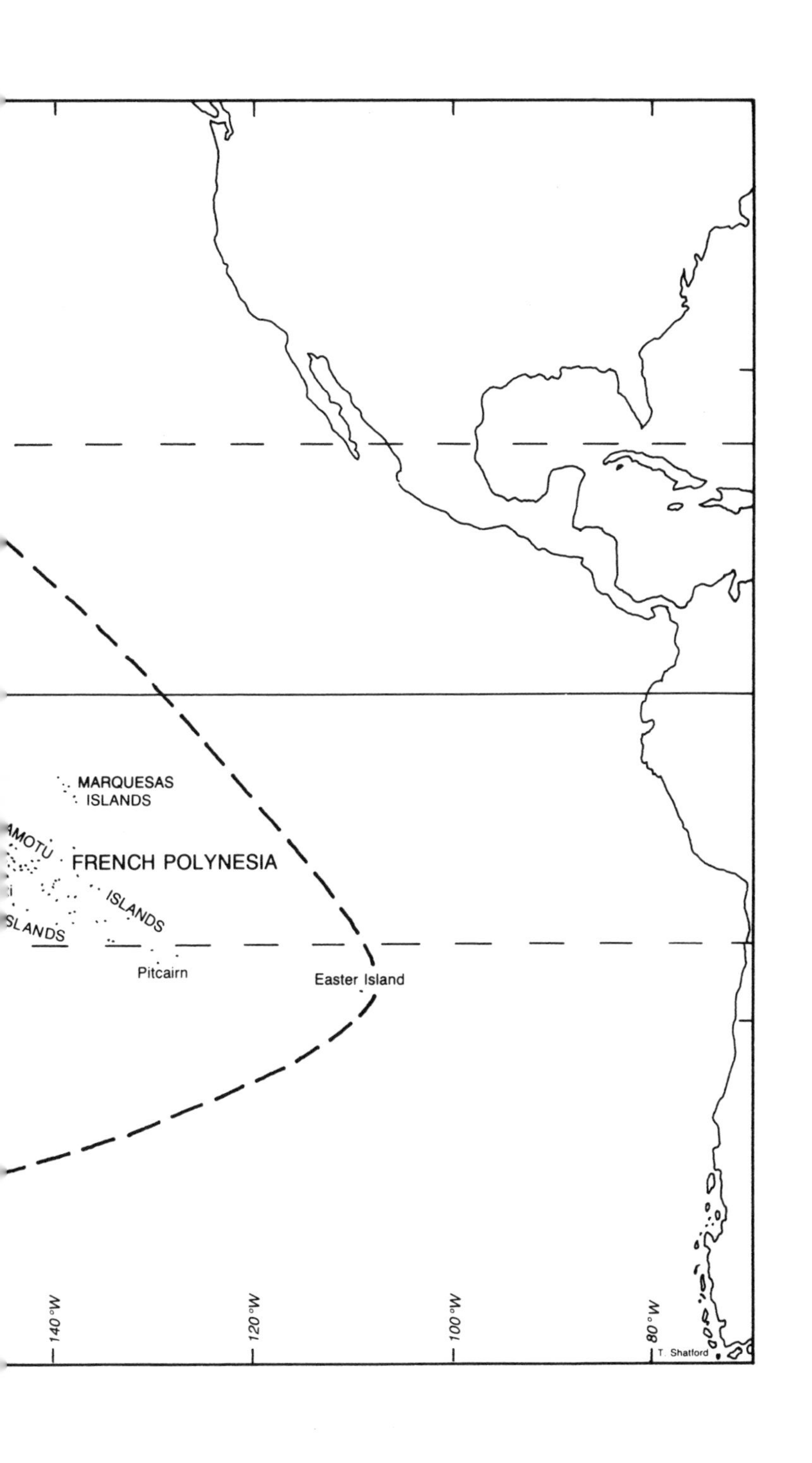
MARQUESAS
ISLANDS
FRENCH POLYNESIA
ISLANDS
Pitcairn
Easter Island
140°W
120°W
100°W
80°W
T. Shatford

PREFACE

The Pacific Ocean, approximately one third of the earth's surface, is the setting for a world of islands which were originally occupied by people who achieved the greatest feats of maritime navigation in all human history. Their colonization of this vast expanse was spread over several thousand years, during which time their cultures developed and diversified into a collection of intricate patterns. Their cultures were not only pragmatic systems of survival, but were also rich in imaginative power and beauty, representing achievements of the human mind, tongue and hand as inspiring as any others in the world.

These diverse peoples, broadly classified as Polynesian, Melanesian and Micronesian, had only desultory contact with Europeans in the sixteenth and seventeenth centuries, with regular systems of contact not becoming established until late in the eighteenth century. Over the next two hundred years, a succession of Europeans representing different facets of European civilization came to the islands, and left an indelible imprint of such objects and ideas as metals, Christianity, disease, medicine, literacy, individualism, money, the state, democracy, and justice.

The islands, their peoples and cultures were changed by their contacts with Europe, and although all relations between islanders and outsiders involved two-way traffic, cultural change has mostly been in one direction only.

By the beginning of the twentieth century all Pacific islanders had come at least nominally under the rule of western powers. Some of them (New Zealand Maoris and Hawai'ians) had become citizens of the colonizing power. The history of colonialism in the Pacific islands shared some of the abuses of human rights common to colonialism elsewhere, but the comparative poverty of exploitable resources liberated colonial regimes from the temptation or necessity to be oppressive. Although there were ugly features of the colonial period of Pacific history, there were also cases of pragmatic moderation and of sincere and effective humanitarian administration.

After the Second World War political change was initiated in most Pacific island territories, with the result that since 1962 most of them have become independent nations. This transition has occurred sometimes earlier and faster than the inhabitants wished, when western ideology has proven a more important factor than island nationalism. The new nations of the Pacific islands, however, have found that political independence has not enabled them to meet all the social and economic goals which they optimistically envisaged. The desire for progress beyond the means of their own resources has induced a dependency and an accelerated rate of social change far greater than during the colonial era before 1950.

The historical literature of the Pacific islands is enormous, possibly greater in relation to population size than any other part of the world. Despite the enormous advances in knowledge of the area in recent decades, this book is the first since 1951 to present a synoptic history of the region as a whole. The book is therefore intended to be an introduction, to make more accessible to a wider and non-specialized readership the richness of the many specialized works on the subject. For that reason, and in deference to the purse or wallet of the reader, references have not been included. The table of further reading at the end of the book lists, without attempting to be comprehensive, a sample of books chosen for being most easily obtainable, or most authoritative. These scholarly works in turn all have extensive bibliographies, which any reader wanting further clarification may consult.

Chapter One

THE ORIGINAL INHABITANTS

When European voyagers first sailed into the Pacific Ocean in the sixteenth century they marvelled at finding populated islands. Subsequent visitors have marvelled at their inhabitants; they have admired the Polynesians for their beauty and stature, their well-ordered communities, their open-handed friendliness, and for the homogeneity of culture, race and language which shows that this people was the most widely dispersed race on earth. Their neighbours to the west, the Melanesians, have also excited wonder: the people exhibit a unique diversity, with 1200 distinct languages (perhaps a quarter of the world's total), cultures so different from each other and from cultures elsewhere that anthropologists have been baffled in their attempts to classify them. These people, less dispersed than the Polynesians, occupy a string of island chains which curve from New Guinea to New Caledonia like an arm protecting the Australian continent. North of the equator, the Micronesians remain for most people the unknown islanders, their homes the myriad sandy atolls which, known simply as 'the islands', form the inspiration of cartoonists and novelists. The Micronesians, like the Polynesians, are spread across a vast area of featureless ocean, and for people so far-flung, display a remarkable homogeneity.

To their earliest European visitors of the sixteenth, seventeenth and eighteenth centuries, these peoples were a double enigma. How could peoples with a strictly limited technology have found and populated such tiny, distant pieces of land? And having colonized these places, why were the most far-flung so much alike, and those most concentrated, so diverse?

To the common-sense mind of continental Europeans, differences of culture and language over distance were to be expected, and roughly speaking, the degree of difference was proportional to distance. Similar peoples lived nearest each other, dissimilar ones furthest away, for that is the cultural pattern of Europe. Similarly, to continental minds, dispersal was achieved by crossing land. When the first tentative maritime explorers had ventured into the Atlantic in the fifteenth century, they found islands which were uninhabited because they were out of sight and reach of a mainland. The natural conclusion to draw was that voyaging necessitated stout ships, extensive preparations, metal compasses and a way of measuring in clear night skies the elevation of the Pole Star.

Thus the early European visitors were intrigued by the ethnographic wonders of the Pacific ocean. Inhabited islands must mean a mainland nearby—just below the horizon—and so they searched for a missing continent, belief in which was reinforced by studies of the ancient geographers. Accounting for the distribution of cultures across this vast ocean led to some of the most ingenious and provoking speculations in the history of science, and in time, the modern science of anthropology was born among, and grew upon, the cultural mysteries of the Pacific islands.

Describing the Pacific and its peoples was logically the first step, and as early as the 1820s the terms 'Melanesian', 'Polynesian' and 'Micronesian' were coined by the French explorer Dumont d'Urville to describe the obvious but blurred differences between East and West.

Polynesia

The Polynesians occupied the eastern half of the ocean: Hawai'i in the north, Easter Island, the Marquesas Islands, Society Islands, Tuamotu and Austral Islands in the east, New Zealand in the south, the Cook Islands in the centre, Tonga and Samoa in the west, Tokelau and Tuvalu (formerly Ellice Islands) in the north-west (see map 1). Further to the west were scattered small communities of Polynesians, called the Polynesian outliers, including Ontong Java, Tikopia, Rennell and Bellona, Nukumanu, Kapingamarangi.

The languages spoken by the peoples of these islands were closely related. Those of the eastern area of islands, from Hawai'i to New Zealand, had sufficient common vocabulary and consistent phonetic characteristics for native speakers of one language to become conversant in another very rapidly. Captain Cook for instance, used a Tahitian as an interpreter in New Zealand. The western languages presented more difficulties for an Eastern Polynesian and diverged between themselves to a greater degree. The accompanying table (Table 1) indicates some family likenesses among the Polynesian languages.

All these languages form one group within the vast and complex Austronesian language family, which also includes most of the languages of Melanesia, the Micronesian languages, and several of South East Asia, including Indonesian and, far to the west, Malagasy.

TABLE ONE

Some words illustrating the relationship between the languages of Polynesia.

English	Tonga	Samoa	Tahiti	N.Z. Maori	Hawai'i	Marquesas
house	fale	fale	fare	whare	hale	hae
island	motu	motu	motu	motu	moku	motu
chief	e'iki	ali'i	ari'i	ariki	ali'i	haka'iki
priest	tufunga	tufunga	tahua	tohunga	kahuna	tau'a
man	tangata	tangata	taata	tangata	kanaka	enata
woman	fefine	fafine	vahine	wahine	wahine	vehine
land	fonua	fanua	fenua	whenua	honua	henua

All Polynesian peoples had the idea of social and political distinctions, and generally speaking the larger and more resource-rich a community was, the more elaborate and complicated were its notions of social gradation and political rank. All societies had chiefs who ruled over communities which had a fairly stable territory, and whose members traced descent from a common ancestor. There was thus some idea of consanguinity between ruler and ruled to reinforce the idea of mutual obligations, but the gulf between the various ranks within one of these tribes was nevertheless profound: rank and status depended first and foremost on inheritance. The standing of both parents was important (generally one inherited political power from the father but rank and social status from the mother), but the hereditary principle was modified by an assessment of suitability. At the time of inheritance the possible candidates and their peers (these might include the sons, brothers, nephews, cousins and uncles of the previous title-holder) would confer and choose a successor. The eldest brother and eldest son might have an advantage, but not an automatic right to inherit. The succession might—and frequently was—decided ultimately only by war between contending factions.

The authority exercised by such a chief was generally absolute: he commanded unquestioning obedience, was the source of law and justice, decided matters of life and death; but if he ignored the advice of his peers and the interests of his subjects, he ran the risk of assassination or civil war. In short, the Polynesian political system may be described as a warrior aristocracy in which custom and tradition were modified by pragmatism.

In this scheme the role of women could be very important. Women often had higher rank than their brothers, but generally did not wield political power, although by force of character a woman might have exerted enormous influence through her brother, husband or son. This was conspicuously the case on occasion in Tonga, Tahiti and Hawai'i around the time of European discovery.

The political units over which these aristocrats ruled varied enormously in size and power. On a small atoll like Tongareva in the Northern Cook Islands, a chief might be little distinguished from his people, command a few dozen warriors, a few hundred people altogether and a few square miles of sandy soil. At the other extreme were the advanced kingdoms of Hawai'i and Tonga, their paramount chiefs commanding thousands of warriors, their own accessibility and freedom limited by an elaborate system of sacred prohibitions and rituals. Their populations were so large, their territories so carefully defined, and their armies so numerous and disciplined, that they came close to being states, held together by something more than the personal prowess and intelligence of a warrior chief. Between these two political extremes were the political systems of New Zealand, Tahiti and the Marquesas, where clearly defined tribes dwelt in territories which might change with their military fortunes, but no tribe was ever able to establish and maintain a lasting hegemony over its neighbours.

In all of these Polynesian societies, the fortunes of the common people compared well with the general lot of humanity. On most islands their physical needs of food and shelter were well-provided for by a generous environment, and there was an absence of infectious diseases, insect pests and dangerous animals. They were, however, subject to the demands and discipline of their chiefs, and these were often very exacting. Life was frequently one of hard labour, experienced perhaps as building, maintaining and utilizing the irrigated agricultural systems of Hawai'i, or working the intensively cultivated gardens of Tonga. It might have seemed leisured to the outsider, but life was rarely idle, and it was arduous to the extent that both men and women aged prematurely, old at forty according to studies of prehistoric skeletons. The industrious lower classes of Polynesia were kept well occupied with food production, canoe-building, house building and maintenance, tool making, and ceremonies; at various times warfare made heavy demands, although it was rarely endemic. Polynesian life, far from being a careless idyll of relaxation and indulgence, was in most places closely regulated by both chiefs and priests.

Religion made its own demands, as well as being the instrument and partner of political authority in maintaining order. The Eastern Polynesians had a multiplicity of gods, which, rather like those of the ancient Greeks, were sky-dwellers who sometimes came to earth, performed deeds among men, and procreated with mortal women. Again like the Greeks, their gods were 'departmental' gods, each having special influence over some aspect of human affairs or nature. In Western Polynesia the Tongans and Samoans had fewer great gods and more spirits, many of them unnamed, who were attached to persons or families rather than to roles as in Eastern Polynesia. In both areas, stories were told of demi-gods, the great culture heroes, of whom Maui was pre-eminent: he was the doer of great deeds, the fisher from the ocean depths of the islands which the people inhabited.

The religious ideas which accompanied these beliefs also resemble ancient European paganism: it was a religion which emphasised power rather than ethics, effectiveness rather than goodness, success rather than rectitude. A religion of pragmatism, its observances were intended to influence the gods to affect events among the people, or to placate the gods to avert misfortune or punishment.

The two key concepts in Polynesian religious life were *mana* and *tapu*. *Mana* in essence meant efficacy: it was the sacred power which a god possessed and by which he was able to act, and some gods had greater *mana* than others. *Mana* was something which men could have as well: a powerful and effective chief had great *mana*; a chief who did not command authority, or successfully wage war, or keep his people prosperous, healthy and numerous obviously had little *mana*, and was apt to be superseded by one who had more *mana*. It was thus a concept which not only helped to explain the way the world was, but which also channelled divine power.

Tapu (*tabu*, *kapu*) has passed into English as *taboo*, but means more than just 'forbidden'. Something which was *tapu* might have been sacred or accursed: as such it was out of bounds to all who did not have a dispensation. *Tapu* thus became a means of social control: a person might be made *tapu* to keep him isolated; a place or thing might be declared *tapu* to protect it or preserve it. People or things frequently became *tapu* after certain specified events. For example, in Tonga someone who prepared a corpse for burial was *tapu* for several months during which time he could not feed himself or handle food. In the more hierarchical societies of Tonga and Hawai'i high chiefs had so many *tapus* associated with them that they became burdensome. The Tu'i Tonga, for example (the most senior chief of all in Tonga), was so *tapu* (sacred) that if he entered a house it became *tapu* (holy and therefore forbidden) for anyone ever again to enter. A Tu'i Tonga for this reason had to be careful where he went and what he touched.

The authorities on matters of *tapu* and *mana* were the *tohungas* (*kahunas*)—priests, wise men, experts, possessors of arcane skills of all kinds (not purely divine matters, but including horticulture, navigation, medicine, tool making and so on). They officiated at ceremonies, interpreted the will of the gods, channelled a god's *mana* into various earthly projects and sometimes possessed considerable temporal power either in their own right, or through their influence over the chiefs. They were not shepherds of their flocks, but a medium of power and authority.

In material culture the Polynesian achievement was distinguished by the care and quest for perfection, yielding objects which combined beauty and utility, reflecting both environment and ingenuity. Stone, shell, wood and plant fibre were made to supply human needs, often at the cost of considerable labour and the exercise of great skill. Tools for gardening were made of wood; tools for wood working were made of stone; housing of timber and thatch of coconut or pandanus leaves; clothing from the soft fibres of plants, for example the braided and knotted flax of New Zealand, and the beaten and glued *tapa* cloth made from bark in tropical Polynesia. Metals and pottery were absent from the Polynesian resource kit: their homelands generally are devoid of metal ores, but many of them have clay. Pottery was known to their ancestors, and continued to be supplied by Fijians to Tongans and Samoans until recent times, so the absence of Polynesian pottery is an inexplicable mystery.

In the material dimension as well as the non-material, a clear East-West division is seen (see Table 2). Eastern Polynesian adzes were tanged (shaped to take a handle), those from the west were not; in the east fishing was done mainly with hook and line, in the west mainly with nets; coiled basketry was used in the west, not in the east; canoe construction differed in a variety of ways, including the fastening of planks, the attachment of outriggers, rigging, ornamentation and paddle shapes. Artistic designs also varied: in the west styles tended to employ straight line geometrical patterns, with an absence of human forms; in the east carvings were curvilinear, and human forms were commonly represented.

Isolated though they were, the Polynesians had distant cultural and racial relationships with their oceanic neighbours, the Melanesians and Micronesians.

Melanesia

Melanesia—the 'black islands' in Dumont d'Urville's terminology—is as remarkable for its diversity as Polynesia is for homogeneity. Its peoples range in stature from tall to short, in skin colour from light brown to deep black, in social organization from near anarchy to hereditary chieftainships. The variety of social organization is bewildering and the number of languages marvellous. Some generalizations are possible, but none of them is universally applicable.

TABLE 2

The West Polynesian—East Polynesian Cultural Division

(Adapted from E.G. Burrows, 'Western Polynesia: a Study in Cultural Differentiation' in *Etnologiska Studier* (1938) 7:1-192.)

	WEST	EAST
ECONOMY:		
Fishing	Bonito hook points with two fastening holes	Simpler form of bonito point
	Reef and net fishing common	Net fishing rare; greater use of bait hooks
Gardening	Sweet potato minor	Extensive use of sweet potato
Food Preparation	Food pounders rare	Stone food pounders widely used
Land Tenure	Strongly hereditary through either mother or father	Chiefs' perogative overrode the hereditary principle
MATERIAL CULTURE		
Tapa	Brief soaking of bark	Long soaking of bark
	Pasting technique	Felting technique
Basketry	Coiled type	Not coiled
Houses	Rounded ends with parallel rafters	Rounded ends with radial rafters in Society Islands
		Rectangular houses in most places
Canoes	Hulls have low ends	Hulls have upraised ends
	Little decoration or none	Carved decoration
	Flange-lashing of planks	Planks lashed straight through, with cover strip
	Indirect outrigger connection	Direct outrigger connection
	Lateen sail	Sprit sail
	Direction changed by shunting	Direction changed by tacking
Adzes	Untanged	Tanged for hafting
	Quadrangular cross-section not dominant	Quadrangular cross-section most common. Triangular cross-section dominant in Society Islands
Art	No human figures	Carved human figures
Music	Slit gong	Drum

TABLE 2 (continued)

	WEST	EAST
SOCIAL PRACTICES		
Kava	Elaborate ceremony	Not ceremonial
Kinship	More complicated terminology concerning gender relationships.	Simpler gender and kinship terminology
	Brother-sister avoidance	No brother-sister avoidance
	Vasu (*fahu*) privileges (for a man's sister's son)	No *vasu*
Rank	Honorific language to address chiefs	No chiefly language
	Infinite subtle gradations	Sharp status divisions
Religion	Tangaloa (Tangaroa) known but not a major god	Four great 'departmental' gods, Tangaroa, Rongo, Tu, & Tane, and many lesser gods and heroes
	Family and animal spirits important	Family patron spirits were known
	'Evolutionary' creation myth	'Procreative' creation myth
	'Pulotu' spirit home, located in the west	'Hawaiki' spirit home located in the east
	God houses	Open sacred court
	Malae: a common meeting place	Malae (marae) a sacred, ritual place, except in New Zealand
Death	Bodies interred	Tree or cave burial. Relics often kept by family

Unlike most Polynesian societies, Melanesians were usually not seafarers. Their horizons were limited to the modest territories claimed by a village community, and few travelled more than a few miles by either land or sea. It was congruent with this immobility that Melanesian society was intensely xenophobic. Strangers were held in the deepest suspicion, so much so that anyone who travelled far from home went at the risk of his life. The extensive trade networks which distributed goods over long distances were either maintained as the linking of innumerable short-distance contacts between neighbours, or by the few communities which were travellers and seafarers, such as the Trobriand Islanders, famous for the Kula ring network of exchange.

Each community therefore was supported mainly by horticulture, usually with just one staple, supplemented by a variety of subsidiary crops. Shifting swidden cultivation was common, but many communities had permanent gardens, especially those few in the New Guinea highlands and New Caledonia which had constructed irrigation systems for cultivating swamp species like *taro*.

In these societies which produced little that could be accumulated (unlike the Polynesians, they had not generally developed ways of preserving food), the possibility of great differences of wealth, and of differences of status built on wealth, was slender. Rich and powerful men were those who by hard work, political marriages and shrewd use of patronage could command a larger than usual capacity to produce food, or construct buildings for public use. Their surplus food production was used to provide public feasting, and secure the social and political support of lesser men. Such a man has been called by anthropologists, a 'Big Man'. Big Men acquired their status: they did not inherit it, and were not elected to it. Instead, they had to scramble by fierce and anxious competition to a position which they had constantly to defend until they retired, died or were eclipsed by another, more vigorous social climber. The authority of a Big Man was an authority based on social status. He had influence rather than power, and the sway that he built up for himself could not usually be transformed into regular political power, or into institutions which would survive his death or retirement. His achievement was purely personal.

Political units in Melanesia, therefore, were kinship units, whereby people lived in small communities composed of kinsfolk. Exogamy sometimes established kinship links with neighbouring communities, thereby ensuring that warfare was minimal between such groups. Violent quarrels and raiding which involved whole villages certainly occurred, and with the deep suspicion Melanesians had for each other, and the almost universal dread and expectation of sorcery, such conflicts were not uncommon. But unlike Polynesian warfare, casualties were generally light, and territory was not at stake. Battles were fought not for conquest, but for the restitution of real or imagined grievances.

In religion the Melanesians were again different from the Polynesians. Lacking the great 'departmental gods' of eastern Polynesia, Melanesian religion was a complicated business of a multitude of powerful, capricious and usually malevolent spirits, demons and ghosts. But as in Polynesia, religious belief and practice were thoroughly pragmatic affairs. The supernatural was feared mainly for the danger associated with it, so religious practice was a matter of ceremonies and rituals intended to deflect evil or to constrain the spirits to allow or promote certain undertakings, often some personal enterprise, or an economic interest such as the growing of yams or the running of fish. Melanesian religion was thus a system of beliefs and rituals for controlling human and natural affairs by manipulating the spirits, and for this reason has sometimes been described as a technology. Worship in the Christian sense was not part of this system.

Closely related to religion were magic and sorcery. These were ways of controlling natural events without working through an intermediate spirit. Men suspected of sorcery were very much feared, and any unwelcome event such as a death or hurricane was attributed to the agency of a sorcerer. Sorcerers did not practise publicly: individuals were suspected of sorcery, but it was not an acknowledged role. There were indeed no religious or magical specialists, no people who could live solely by the practice of their mysterious arts; Melanesian religion had no priests just as there were no specialists of any other kind.

To the Europeans who first saw them, the Melanesians seemed a wretched, barbarous race in the extreme, although there was much to admire in aspects of their social organization—in the paramountcy of kinship obligations for example, or the achievements of building, art and narrative. Unlike the Polynesians whose environment was insulated by successive ocean passages of hundreds of kilometres, the Melanesians occupied a chain of islands which stretched all the way to the shores of Asia and Australia, with no great barriers to the passage of a rich variety of life forms. The Melanesian islands were home to more various populations of plant, animal and insect life, and offered a wider range of ecological types than the islands of Polynesia. The negative aspect of this variety was the presence of pests, parasites and diseases which plagued the life of the people, and from which the Polynesians were blessedly free; foremost among the curses suffered by the Melanesians was malaria. Life was accordingly short and hard, especially for those inhabiting the hot, humid coastal regions of their islands.

The absence of large political units, the fear of sorcery, xenophobia, together with the effect of endemic illnesses on temperament, all probably contributed something to the diversity of Melanesia. The protracted isolation of small groups is probably more responsible than any other single factor for the enormous range of physical, cultural and linguistic types, and for the absence of any discernible correlation in the variations of different characteristics. Each community over time developed its own idiosyncrasies until at length clear patterns became lost. Early anthropologists supposed that the variations were due to successions of different populations filtering into and through the area. Current thinking is that such waves of immigration are improbable, and probably could not account for the enormous range of differences anyway.

Amid all this cultural chaos one thing has been established, and that is that most of the twelve hundred or so Melanesian languages belong to the one large language group: the Austronesian language family of which the Polynesian languages all constitute one subgroup. The non-Austronesian languages of Melanesia (formerly called Papuan) are mostly found in New Guinea, with some in the Solomon Islands. So far no-one has been able to detect any affiliation for these languages with languages from outside the region, and they are only very distantly related to each other.

Micronesia

The third major culture area of the Pacific is Micronesia, which, superficially at least, resembles the Polynesian type rather than Melanesian (see Table 3). This resemblance led some earlier scholars to suggest that Micronesia was a blend of Polynesian and Asian influences. Physically, the Micronesians resemble the gracile forms of East Asia, becoming progressively darker and stockier to the east. In material culture, the two areas show some striking similarities, such as shell adzes and fishing gear. Culturally, however, Micronesia was more heterogeneous than Polynesia, and generalizations about Micronesian society immediately call to mind a cloud of exceptions and qualifications.

As with the other two cultures a subsistence economy with technological resources of only plant materials, stone and shell does not permit a great variety of wealth or ease. Social differentiation depended on inherited rank, but the Micronesian ranking system was so complicated that no two people would be exactly on the same level. Some communities had members of such exalted rank that they had an almost kingly status and authority; elsewhere, government was in the hands of a council of high-ranking men.

Notwithstanding the complexity of the ranking system, most communities had two or three social classes, or more correctly, grades. Cutting across these grades was a principle of dualism: two lines of titles both ranging in rank from high to low, sometimes residentially segregated. Every member of a community was thus classified by descent into one of two groups. For this purpose, as well as for inheriting property, matrilineal descent is usually regarded as typical of Micronesia, although patrilineal and mixed groups may also be found. With this type of social and political organization, rivalry within communities and competition between them was intense, and warfare—at least at the time of European contact—was common.

The material culture of Micronesia shows the influence of contact with the adjacent regions of Asia in pottery and in looms for weaving which were both present in well developed forms. Seagoing vessels were probably the most superior in all Oceania, with large dual-hulled, plank-built canoes, and an elaborate knowledge of sea- and star-lore which made the Micronesians more accomplished seafarers than any of their neighbours. Their elaborate fishing tool-kit provided for the harvesting of both reef and ocean, whereas in Polynesia and Melanesia the pattern was generally inclined towards one or the other.

In religion, the Micronesian beliefs seem to have had most in common with Western Polynesia, with a collection of spirits and ghosts, some of whom were the patrons of various crafts and activities.

TABLE 3.
Comparative Table of Oceanian Cultures

	MICRONESIA	POLYNESIA	MELANESIA
Social organization	Matrilineal emphasis	Ambilineal	Matrilineal societies
	Patriarchal (dualism)	Patriarchal	Patrilineal societies
	Club houses	Usually three classes	Fragmented social units
	Two or three classes		Men's club houses
			Classless
Political organization	Ramage	Ramage	Egalitarian descent
	Aristocratic	Aristocratic	'Big Man' pattern
	'High island' societies more hierarchical than atoll societies	'High island' societies more hierarchical than atoll societies	Hereditary chiefs in some societies, but not usually markedly hierarchical
	Warrior ethic	Warrior ethic	Warrior ethic
	Decision by council	Chiefs autocratic	'Consensus' rule
	Politico-military alliances between lineages	Political units larger than lineages	Small units—village focus

TABLE 3 (continued)

	MICRONESIA	POLYNESIA	MELANESIA
Law	Arbitrary Supernatural and secular sanctions	Arbitrary Supernatural and secular sanctions	Arbitrary Stronger supernatural basis, with sorcery as means of punishment
	Application varied according to personal rank	Application varied according to personal rank	More legalistic
Social rituals	Kava drinking Feasting Competitive giving Elaborate display	Kava drinking Feasting Competitive giving Elaborate display	Betel nut chewing Feasting Competitive giving Elaborate display Head hunting (some)
Religion	Tapu/mana complex Variety of spirits, gods and ancestors	Tapu/mana complex Anthropomorphic sky-gods, 'departmental' (sea, forest, war, etc.) (Eastern Polynesia) Creator gods; ancestral spirits and household gods	Tapu/mana complex Creator-regulator gods in places; ghosts and spirits, capable of evil
	Ritual was placatory not worship	Supplication and bargaining, not worship	Not worshipped but placated & manipulated by ritual
	Use of magic	Sacrifice (including human in many places)	Magic and sorcery practised extensively
	Shamans, diviners, mediums and sorcerers	Priests, prophets and chief-priests After-life for chiefs only	Sorcerers but no specialist priesthood
Territory and Land tenure	Territory occupied by a lineage	Lineage definition of territory giving way to political definition	Territory occupied by kinship group
	In all three regions there were varieties of group or individual use-rights under the control or stewardship of community leaders.		

TABLE 3 (continued)

	MICRONESIA	POLYNESIA	MELANESIA
Settlement	Extended	Usually extended; some hamlets	Nucleated, concentrated villages
Economy	Rich marine exploitation	Rich marine exploitation	Limited marine exploitation
	Swidden horticulture (often female role)	Intensive horticultural development (male role)	Swidden horticulture (variously male and female)
	Food preservation	Food preservation	Generally no food preservation
		Irrigation or other major works	Irrigation works in some areas
	Craft specialists	Craft and ritual specialists	Usually nonspecialist
Trade, Navigation and Mobility	Atoll dwellers highly mobile. Long voyages for trade, socializing and crisis relief	Extensive communication within contact zones. Ancient long-range voyaging. Trade, social and political reasons	Some societies had a maritime capacity; trade was mostly with immediate neighbours. Mobility generally closely restricted
Values	Intensely competitive	'Communal' or competitive depending on scale of reference group (class, family, island) and the social or political context	Strongly competitive, especially in Big Man system. 'Communal' elements on occasion
	Hospitable	Hospitable	Xenophobic, suspicious

In language, as in other things, Micronesia seems to occupy some midpoint between the extremes of Polynesia and Melanesia; less numerous and perplexing than the latter, more divergent than the former, but still representing one or more branches of the great Austronesian language family.

The study of the cultures and peoples of Oceania has now absorbed the attentions of three generations of anthropologists in large numbers. The reason for all this attention is partly because of the apparent neatness with which the populations of the Pacific fall into one of three categories. Within each category there is an intricate network of divisions and continuities. Sometimes the continuities extend across the great cultural divides. With many thousands of islands the variations on the basic patterns of culture are practically infinite and pose an endless series of questions about human organization, human creativity and resourcefulness, and cultural history. The peoples of the Pacific have devised the most heterogeneous collection of cultures and languages in the world; they have colonized the most remote pieces of land on earth, across an ocean which covers one third of the globe. The story of this enterprise, and how the people survived and flourished is only partially known, but is one of the great epics of human history.

Chapter Two

AUSTRONESIAN COLONIZATION

'Where did they come from?' was the question asked by the first European explorers, a question asked often and answered in many different ways ever since. The crux of the problem, as it was usually posed, was the Polynesian distribution. Accounting for the settlement of Melanesia seemed comparatively straight-forward: the Melanesians had occupied a chain of elongated islands which seemed to point across the narrow ocean passages to the next land. The Micronesians on their innumerable, tiny specks of land also seemed quite readily to have flowed from the adjacent Asian mainland. Explaining how they actually got to their island homes was a difficulty, but only a technical one. The Polynesians presented the real problem. The relative homogeneity of their cultures and languages implied that their geographical dispersal was fairly recent, and that it had taken place fairly quickly. But the most obvious migration route, out of Asia, via the Melanesian islands which seem to point the way, was occupied by a population whose extreme diversity implied an enormous antiquity, and whose apparently xenophobic savagery discouraged sojourners. In other words, the most likely route between the Polynesian homeland and their islands was blocked by a tenacious people who were there first.

That observation was the starting point for the many ingenious theories about Polynesian origins; and so intriguing was the problem that for many decades the central problem of Pacific anthropology was accounting for the Polynesians, while study of the Melanesians and Micronesians was neglected. How, it was asked, could the Polynesians have got through or past Melanesia without becoming Melanesian on the way? One answer was to say that this seafaring people moved quickly, merely skirting Melanesia, and left only a few traces of their passage on the north-eastern coasts and outlying islands, in the languages and cultures of pockets of population: hence the so-called Polynesian outliers.

Another answer which seemed more plausible, because it seemed less likely to imply an organized, migratory expedition of vast size, was that favoured by the distinguished New Zealand scholar, Sir Peter Buck: a route through Micronesia. This theory was attractive because it did not require the Polynesians to have kept themselves segregated from the other populations during their passage, as did the Melanesian theory. Moreover, similarities in religion and material culture, and the idea of an aristocratic society, seemed to favour Micronesian rather than Melanesian influence in Polynesia.

The third possibility was for a non-Asian origin which would allow the Polynesians to avoid both Micronesia and Melanesia. The best known, though not the first, proponent of this theory was Thor Heyerdahl. His earliest view was of a South American origin via Easter Island, and was supported by the presence in Easter Island and elsewhere in Polynesia of plants of South American origin (notably the sweet potato, cotton, gourds and freshwater reeds), the use of the names Tiki and Ra in the religion of both regions, and some similarities in stone-masonry techniques.

Heyerdahl's later theory acknowledged that the Asian affinities were too numerous for a South American connection to be more than an influence. Finding some cultural parallels between the Indians of the American north-west and the Hawai'ians at the northern apex of the Polynesian triangle, and again trying to avoid Melanesia and Micronesia, he put forward this ingenious idea: the shortest route between any two points on the globe is not necessarily the straight line of the Mercator-projection map, but a 'great circle' route: thus the shortest route from South-East Asia to America is via the North Pacific, past Japan, the Aleutians and Alaska, to a landfall in British Columbia or Washington State. From there, Heyerdahl's Polynesians, with the help of the favourable north-east trade winds and ocean currents, were able to find Hawai'i and disperse from there into the rest of Polynesia.

Heyerdahl's theories won a large popular audience; anthropologists were less impressed, even after he modified his ideas in the light of new information. Yet given that extraordinary navigational feats were required of the Polynesians whichever theory was adopted, and given the existence of some American traits in the Pacific which no-one has yet explained away, the theory was not as outrageous as many claimed it to be. It certainly goaded other anthropologists to examine their data more carefully. Heyerdahl's theories have now been shown to be wrong as an explanation of Polynesian origins; as a possible explanation for some details of Polynesia culture and ecology, however, Heyerdahl's ideas continue to deserve respect.

A new approach to the question of origins began in 1959 with a modest article by one of the most distinguished of Pacific anthropologists, Kenneth P. Emory, of the Bernice P. Bishop Museum in Honolulu. Emory suggested that the Polynesians as such did not come from anywhere—that there was, indeed, no mass migration: the Polynesians, he suggested, grew from a small population of mixed origins, and developed their distinctive racial and cultural characteristics in the Western Polynesian area (Tonga, Samoa) whence they spread by stages over all the island groups of the eastern Pacific.

At the time, few scholars noticed the suggestion, but over the next two decades the idea was confirmed and developed by intensive research in two disciplines: linguistics and archaeology. Linguists, working with a variety of different methods (two main ones: the comparison of structures and grammatical rules between languages, and a comparison of vocabularies) have come to broadly similar conclusions although differing in detail. The area of agreement is that the Polynesian languages are related more closely to some Melanesian languages than to the Micronesian languages, and that all belong to the great Austronesian language group. Polynesian has a 'fraternal' relationship with several of the languages of Eastern Melanesia (mainly of Vanuatu, formerly known as the New Hebrides); beyond that the direct relationships with other languages are shared by several Melanesian tongues, and eventually by all Austronesian languages.

The early seafarers whose descendants became the Polynesians were therefore speakers of one of the languages of Melanesia. But that cannot be the whole story, for in their physical type and in their material culture the Polynesians seem distinct from the usual Melanesian patterns. Besides spreading their language, however, these seafarers also distributed a distinctive style of pottery, first found in New Caledonia early this century, but later found in numerous coastal sites in Vanuatu and New Caledonia, and as far north as New Britain and New Ireland (see Map 2). This pattern with its distinctive manufacture (no potter's wheel was used) and geometrical surface decorations, was dubbed 'Lapita' ware, and its manufacturers, Lapita people. Pottery was known in various parts of Melanesia and Micronesia, so the existence of Lapita ware raises no particular question. The problem is, how did Lapita ware travel to Fiji, Tonga and Samoa, where archaeologists have shown it to have arrived by 1500 B.C. and why were its carriers physically different from the other peoples of the region?

The paramount seafarers of the pre-European Pacific were the Micronesians, and here the old theories of a Micronesian migration route still have some validity. But the earliest settlements in what is now called Micronesia seem to be roughly contemporary with

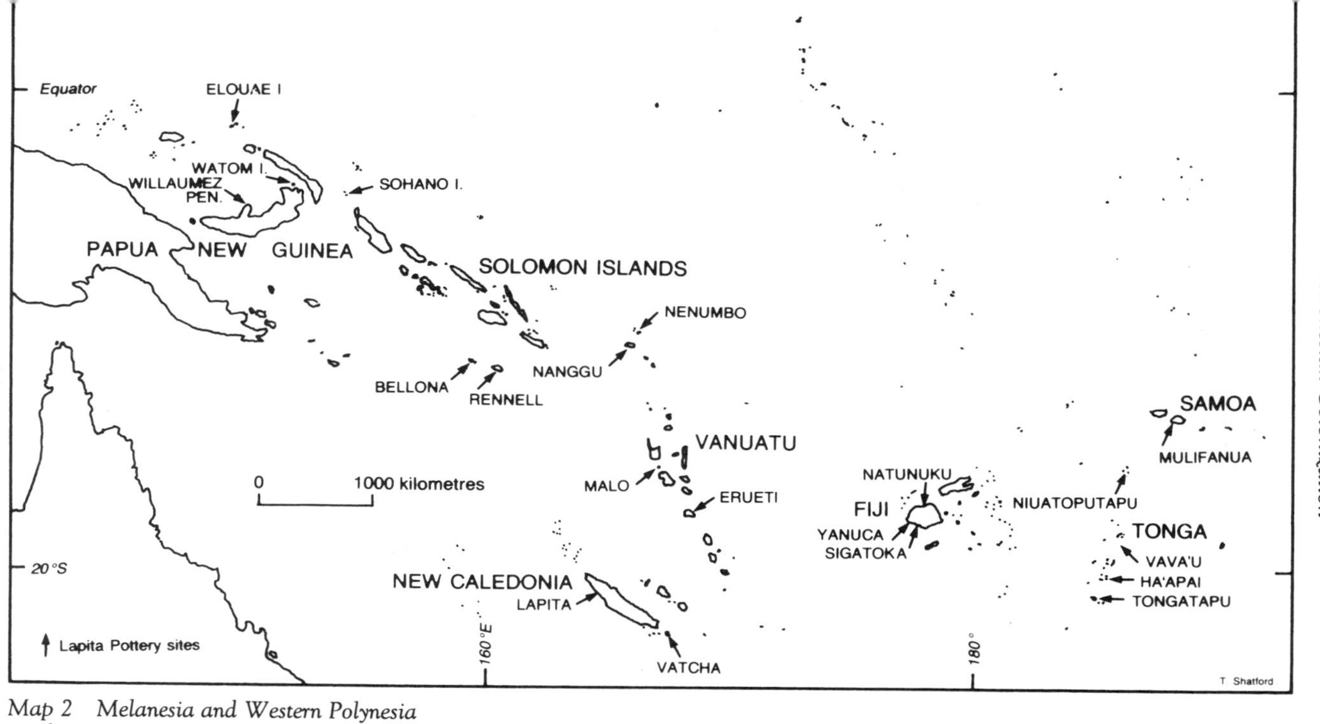

Map 2 Melanesia and Western Polynesia

The arrows indicate the more important sites where Lapita pottery has been excavated. Because these sites are so widely distributed in Melanesia, it is unlikely that they indicate a Polynesian migration route; but it is probably true that they do mark settlements by people who were culturally identical to the ancestors of the Polynesian people.

the earliest Lapita sites in Melanesia and Western Polynesia. So the Lapita people were not Micronesians. On the contrary, the people who later became 'Micronesians' were a mixed people who probably received their navigational capabilities from the same unknown source as the people who later became 'Polynesians'.

The island groups of Tonga, Samoa and Fiji were thus settled at about the same time (that is, probably within the time span of a few human generations around 1500 B.C.), by a highly mobile population which ranged widely over the western Pacific. Having reached the Fiji-Tonga-Samoa area, the settlers then lost contact with the islands to the west. For perhaps a thousand years, these people developed a distinctive culture based on the resources available close at hand, and gradually changed their pottery styles until they eventually abandoned its manufacture altogether. Their sea-going capability, however, was not forgotten.

A new phase of migration began, perhaps around the beginning of the Christian era. We can only speculate about its cause, but pressure of population on limited land is a possible though unlikely reason. Expeditions well equipped with food plants, domesticated animals (the pig, the dog and the fowl), craft specialists, and, of course, both women and men, arrived almost certainly from Samoa, at the Marquesas, a distance of over 3000 kilometres, against the prevailing winds and ocean currents, certainly by the fourth century A.D., probably earlier. If land shortage was the problem, many expeditions must have set out, in which case more than one would be expected to have arrived in the island zone of the eastern Pacific. As this first colonization of the eastern Pacific, in the least accessible group, is likely to have been a unique event, population pressure is an unlikely explanation.

The priority and uniqueness of the Marquesan colonization is attested by both archaeological and linguistic evidence. The first dated settlements in Eastern Polynesia are in that group and its early artefacts have the closest resemblance to western Polynesian types so far found. Its language seems to be ancestral to the other languages of eastern Polynesia, and is also the one most closely related to the Samoan parent.

From the Marquesas the settlement of eastern Polynesia followed fairly quickly, that is over the next few hundred years: quickly enough indeed to suggest that pressure on land was again not the major reason. Expeditions of migration set out from time to time, and in due course came to Easter Island, Tahiti, and the Hawai'ian Islands. Tahiti in turn became a base for further expeditions, to Hawai'i again, the Cook Islands and New Zealand (see Map 3). Before long, by about 800 A.D., all the habitable land in the eastern Pacific

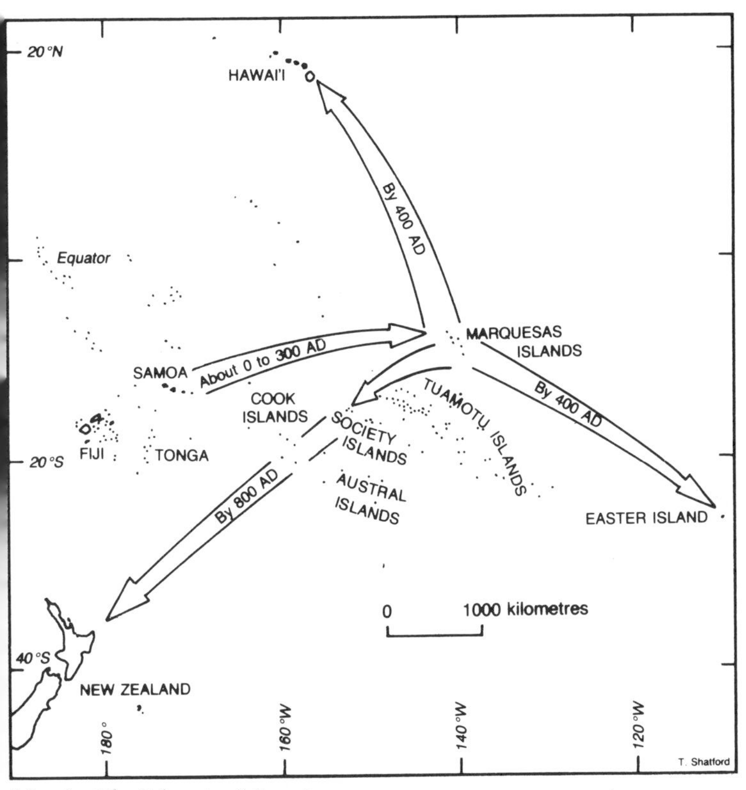

Map 3 The Polynesian Migrations

Present linguistic and archaeological evidence suggests this pattern of movements of colonization, with their likely dates. This scheme does not exclude the likelihood of multiple voyages or reverse movements, or of the possibility of subsequent migrations from within Polynesia in later centuries. The fine details of specific departure points will probably never be known, nor will the precise dates and sources for all islands.

had been found and occupied. Some of these lands were extremely small and remote—and on some of them, such as Pitcairn Island or the Line Islands, the human population disappeared again, its former presence known only by the tools and workings which remained.

Further to the west, small communities of Polynesians appeared in various parts of Melanesia and Micronesia. Although thought by some scholars at various times to be remnants of the eastwardly moving Polynesians, linguistic and archaeological research has shown them to have been settled from mature, well-established Polynesian parent communities. Samoan influences seem most common. While most of them show signs of settlement or resettlement within the last seven hundred years, others, such as Anuta and Tikopia have been inhabited by Polynesian-related peoples for over two thousand years. This occupation has not been continuous in all cases. In addition, the Loyalty Islands and other communities in Melanesia, even as far west as Port Moresby in Papua New Guinea, show unmistakable signs of a Polynesian heritage.

Of the settlement of Melanesia and Micronesia, much less is known. Less thoroughly penetrated by Europeans during the nineteenth century, they were less closely investigated, and in the twentieth century, research into the prehistory of both regions has been slower and less intensive.

The challenge which Melanesia in its wonderful heterogeneity presented, was to explain how such diversity came about. The popular early attempts invoked multiple migrations, with consequent shuffling and jockeying for position by the various immigrant groups, to produce the subsequent mixture. Taken to its logical extreme such a theory would become incomprehensibly complicated. It was also undermined by the fact that the population of Melanesia, despite its differences, did not really lend itself to the identification of a multiplicity of different races. Therefore, if some of the diversity of Melanesia was to be accounted for by other factors (for example, prolonged development in isolation of small communities from small initial populations) then why not all of it?

The most likely explanation is not that there were any mass migrations, but that there was a filtering of people through the South-West Pacific in at least two stages: first, the so-called Papuans speaking languages very distantly related to each other, and not at all related so far as is known to the Austronesian group. These people are mostly found in the highlands of New Guinea, with pockets of them in the Solomons. So far it has not proved possible to identify these people with a particular assemblage of artefacts or archaeological sites: their languages and their distribution imply, however, that they were the earlier population stream; the oldest archaeological sites, in New Guinea, have been dated in the highlands at about 25,000 years, but human occupation could well be twice that age.

The second human stream therefore seems to have been the Austronesian-speaking Melanesians, who migrated in small groups over an extended period of time. The precise geographical origin of their ancestors outside their present distribution is not known. The making of pottery is associated with these people, and was present as early as 4000 years ago, but it seems likely that the

Melanesian migrations were earlier even than that. Linguists suggest that the fragmentation of the Austronesian languages of Melanesia implies a dispersal five to six thousand years ago. Within that time there has certainly been a good deal of movement within Melanesia which has obscured a definitive answer.

One old theory, propounded in the 1920s by the pioneer anthropologist, W.H.R. Rivers, has received perhaps less attention than it deserves. This is that there were three discernible stages in the Melanesian inflow, each stage contributing something distinctive to later Melanesian culture. This theory, based on the intensive comparison of kinship structures, posits a number of correlations: first, the use of the sitting position in the burial of the dead; second, the use of kava as a ceremonial drink; and third, the chewing of the betel nut. Archaeological investigation alone is not likely to be capable of either confirming or refuting this hypothesis, as there is an absence of distinctive artefacts which can be associated with each culture and which reach back continuously to an early settlement. By the same token, these successive migrations must all have been made by closely related peoples, speaking closely related languages. The distribution of the traits mentioned is suggestive, and calls for an explanation.

Of the Austronesian colonization of Micronesia, even less is known than of Melanesia, but neither does Micronesia appear to present the same complexities or problems as the neighbouring regions. Common sense seems to argue for a movement of peoples from Eastern Asia, and the physical types of the Micronesians and such artefacts as pottery and the loom confirm it. There are, however, complications, revealed particularly by the linguistic work of Isidore Dyen, who has suggested that the most likely homeland for the Austronesian languages is eastern Melanesia, not east Asia. This argument is based on the principle that the region of the greatest diversity of a phenomenon is likely to be the source of migration (on the grounds that only part of a population is represented in any migration, whether it be plants, insects, people or languages). Dyen's analysis, using a prodigious volume of data, is extremely complicated and is not readily accessible to a layman; moreover, it is possible that there are other reasons for the linguistic diversity of eastern Melanesia. Dyen's theory, however, creates problems for the anthropological and archaeological data, which will not be resolved until Micronesia is more fully investigated.

The antiquity of human occupation of Micronesia so far seems surprisingly short. The Marianas—the most north-westerly group of islands, nearest to Asia—were occupied by about 1500 B.C., contemporary with the early Lapita people. About two thousand years later another cultural tradition appears, implying perhaps a second settlement. Elsewhere in Micronesia, in the Caroline islands, settlement seems only as old as the second Marianas culture, but is not the same as it. The evidence is simply too sparse to attempt a reconstruction of the distant Micronesian past. Asian influences there certainly were; a Melanesian connection is also definite; traits are also shared with Polynesia; the only conclusion to be drawn is that the Micronesians are a mixed and unevenly blended people.

The tiny, multitudinous, scattered islands of Micronesia must have been settled much less easily than the tall continental island chain of Melanesia. This geographical contrast implies some advanced seafaring capability as a precondition of colonization. It seems logical to suggest, therefore, that Melanesia was settled first, and that the same—or a contemporary—movement which brought Lapita pottery to Vanuatu, Fiji and Tonga, also took people to Micronesia. So far, no-one knows for certain where that movement began, but the pottery appears to have been carried by people who were not racially identical with modern Melanesians, although to judge from the languages spoken by their descendants, they spoke a Melanesian tongue.

The middle of the second millennium B.C. therefore, was a period of comparative ferment in the Pacific as it was elsewhere in the world: a maritime-capable people traversed great ocean distances of the western Pacific linking eastern Micronesia, eastern Melanesia, Fiji and Tonga in a great movement of exploration and colonization which was the boldest exercise in seafaring so far undertaken by the human race, and although it did not involve large numbers of people, it had enormous implications for subsequent cultural history.

That burst of activity was followed by another between one and two thousand years later, with the colonization by people from Samoa, of the Marquesas far to the east. Within a few hundred years most of eastern Polynesia had been settled. Following that, there seems to have been a lull in ocean voyaging, and the various island communities settled down to develop their own cultural patterns.

A final efflorescence of voyaging and interisland contact is suggested by archaeology, linguistics and legend for a period roughly from 1100 A.D. to perhaps 1500 A.D. Archaeology reveals a simultaneous cultural upheaval in Southern Papua, Vanuatu and Fiji; some of the Polynesian outliers in Melanesia were settled during this time; it is also the period of the earliest carbon dates for the eastern Caroline Islands, and a period of further voyaging between Tahiti and not only Hawai'i but also possibly New Zealand. The techniques and vessels of these voyages—and therefore the possibility of the voyages themselves—has long been the subject of academic debate. Could non-literate, pre-mathematical, non-metallurgical people have made deliberate, two-way voyages over such vast tracts of ocean to such tiny landfalls? Could not the islands have all been settled by castaways or by other voyagers of no return? The answer at the end of decades of protracted argument seems to be that deliberate and accurate voyaging was possible. No other explanation seems consistent with the total transfer of cultures which took place in Polynesia, or with the evidence of tradition. Research into indigenous vessels and techniques of sailing and navigation supports the belief—incredible to the first European explorers—that such feats were possible for Pacific islanders of the past.

During the time of European contact some Pacific islanders were found to have craft which are properly called ships: twenty-five or more metres in length, built of planks fastened securely with ropes of coconut fibre, propelled at least in the western half of the Pacific by huge fore-and-aft sails which were very efficient. The men who managed these craft were experienced, knowledgeable and capable seamen, much in demand as sailors with European commercial shipping. Specialist navigators were found to have a knowledge of stars and their movements, of wind and ocean currents and wave patterns to a degree which enabled them to find their way at sea.

This knowledge and capability, however, is known from experience of the last two hundred years: what of the voyages before that time? Recent studies show at the very least that those sceptics who argued that such navigational feats were impossible, were wrong. The skills found to exist in the eighteenth century must have existed before that time, simply because of the facts of the distributions of cultures, plants and animals. Chance, one-way drift voyaging cannot adequately account for the thoroughness of ancient colonization. Moreover, the traditional evidence suggests that by the eighteenth century, seafaring was in a state of relative decline. Pacific islanders were more dependent on the sea in the distant past, and therefore must have had at least as great a mastery over it.

Nevertheless there was taking place in the eighteenth century a process called by one scholar, G.S. Parsonson, the 'nautical revolution'. The seacraft of the 'fringe' areas of Polynesia—Hawai'i, New Zealand and Easter Island—were inferior to those of the more central islands. This decline can easily be explained in the case of New Zealand by the sheer mass of land, which rendered the preservation of ocean voyaging skills unnecessary, and in the case of Easter Island by its extreme isolation from other land. But in Hawai'i seamanship continued to be valued, and so the less advanced Hawai'ian craft are probably representative of an earlier phase of Polynesian history. The Hawai'ians had robust double canoes, equipped with a sail of the 'square' type, but not square in shape, a sail ill-adapted for tacking or sailing up-wind, but probably similar to the sail of the earliest voyages. The Tahitian sail was closely related, but the surviving New Zealand style was even more primitive in design, suitable only for a following or near-following wind.

In western Polynesia a new sail was coming into vogue at the time of first European contact in the seventeenth century. This was the more efficient 'fore-and-aft' sail, almost identical to the lateen sail which the Arabs had introduced to Europe a few centuries before. It had become standard equipment throughout Micronesia, and had spread to the Gilbert Islands (Kiribati) whence it was passed to Fiji. From Fiji it became known in Samoa and Tonga, and by the eighteenth century it had become known, but was still rare, in the Tahiti-Tuamotu sailing area.

Together with the diffusion of this radical and versatile sail came modifications in hull design and sailing technique: asymmetrically-shaped hulls were a logical development, as was the adoption of complementary, non-identical hulls for constructing the large catamarans. These modifications capitalized on the advantages of the new sail. The earlier twin-hulled ships of the Polynesians were made with identical hulls, such as the Hawai'ians were still using in the late eighteenth century. The new style ships—called *drua* in Fiji—were larger, more seaworthy, and had greater carrying capacities than the earlier *camakau* which probably represented the typical vessel of the previous great era of voyaging (approximately the eleventh to fifteenth centuries). The largest of these new-style vessels were up to thirty-five metres long and their carrying capacities were many tons. Instances are known of them carrying 500 to 600 people, although voyages with that number are not likely.

These innovations were both the means and the result of cultural diffusion throughout Oceania during the previous few centuries—a distant consequence presumably of Arab trade with Indonesia, and a link between Polynesian and Eurasian history. Therefore, it should not be supposed that the most efficient sea-craft seen by early European visitors represent the vessels used for the original migrations. The earliest seafarers of the Pacific had smaller, simpler and less efficient vessels, but they were adequate to achieve an extraordinary task of colonization. The seamanship, knowledge of sky and sea, and willingness to go voyaging probably changed less in three and a half thousand years than did the equipment used.

The maritime technology and techniques of the ancient colonists will never be known precisely, but their achievement speaks for itself. They were peoples of the sea.

Chapter Three

POLYNESIA: THE AGE OF EUROPEAN DISCOVERY

By the eighteenth century, most Pacific islanders had been in possession of their lands for periods of between one thousand and five thousand years, and in parts of Melanesia, for a vastly longer time than that. During that time they had developed a variety of cultures, rich in oral literature and ceremony, artistic and utilitarian in their material forms, and with a variety of social and political systems ranging from egalitarian to hierarchical. Few islands or island groups were entirely cut off from other Pacific peoples: voyaging for trade or other purposes kept most people in sufficient contact with other groups so that the number of communities who, like the Easter Islanders, believed that the world was only as big as their own part of it, and that they were the only human beings in it, was few indeed. Nor were the Pacific islands entirely cut off from the influences of the outside world, as the diffusion of the fore-and-aft sail shows.

Stable as the cultures of the Pacific were, there were times of change and upheaval, some of which have been briefly mentioned in the previous chapter. By the eighteenth century the previous stability was breaking down at least in Polynesia, and new forms and political institutions were emerging. These changes were soon to be absorbed and overshadowed by introduced changes from regions beyond the Pacific.

There is some knowledge of these late pre-European developments in Fiji, Tonga, Tahiti and Hawai'i. Tonga and Fiji were to some extent under each other's influence, but with the other places there was no apparent relationship, although there were some features in common. In all of them, for example, the beginnings of the idea of political centralization can be seen; indeed, Tonga was already a unitary state, and in the others, there seems to have been an awareness that the ultimate goal of political ambition was shifting from an emphasis on status, titles and hegemony, to dominion of a more direct kind. If this transition was to be achieved, then some basic assumptions in Polynesian politics were likely to change: kinship as a basis of political alliances and delegation would have to be abandoned; territory rather than descent would have to become the defining principle of group identity; *mana* might have to be replaced by a more secular concept of political legitimacy, and *tapu* replaced by a more systematic process of law. In short, politics and religion might need to be divorced. In Tonga where unification had been long established, the priests were very much subordinate to the chiefs, some of whom were openly sceptical. In Hawai'i and Tahiti there was tension between chiefs and priests, the power of the latter having grown great enough to rival their masters.

Political change in these parts of the Pacific was beginning to look like the early stages of state formation. With the coming of Europeans at the end of the eighteenth century, that process was to be accelerated. In Fiji, the traditional skirmishing and symbolic wars between petty communities gave way to wars which aimed at exterminating or absorbing and supplanting the enemy, and enlarging the territory and status of the victor. A principle of regional conquest and wider hegemony was becoming established. This development took place through the rivalries of three districts, Verata, Rewa and Bau, on the eastern side of the large island, Viti Levu (see Map 5). Verata had for some time exercised hegemony over the northern and eastern coast of Viti Levu, collecting tribute from time to time, and though still powerful, was nevertheless in decline. South of Verata was Rewa, occupying the rich river delta of the same name: large in population, rich in timber, with good soil and fishing areas, and ambitious in its leadership. Bau occupied a small wedge of land between these two giants.

Elsewhere in Fiji other large power blocs were developing. To the north on the other large Fijian island, Vanua Levu, Cakaudrove was similarly establishing a hegemony. To the east, in the islands of Lau, a people with a small land-base was also making claims of prominence. These four power-bases were all soon to be overshadowed by the extraordinary, dramatic rise of Bau, with the smallest territorial base of all. The basis of Bau's success was twofold: the exploitation of concepts of rank and prestige through strategic intermarriages between the chiefly families of the most powerful tribes in the group, and the imaginative and skilful use of sea power, using the great twin-hulled *drua*, with its versatile fore-and-aft sail. Bau, perforce, had to be a sea power; its greatest rivals were land-powers.

Meanwhile, in the adjacent island group of Tonga, the long established tranquillity and good order commented on by the

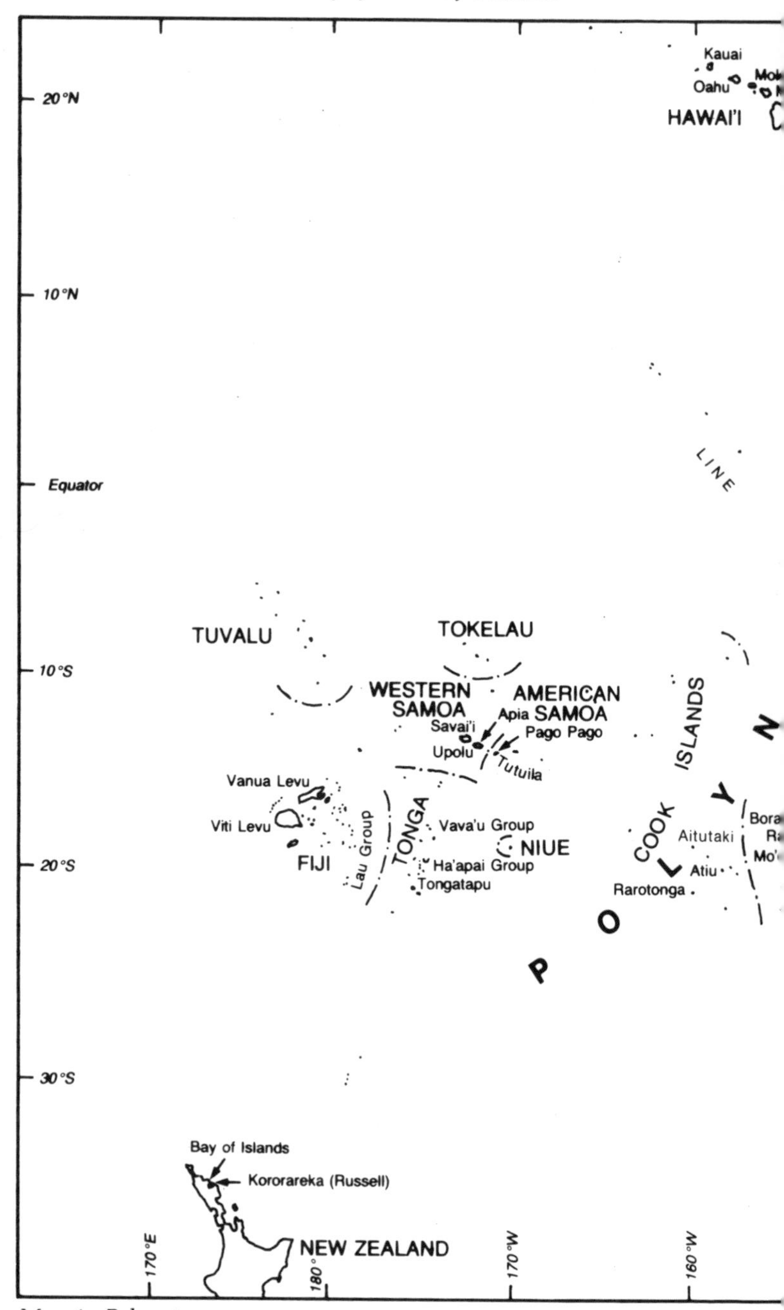

Map 4 Polynesia

Polynesia: The Age of European Discovery

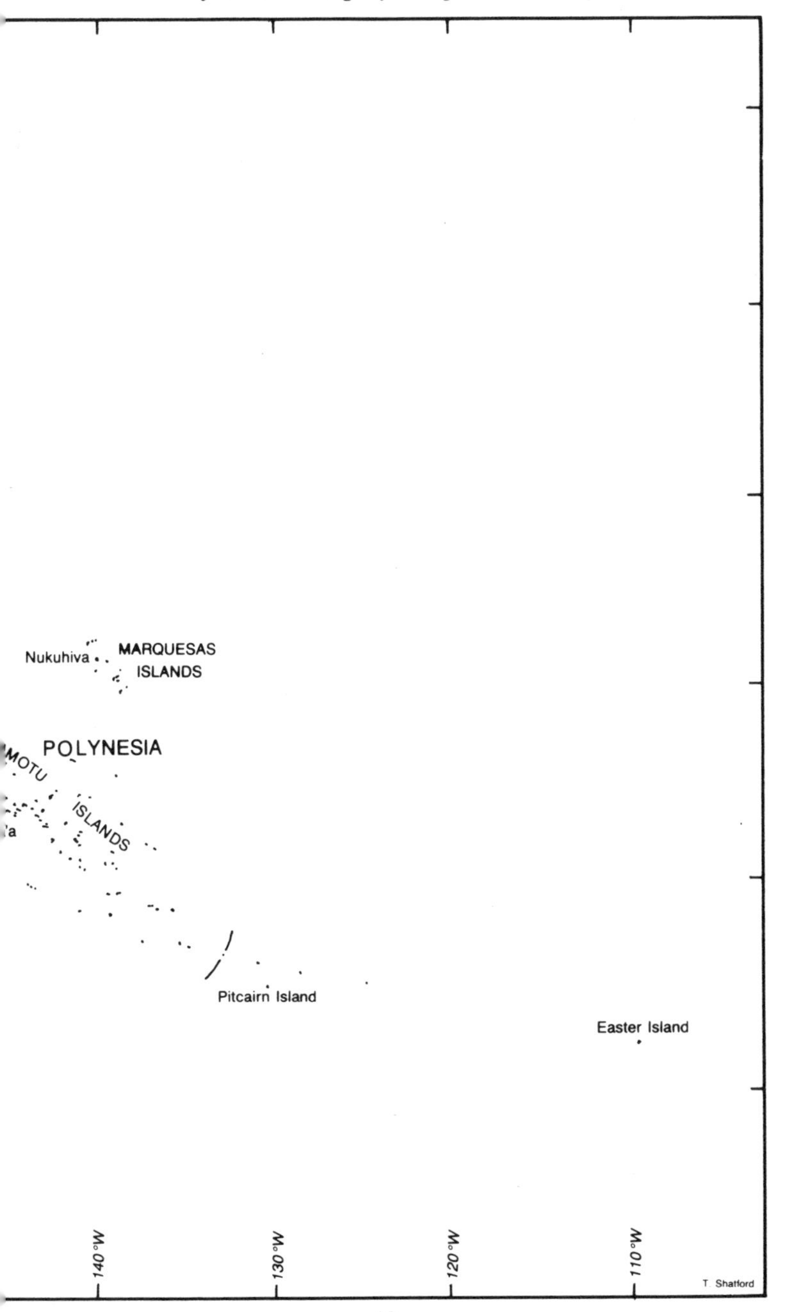

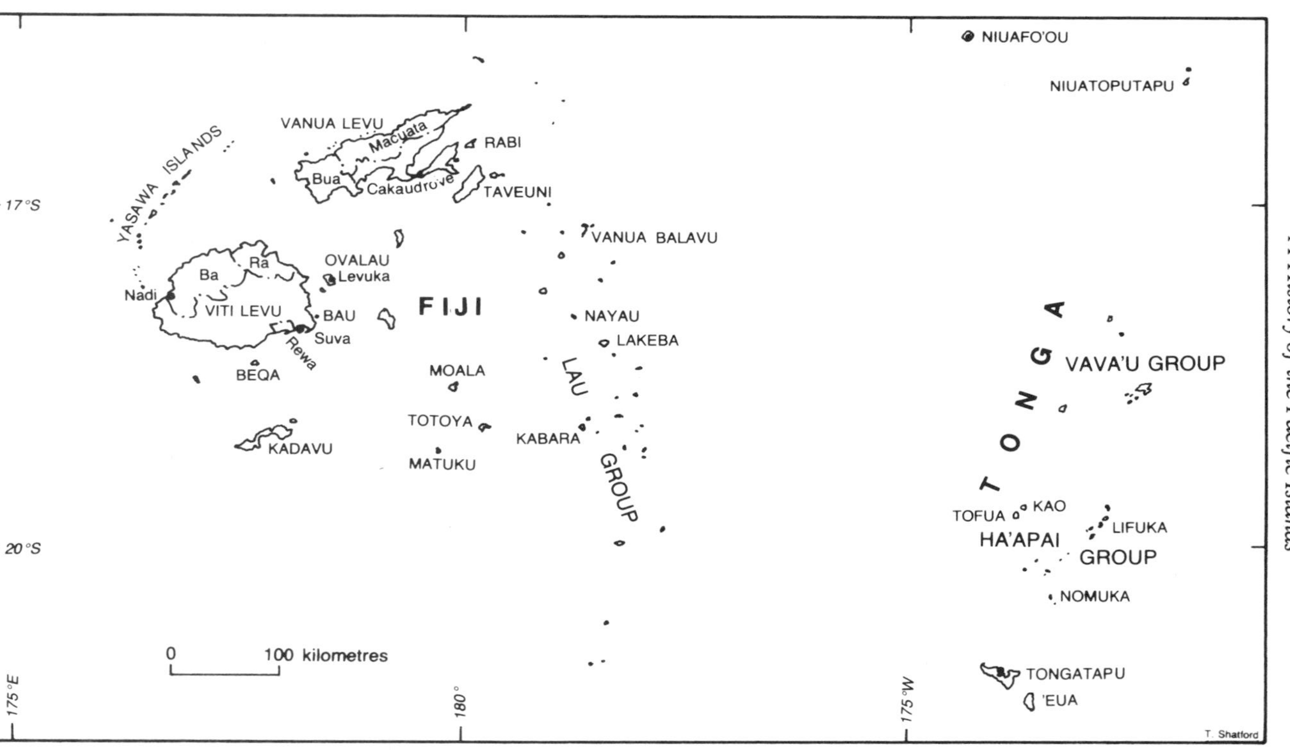

NIUAFO'OU
NIUATOPUTAPU
VANUA LEVU
Macuata
RABI
Bua
Cakaudrove
TAVEUNI
YASAWA ISLANDS
17°S
VANUA BALAVU
OVALAU
Levuka
Ba
Ra
Nadi
VITI LEVU
BAU
FIJI
Suva
Rewa
NAYAU
LAKEBA
BEQA
MOALA
LAU
TOTOYA
KABARA
KADAVU
MATUKU
GROUP
TONGA
VAVA'U GROUP
TOFUA
KAO
LIFUKA
HA'APAI
GROUP
NOMUKA
20°S
0
100 kilometres
TONGATAPU
'EUA
175°E
180°
175°W
T. Shatford

explorer Tasman in 1643 was being disturbed by an aristocratic revolution. Tonga, alone among the island groups of the Pacific, had established a unitary, centralized political system under a single monarch. Tradition and genealogies suggest that this development took place in the tenth century A.D., and by the time of the visit of the Dutch explorer Abel Tasman in 1643, there were signs of a long-established peace. This peace evidently continued for another century and was then disturbed apparently by dynastic ambitions. The eighteenth-century European visitors to Tonga had great difficulty understanding the political system and it may be doubted whether at that time many Tongans understood it either. This was because of the revolution in politics which occupied much of the eighteenth century.

The paramount chief of all Tonga, the Tu'i Tonga, had long since become a mainly ceremonial figure, elevated by his unapproachable sanctity far above the day-to-day routine of administration. The conduct of affairs was placed in the hands of a hereditary chief, the Tu'i Ha'atakalaua. Some authorities, deriving from nineteenth century traditions, aver that the Tu'i Ha'atakalaua, like the Tu'i Tonga, had long since been elevated to ceremonial impotence, and his political role taken over by the Tu'i Kanokupolu. There is reason to believe, however, that this scheme, far from being the traditional order, was actually the object of eighteenth century intrigues. Alternatively, the Tu'i Ha'atakalaua lineage might have been making a bid to regain its lost power.

At all events, during the second half of the eighteenth century the former peace of Tonga was lost, warriors regained their former status, arbitrariness in the exercise of power crept back in, and there was a series of irregular successions to the major titles, including even the possession of the powerful Tu'i Kanokupolu title by a woman, Tupoumoheofo.

Civil war finally broke out in 1799 between the major lineages of the large island of Tongatapu. One faction allied itself with the sea-borne peoples of the smaller northern islands, so that soon most of Tonga was involved. Neither side was able to prevail until 1852, when a chief from Ha'apai, Taufa'ahau, who had combined a strong genealogical claim to the important Tongatapu title of Tu'i Kanokupolu with an imposing and brilliant personality, asserted his supremacy over all rivals to become king, and the founder of the present dynasty.

In Tahiti the political changes were connected with religious changes. The old Eastern Polynesian religion of departmental gods was challenged by a new god from Ra'iatea, sponsored by an ambitious chief with politically astute priests. This new god, 'Oro, had a greater appetite than its rivals for human sacrifice and its sponsor was able, by a combination of terror and the manipulation of titles, to challenge the *status quo* of the great island of Tahiti which exercised a loose pre-eminence over the whole Society Islands group.

The nature of politics in the Society Islands was therefore changing. Power, both ritual and temporal, was becoming increasingly the object of ambition of the chiefs. In the course of this new competitiveness, new titles were created and became in turn the object and means of further chiefly aggrandizement. The ultimate object of ambition was the title Te Nui e A'a i Te Atua, which was particularly associated with 'Oro and was symbolized by the possession of a special girdle of red feathers. This title and its insignia had become so potent that it threatened to overshadow the former multi-tribalism of Tahitian society, and to replace it with a centralized authority.

This indeed was the purpose of a chief called Teu. Alleged by some to be descended from a relatively low-born Tuamotuan, Teu could in fact claim descent from the great Ra'iatean family of Tamatoa, which endowed enormous prestige. By a protracted and subtle process of alliances and marriage, and some warfare, Teu's family by the 1760s had become the leading title-holder in the Te Porionu'u district of Tahiti, and was in a strong position to win the prized red feather girdle. The next step was to ensure that overwhelming alliances between other claimants could be forestalled. In the last and greatest step, Teu and his son Tu failed, and at that point their fortunes became entwined with those of a succession of European visitors who by chance, came to this district of Tahiti. Over the period of two generations, this family's fortunes had a succession of rises and falls until Tu's son, known as Pomare II, modified the old goal, adopted Christianity, conquered his opponents in 1815, and established a tenuous political centralization, with Christianity occupying a similar political role to that previously possessed by the cult of 'Oro.

In the Hawai'ian Islands, a remarkably similar process was in train, but here the religious overtones involved traditional gods: the god of war, Ku, and the god of peace, Lono. Ku won, and Hawai'ian politics then became more clearly a question of naked power between strong tribal groupings which had already established strong, centralized authority.

For some centuries, the size of political units in the Hawai'ian group had been increasing, until by the eighteenth century, the existence of a single paramount chief over each island was accepted as the normal state of affairs. This indeed was the condition of limited centralization which the Society Islands were approaching during the eighteenth century. Ambitious Hawai'ian chiefs, not satisfied with limited worlds to conquer, aimed at uniting several islands under a single rule: the object of warfare was not simply to establish hegemony, collect tribute and acquire titles, but to conquer and to exercise control. In this process Hawai'i and Tonga were foremost in Polynesia.

By about the middle of the 1770s, the several islands of the Hawai'ian chain had been consolidated into three kingdoms, and the men who had made them were growing old. Within ten years, all were dead, and in all cases the succession was either disputed, or was divided between two heirs. Within a short time, civil war occurred within all three inheritances, and the winners, the new generation of paramount chiefs, then looked afresh at the territories of their neighbours. A new round of warfare broke out, overlapping with the internal wars and confusing the details. After some see-sawing of fortunes, one great chief, Kamehameha, having made good his claim to the island of Hawai'i by rank, warfare and murder, achieved the systematic conquest of most of the island group by 1796. The extent of his dominion was unprecedented, and to retain it he had to break new ground in government. The limiting factors in the sizes of the kingdoms of the predecessors were three: the uncertainty of communications, the danger of chiefs close to power making a bid for supremacy, and the danger of chiefs in remote parts asserting their independence, and attracting to them others who were impatient of control.

Kamehameha solved this problem (common to all kingdom builders in Polynesia) by some unusual expedients of his own and by the use of the European settlers ('beachcombers') who had assisted him in his wars. He appointed to positions of authority these men, and Hawai'ian commoners, who depended for their standing entirely on him. He bound them to him by marriage, and he listened to their advice, but retained power firmly in his own hands. For a quarter of a century he maintained the largest and most stable kingdom to be established by a Polynesian, and did it during a period of profound social change occasioned by rapidly accelerating contact and commerce with adventurers from Europe and America.

When Europeans came to Polynesia in the eighteenth century, therefore, they came to societies which were already undergoing some major changes, and they found communities and factions poised to take advantage of the destabilizing influence of the newcomers.

The Europeans themselves were sent to the Pacific by complicated sequences of events in their own homelands. From the end of the fifteenth century, the political and intellectual storms called the Renaissance expanded the portions of the globe into which Europeans began to carry themselves. In 1521, Magellan traversed the Pacific trying to circumvent the restrictions imposed on Spain by the Treaty of Tordesillas of 1494, and at the same time to satisfy his own obsession about the shape of the earth. Within a hundred years, the Pacific had been crossed several times by Spaniards and by buccaneering Englishmen motivated by the desire for wealth and political advantage; only a few of them, however, and they Spanish, had envisaged European colonization.

By the beginning of the seventeenth century, the Dutch, having freed themselves of the Spanish yoke and successfully asserted their prowess as seamen and traders against their rivals and former allies the English, also began to look to the Pacific for access to rich markets and cheap sources of trade goods. Three great voyages, Schouten and Le Maire in 1616, Tasman in 1642-43, and Roggeveen in 1721-22, were failures from a commercial stand-point, but added to the growing intellectual mystery about this unknown third of the earth's surface.

The eighteenth century, a time of vigour in Europe as in Polynesia, brought about a conjunction of four powerful interests: military, scientific, commercial and ideological. The last great attempt to deal the Spanish a serious military blow by sailing upon the Pacific Ocean was executed by Captain George Anson in 1743, one hundred and sixty-five years after the Elizabethan, Francis Drake, had first boldly shown the way. Anson's expedition, culminating in the conquest of Manila, was scarcely less sensational, and re-awakened a British awareness of the vast ocean and its possibilities. The extensive and largely French commerce with the Spanish settlements on the west coast of South America pointed at a time of international tension to the importance of controlling the entrance to the great sea; growing suspicions of the presence of a great southern continent hinted at strategic and commercial opportunities to be won, or at least denied to others. Accordingly, twenty years after Anson's voyage, and at the end of yet another European war (the Seven Years' War), Captain John Byron was sent in 1765 to secure the Falklands Islands, and from there to search both for land and for the much desired north-west passage between the Pacific and Atlantic Oceans.

The belief in the existence of a southern continent (which Byron was instructed to find) had long been noticed in the works of the ancient geographer Ptolemy, and, added to by the misrepresentation of Marco Polo's Asian adventures in the thirteenth century (the land of 'Beach'), was finally given an air of possibility by the voyage of the disastrously visionary Spaniard, Pedro Fernandes de Quiros. Quiros in the course of two Pacific voyages (the first with Mendaña's second voyage of 1595, and the second an attempt to continue Mendaña's work in 1606) convinced himself from imagined sightings and from the inference that Polynesian-inhabited islands must imply a nearby mainland, that a great southern continent certainly existed.

Quiros himself had inherited the idea from Mendaña, who had been sent in search of it in 1567. The trail had been started by Pedro Sarmiento who had evidently connected the bar-talk of sailors with Inca traditions of land to the westward, and persuaded the governor of Peru to send an expedition. Sarmiento himself had to endure the humiliation of accompanying the expedition as the subordinate of the young, inexperienced and incapable Mendaña, the governor's nephew.

Seventeenth and eighteenth century 'sightings' in the extreme south-east Pacific, and Tasman's discovery of a west coast of a large fertile, inhabited land, (New Zealand, and not a continent) gave further evidence to the speculative geographers who wanted to know the features of the earth. Several of these, Charles de Brosses, John Campbell, and Alexander Dalrymple, advanced reasons for searching for a sixth continent until it eventually caught the imagination of influential opinion.

The result was several voyages in the 1760s; indeed, this decade was the watershed in Pacific exploration. Up till then, Pacific navigation was attended by the most appalling suffering and mortality. The first difficulty was the sheer size of the ocean and its remoteness from Europe: it was a long voyage of several months (eight months for Schouten and Le Maire in 1615, five for Cook in 1768) just to reach the entrance to the ocean, which for all voyages before 1773 (except for Tasman in 1642-43) was via Cape Horn or the Straits of Magellan. Deteriorating food and water, diminishing supplies of both, increasing illness (especially scurvy), fatigue, the decay of ships and equipment, and the problem of maintaining morale and discipline among tired, sick, bored crews, made these voyages dangerous. By the time a ship-master had reached the Pacific, he had little opportunity or time for exploration, and so the tracks of most voyages across the Pacific followed a monotonously similar course, which uniformly avoided major discoveries. The second difficulty was the imperfect state of navigation: latitude could be fixed only approximately by most navigators, despite the improvements in instruments over two hundred years; longitude was mainly a matter of dead-reckoning, and subject to enormous errors. Until reliable chronometers became available, the accurate fixing of longitude depended on long and laborious mathematical calculations and accurate astronomical observations. Few navigators could achieve reliability in these procedures.

By the 1760s, however, improvements in the design of ships, rigging and instruments made exploration less hazardous. Some mariners knew how to avoid scurvy even if most did not, and a spirit of scientific inquiry was in the air. The English sent Byron on a voyage which although strategic in intention had a scientific afterthought. Byron was followed in 1767 by an expedition of two ships, commanded by Samuel Wallis and his lieutenant Philip Carteret, to find what Byron had failed to find—the missing continent. At almost the same time, the French sent Bougainville on a duplicate of Byron's voyage, namely, to secure the Falkland Islands and to explore the Pacific Ocean. That was the extent of the similarity between Byron and Bougainville: the latter had a scientist's curiosity and an explorer's imagination, whereas Byron had had neither. Wallis and Bougainville within a few months of each other discovered the land which was to intrigue the armchair and coffee-salon philosophers for decades—Tahiti.

Tahiti was discovered at a time when political philosophers were much concerned with speculations about life 'in the state of nature' as a starting point for thinking about what sort of government and laws were necessary or best. If one knew what the original state of Man was, then many mistakes could be avoided. While many 'natural states' had been discovered, and many more imagined from the time of Sir Thomas More to that of Voltaire and Rousseau, none seemed to give such evidence for optimism about human nature as did Tahiti, as reported by Wallis and Bougainville. Tahiti thus acquired and held a place in the romantic imagination of Europe which has never been rivalled.

The discovery of Tahiti with its abundant natural resources, and its apparently hospitable and peaceable inhabitants was timely. A voyage was being planned under the auspices of the English Royal Society and the Royal Navy primarily to make astronomical observations which, amongst other things, would assist navigators to fix their longitude more accurately. In particular, the transit of the planet Venus across the face of the Sun was to be observed, to provide information to assist the calculation of the distances between the Earth, Venus and the Sun. This observation was possible only twice every hundred or so years (the next transits occurred in 1874 and 1882). Observers needed three points of observation as distant from each other as terrestrial geography would allow. Tahiti was almost ideally located, and the reported qualities of the land and people made it a perfect choice.

The finest cartographer in the Royal Navy, and master of a

surveying vessel, James Cook, aged forty, was chosen to lead the expedition for which he was commissioned as a lieutenant. Although the primary objective of Cook's voyage was astronomical observation, the Admiralty took advantage of the opportunity to satisfy lobbyists with other interests. He was to solve the mystery of the great southern continent, and to record information about the peoples and natural productions of any lands to be found on the voyage. An influential young scientist, Joseph Banks, saw the possibilities for science, and secured a place for himself and his assistants on the expedition. Cook was given wide powers in planning: he chose his own vessel (a steady, shallow-draft, North Sea collier), had her modified, personally oversaw the modifications and fitting out of the vessel, and paid particular attention to the food and accommodation of his crew to ensure their good health and morale throughout the long voyage. Aware that the principal limiting factor in all previous Pacific voyages so far had been the enormous distance and time involved, he therefore aimed at minimizing their effects: scurvy in the crew, wear-and-tear on ship and rigging, and the wood-consuming worms in the hull.

Cook's three great voyages from 1769 to 1780 were extraordinary. They added more to geographical knowledge than any other project of investigation had done before (and perhaps since), collected an enormous bulk of information about the peoples of the Pacific, and they did so at extraordinarily little cost in human life, both among his own crews and among the Pacific islanders. In his three voyages, Cook had not a single man die of scurvy, and he established generally safe and friendly relations with the people wherever he went—notwithstanding the fact of his own death at the hands of the Hawai'ians in January 1779. Cook's journals are the starting point for all studies of the history and culture of four major island groups in Polynesia (Society, Tonga, New Zealand and Hawai'i) and of eastern Australia, Vanuatu (New Hebrides) and New Caledonia.

On his first voyage Cook sailed directly for Tahiti via Cape Horn. He spent four months from April to August 1769 in Tahiti and the adjacent islands, engaged with his staff in multifarious scientific enquiries. Cordial relations with the Tahitians were firmly established and maintained despite the constant attempts at theft, and Cook's equally constant insistence on punishment and restitution. Having accomplished the first and major part of his assignment, Cook then turned south, to clear up the matter of a great southern continent. Having already sailed over the ocean where part of this continent was supposed to exist, and being convinced by the behaviour of the sea that an extensive land mass was not likely for some considerable distance, he steered south and then west to meet the land which Tasman had reported, and which was thought to be the continent's western margin. That land, New Zealand, Cook circumnavigated and charted in detail over the next six months—October 1769 to March 1770.

Cook had thus satisfied his instructions. He had not, of course, proven absolutely that a continent did not exist, but he had shown that it was not where it was thought to be, that New Zealand was not part of it, and that if it did exist, it was very much smaller and further to the south than the speculative geographers expected.

Cook's task now was to get his crew and his findings home, but there was another southern continent about which he was curious, and he now sailed west to determine the facts about its easterly extent. Thus, in an adjunct to an already remarkable voyage, Cook set out and performed another monumental piece of exploration—charting eastern Australia—which, had it been his only achievement, would have been sufficient to mark him as an exceptional navigator, ship-master, and cartographer.

Neither this part of the voyage nor the journey home to England was without mishap or drama. Perhaps the most ironic and unhappy development was the death of twenty-nine of his crew and supernumeraries from the mosquitoes and the insalubrious air and water of Batavia (now Djakarta) in the East Indies, where he had to pause for an extensive re-fit. Among several men whose early deaths are much to be lamented as a loss to scholarship, was Tupaia, a Tahitian priest and navigator who had joined the expedition as a refugee from the political disturbances of his homeland. Tupaia, an intelligent and knowledgeable man, was an invaluable interpreter in New Zealand because of the closeness of the Tahitian and Maori languages. He had given enough information, particularly about Tahitian geographical and navigational knowledge, to suggest that he might have given much more. This was a loss to scholarship which was never to be made good: there were to be no more Tupaias.

Cook in his modesty, scarcely realized the magnitude of his achievement; nor was he prepared for the sensation his reports would cause. On the contrary, he seems to have thought his achievement quite mundane, and was more conscious of how much more remained to be done, than of what he had accomplished. Accordingly, even before his arrival in England, his mind had turned to planning another voyage to deal with the many questions started by the first.

Science and national pride (the French were on the ocean again by the time Cook had returned) joined together to urge another voyage. In July 1772 Cook sailed again, this time with two ships, but without the agreeable and indefatigable Joseph Banks. This time he would settle beyond doubt the question of an undiscovered southern land mass, and satisfy himself about other lands reported to exist in uncertain places in the south Pacific, places already discovered by the Spanish in the sixteenth century, and by the Dutch in the early seventeenth and early eighteenth.

This voyage, although it added less coastline to the map of the world, was even more remarkable than the first. This time he approached the Pacific from the west—Tasman's route. After leaving Cape Town in December 1772, he steered south and crossed the Antarctic Circle—the first voyager known to have done so—on 17 January 1773, thus reaching further south than the most northerly parts of Antarctica. Retreating northwards before the impenetrable ice, he disproved the existence of rumoured Indian Ocean lands, and then sailed eastwards in the high and stormy latitude of 60°S for nearly two months, during which voyage he kept his crew dry and healthy.

Further explorations of New Zealand and a closer acquaintance with the Maoris followed, and while winter prevented further southern voyaging, Cook took the opportunity to rule out the possibility of a continent south of Tahiti. He then visited the Society Islands again, the Cook Islands (not given that name by the modest explorer) and Tonga, before returning via New Zealand to Antarctic waters for the summer of 1773-74. In two deep probes he crossed the Antarctic circle twice, and reached 71°10'S before being forced back. There was now no room for any idea of a southern continent: Cook had demolished it, but he was not yet finished with the Pacific. Sheer prudence in any case prevented an immediate return to England via Cape Horn; so Cook planned another great circuit through the south Pacific, during which he found open ocean where sightings of land had previously been reported in the eastern Pacific; he then relocated Easter Island which had been discovered fifty-two years before by Roggeveen, confirmed the location of the Marquesas (found and lost by Mendaña in 1596), and returned again to Tahiti.

From Tahiti he visited Tonga again and renewed his friendship with the chiefs; he then skirted Fiji on the way to the lost lands of Mendaña, Quiros and Torres, which he charted and named the New Hebrides. Further south he made another new discovery, mapped the northern half and named it New Caledonia. Time was again robbing him of more complete discoveries. By now he had been more than two years away, and so, after further refreshments in the now familiar shores of New Zealand, he steered for Cape Horn. Even yet, Cook was not finished: on his way home, he did not neglect an opportunity for more complete exploration, crossing the South Atlantic in latitudes between 55° and 60° in order to clear the map of more fanciful sightings before turning north for Cape Town and then for home.

Cook's second return created as great a sensation as the first: the British government, now enthusiastic at what could be achieved by properly planned and skilfully-led expeditions of discovery, resolved on another in which the interests of commerce, strategy and science might join together, as they had done in the time of Byron, which, though a mere dozen years before, belonged in technique to a different era. The particular objective of this voyage was a dream older than the quest for a southern continent: the existence of the north-west passage which had been sought by Elizabethan seamen. Was there, the Admiralty and the Royal Society wanted to know, a direct link between the North Atlantic and the North Pacific? Where were the western and northern limits of the American continent?

Again Cook sailed via the Indian Ocean, and visited the now familiar places of New Zealand, Tonga, the Cook Islands and Tahiti. He refrained from mapping both Fiji and Samoa, of which the nautically-minded Tongans had told him, and made his way to new waters in the North Pacific.

Much of Cook's achievement so far had been in locating or dismissing lands previously reported: he found few places by chance. A major discovery which had possibly been made already by Spaniards awaited him in the North Pacific. Cook could well have had some knowledge of rumoured Spanish discoveries, and thus had some clue. Either by design or chance, however, Cook came upon the Hawai'ian chain on 18 January 1778. His journals are the earliest written records of the Hawai'ian people, the base line for all subsequent inquiry.

Cook did not stay long in Hawai'i, but continued towards the American coast to get on with the main object of his voyage, namely to dispel more errors about geography. He spent the northern summer making notes about the American Indians whom he encountered and mapping the coast as far as Bering Strait and into the Bering Sea, reaching 70°44' north latitude. For the winter he returned to Hawai'i, now named by him the Sandwich Islands, where he could both rest his crew and add further to geography and anthropology.

It was here on 14 February 1779, that Cook, experienced in the ways of Polynesians, accustomed to dealing with theft and with threats of violence, and distinguished above all explorers for the good relations with the people among whom he travelled, was killed in the sort of quarrel which he had survived several times elsewhere. The shock of the sudden and unexpected death of this extraordinary man seems to have been as great for the Hawai'ians as for his own crew. Both races recognized his greatness; both were incredulous at what had happened; both were subdued in the aftermath. Cook's work, however, was complete: he had shown for all time the extent and boundaries of the great ocean; he had banished mythology and vagueness from Pacific geography and given a definite location to most of the major island groups (the modern map of the Pacific is not very different from Cook's map); he gave to Europe an extensive collection of objects and observations on the natural history of the Pacific of immense scientific interest; he collected a detailed set of observations on Polynesian society long before the science of anthropology was established. His career as an explorer lasted only ten years: no explorer of his time, or in all recorded history, achieved more.

The secret of his success was his close attention to detail in all things. This attentiveness was nowhere more evident than in his maintaining a fit and healthy crew in well-maintained vessels during voyages which lasted for years. In this too, Cook's achievement shines alone in the history of sea-faring; without this, he could have achieved little else.

For the Pacific islanders who knew him, Cook was the representative of European civilization and humanity, and he was remembered with affection. In the late twentieth century he is often said to have been severe in his treatment of Pacific islanders, but the precedents which he established of fairness, firmness and compassion were to be remembered as such for many years; so that for decades afterwards it would be a proud boast to be able to say that one had met or known Captain Cook; indeed, the Hawai'ian who killed him is known to have regretted the act for the rest of his life. The next Europeans to come to the Pacific did not need to apologise for coming in his wake, nor be apprehensive of what he had taught the islanders to expect of Europeans. Unfortunately, few of those who followed him were able to act as he did, and less noble behaviour was quickly adopted on both sides.

The Age of Exploration, however, was not yet over, and as far as scientific expeditions were concerned, the traditions and procedures established by Cook continued. Before the end of the eighteenth century, there were four more expeditions; three French, including that of La Pérouse (also one of the greatest of his profession), and another English, led by Vancouver, who had sailed as a midshipman in Cook's second voyage. The nineteenth century was to open with a major Russian expedition, and in the succeeding decades, more French and Russian voyages were to follow. The Americans joined the contest for scientific distinction with the Wilkes expedition of 1838-42. The British largely withdrew from exploration, occasionally sending a ship to circumnavigate on a surveying errand, including that which carried Charles Darwin as naturalist from 1832 to 1836. The last great British expedition was that of the 'Challenger' between 1872 and 1876, and which also had an association with a later transit of Venus. These errands had scientific purposes other than the location of lands; exploration of the great sea, its weather patterns, its life-forms and its floor still continues, but with less human cost and less romance than formerly.

Within the limits of his era, Cook had not left much for his immediate successors to do besides fill in the gaps which his life had been too short to eliminate. Most of those gaps were to be filled, not by professional explorers pursuing geographical knowledge for its own sake, but by men with commercial motives: sandalwooders, sealers, traders, whalers—all of whom contributed something to the growing contact and mutual knowledge of Pacific islanders and the other communities of mankind.

Chapter Four

POLYNESIA: TRADE AND SOCIAL CHANGE

The process of cultural and racial contact begun with the explorers was soon to accelerate and bring about profound and permanent changes in the societies and cultures of the Pacific islands. The most noticeable, immediate vehicle of these changes was violence.

In only a few cases of contact between explorers and islanders had violence not been present or threatened. Men on both sides came from militaristic societies in which recourse to violence was a traditional solution to conflict, or in which strangers were held to be outside the usual ethical and legal limits so that any measures against them were considered acceptable. In addition, much of the bloodshed of early contact was due to European arrogance and pride, and to the cheapness of human life in an age of short life expectancies and innumerable hazards. It is difficult to find cases in which violence broke out despite goodwill on both sides. Goodwill, tolerance and forbearance were not typical of any of the communities, Pacific or European, which were coming into contact, although such sentiments were of course adopted as policies by various leaders.

The commonest cause of bloodshed was dispute over property, especially in Polynesia. Contrary to common belief, this was not really due to a conflict of values. Private property and rights of property did exist in Polynesia; people often had certain rights to property which was generally acknowledged to be someone else's, but those rights were not undefined or unlimited. Thus, when light-fingered Polynesians helped themselves to the movable property of navigators, it was not because they did not understand what was meant by 'belonging'. They understood that all too well, and wanted certain things to belong to themselves, or to their communities. Such was their persistence that their European visitors in an extremity of exasperation often resorted to gun-fire to protect their rights as they saw them. Even Cook, that most forbearing of visitors—usually patient, resourceful and consistent, sensitive to the perceptions of the islanders, successful beyond all others in establishing peaceful, workable relationships—was sometimes reduced to his wit's end to try to control the endless threat to his limited resources. Most mariners were less humane than he, most more easily unbalanced by the awareness of the dangers they faced. Accordingly, race relations were a volatile blend of cordiality and suspicion, friendship and bloodshed. The seemingly friendly, hospitable Polynesians were found often to be plotting treachery, and sometimes in the act of executing it. The supposedly enlightened, Christian Europeans for their part, often did not respect Polynesian ideas of property or propriety and were thoughtlessly apt to kill and maim.

With more intimate contact there was perhaps more misunderstanding, but greater harmony of interest. Polynesian women—especially those of Tahiti—were seen by the Europeans as having loose morals, or none at all. Europeans for their part have been charged with corrupting the natives and introducing disease and commerce where previously only love and fun had reigned. In fact, numbers of Polynesian women were exuberantly available, and they or their menfolk quickly realized that this was the most expedient way to gain possession of the much desired foreign objects. Prostitution was not an indigenous institution, but sexual hospitality was, and the latter, when joined to the desire for property, quickly evolved into commerce. It was an arrangement which gave mutual satisfaction, and like so many changes from this time on, while not exactly introduced by the strangers, could not have developed in their absence.

Inevitably, commerce of all kinds was to have distressing consequences at many different levels in island society. This was an unavoidable consequence of contact, and requires no imputation of greater vice, innocence, or vulnerability to either party. Each party in any transaction sought to extract whatever possible advantage might be gained. Unhappily for them, the islanders were to be the greater losers, and the cost was to be measured in loss of population, and in diminished health, happiness, social integrity and economic independence, and eventually, in the loss of political independence.

At their first contact with Europeans, most islanders recognized the superiority and merits of iron and cloth. What could they offer in exchange? The islands of Melanesia were later to yield mineral wealth; the atolls and volcanic islands of Polynesia had nothing to offer but hospitality and refreshment.

Within a few years of Cook's death in Hawai'i these last-discovered islands were to become the first resort for European shipping. The discovery of fur seals on the American west coast by Cook's third expedition led almost immediately to a succession of voyages to the North-West coast, using Canton as both base and market. For these voyages, Hawai'i was an almost ideal refreshment place and wintering resort. Water and fresh food therefore were the commodities most in demand. Women were next. The Hawai'ian demand for western goods quickly became sophisticated: nails, hoop-iron (for fashioning into adzes) and cheap cloth were soon superseded by the demand for muskets, powder, small artillery, and even for ships' boats. The trade was quickly brought under the strict control of a district or island chief who decided what produce should be sold, and for what price, and selected and retained the items to be bought. From 1786 to 1796 these goods were overwhelmingly military, a fact which for a time made Hawai'i a dangerous place not only for ships but also increasingly dangerous for the Hawai'ians themselves, since the military and political ambitions of their chiefs were pursued as ruthlessly as before but with greater effect.

Fur traders visiting Hawai'i for refreshment in this way found another commodity which was to play a major role in Pacific commerce: sandalwood. Sandalwood was much in demand in China for incense, and although the early shipments from Hawai'i were of poor quality and therefore not continued, it was a trade which was later to assume the first importance. In the meantime, and for nearly thirty years, Hawai'i was to sustain an erratic flow of western voyages on the provisioning trade.

At the same time that Hawai'i was becoming well known to North Pacific voyagers, an unusual commerce was being planned for Tahiti. The British government, seeking a high quality food staple for the West Indian slave plantations, was impressed with the merits of the Pacific breadfruit tree.

In 1787 one of Cook's former officers, William Bligh, was sent in command of the *Bounty* to Tahiti to obtain a cargo of breadfruit seedlings which could be transplanted on the islands of the Caribbean. The expedition was initially a great success: Bligh was already known to the Tahitians as a companion of Cook, and had acquired sufficient command of the Tahitian language for his purposes.

On Tahiti the courtly process of reciprocal gift-making was conducted between Bligh and the chiefs, while for the sailors the prostitution trade quickly revived. As Bligh himself observed, 'As there was great probability that we should remain a considerable time at Otaheiti, it could not be expected that the intercourse of my people with the natives should be of a very reserved nature', whereupon he had his surgeon examine the entire crew for venereal disease, of which all were reported to be quite free. (A similar examination on leaving Tahiti revealed two cases of infection.)

For just over five months, Bligh and his crew stayed at Tahiti and visited the adjacent islands while the cargo of breadfruit saplings was prepared, potted and loaded. During this time, friendliness and good order were maintained between the English and the Tahitians. The old problem of theft was reduced to negligible size, and when the departure was finally made, there was every sign of deep regret on both sides. As Bligh later noted, 'to the friendly and endearing behaviour of these people, may be ascribed the motives for that event which effected the ruin of an expedition . . .' Three weeks later, on 28 April 1789, the famous mutiny took place, and the South Pacific acquired its first-recorded permanent European residents. There can be no doubt that the social and physical climate of Tahiti had finally asserted its victory over naval discipline. It was Tahiti's tragedy that it exercised such an appeal to Europeans.

While Bligh was engaged on this voyage, a European colony was being established on the east coast of Australia. Although the prime motive was the removal of convicts from Britain, the new colony was also expected to generate some commercial merits. Convict ships coming to Australia were licensed and equipped for whaling so that they would not need to return to England in ballast, and Cook's reports of the timber of Norfolk Island, and the timber and flax of New Zealand were remembered with hope.

Besides being instructed to encourage these commercial possibilities, Captain Arthur Phillip, the first governor of New South Wales, was recommended to look to the 'adjacent islands' for livestock and for female companions for the convicts. Phillip promptly recognized the impracticability and inhumanity of the last suggestion, and did not act on it.

The effect of the establishment of the colony in 1788 was to increase the traffic of shipping in the Pacific, and diversify the range of people with whom the Pacific islanders came into contact. What the North American fur trade did for Hawai'i, the foundation of New South Wales was in time to do for the South Pacific. It took more than a decade, however, for the influence of New South Wales to extend far: for most of that time the settlement was on the edge of survival, and preoccupied with establishing agriculture.

Between Bligh's visits to Tahiti in 1788-89 and his next visit in 1792 on the same errand, several ships called there, some on further voyages of exploration and others taking a southern route to the North Pacific. The intensity of this contact prompted the explorer Vancouver to observe in 1792 that the Tahitians had already become dependent on imported iron, utensils and cloth, remarking that the native equivalents were scarcely to be seen any more. The report is indicative more of the vigorous demand for the labour-saving and convenient imports than of the sudden extinction of native skills, but it was also indicative of the willing commercial partnership which was soon to develop.

Regular commerce with Tahiti did not begin until the new century. By this time New South Wales was securely established, a small shipbuilding industry had begun and a class of traders emerged from among the emancipated convicts and the few free settlers. The beginning of commerce, however, depended on official initiative, and in 1801 a naval vessel, the *Porpoise*, was sent to bring a cargo of salt pork from Tahiti. The trade thus begun was to continue for thirty years, and together with supplying provisions for whalers whose regular visits had begun in 1800, this trade was to be the main source of foreign goods for the Society group.

The Tahitian pork trade, and to a lesser extent the whaling at this time, led to a general increase of traffic which meant that inevitably, other islands would be visited. And so, starting in 1800, ships began calling at Tonga, but no sustained trade developed because of the civil war being waged on and off. In the absence of the former firm government, Tonga now became a dangerous place for shipping.

At the same time, a couple of chance visits to the adjacent islands of Fiji led to the discovery of good stands of high quality sandalwood. Beginning in 1804 and continuing for about twelve years, ships trading in sandalwood made regular visits to Fiji, especially to the northern island of Vanua Levu, where it was necessary to stay for weeks at a time, entering into close and protracted relations with the Fijians for the procurement of cargoes, and thus for a time, distorting the process of Fijian politics. The district of Bua thus temporarily rose to prominence on European wealth and firearms, before the cutting out of the timber dropped it back to the second rank of Fijian power, and ultimate eclipse.

About the time that Fijian sandalwood was becoming harder to obtain, the same commodity was found in the distant land of the Marquesas, far out in the eastern Pacific. Since the early 1790s, the Marquesas had become a provisioning base for a small but steady stream of whalers and north-bound traders. During the War of 1812-14, the islands were used as a base by Captain David Porter of the United States Navy to harass British shipping. In the last months of the war, one of the captured ships escaped, and after it reached Sydney, probably with news of the Marquesan sandalwood, the first of the sandalwood expeditions set out, returning to Sydney with a sandalwood cargo in February 1815.

The Marquesan sandalwood trade was as dangerous as that of Fiji with the continual threat of massacre and plunder by the islanders The wood was gone by 1820; for the next forty years or so, the Marquesans provided supplies for an increasing fleet of whalers and a turbulent home for an enlarging and transient set of deserters and malcontents who wanted relief from shipboard life, or who were abandoned by their captains.

By the time the Marquesan sandalwood trade was flourishing the same commodity was being revived in Hawai'i after a false start in the 1790s. Since Kamehameha's great victory in 1796 and the establishment of a unified government over most of the group Hawai'i had become a much safer resort for the traders in fur seals and the ever-widening American trade. Regulations and a guide to prices and values were laid down, and firearms were not to be traded except to Kamehameha himself or his agents. This stability combined with Hawai'i's favourable location in the North Pacific quickly made Hawai'ian society the most acculturated in the Pacific blacksmiths, rope-makers, boatbuilders and other tradesmen were to be found working expertly with European methods and tool less than thirty years after Cook's last voyage.

The further growth of commerce, however, was seriously retarded by the War of 1812-14 between Britain and the United States In 1812, Kamehameha had entered into a contract with two English partners, Cox and Winship, to export sandalwood to China, but this contract lapsed with the virtual cessation of trade during the war. After the war, the trade in sandalwood in Hawai'i, as in the Marquesas, became the main foreign trade, coinciding with the end of the Fijian trade.

To a greater extent even than with the provisioning trade Kamehameha made sandalwood a government monopoly. His own political achievements meant that unlike the chiefs of Fiji and the Marquesas, the Hawai'ians did not need to dissipate their asset on muskets and powder. Kamehameha instead bought the ware of peace—less destructive but not always more productive than th other kind. Among the many useful things he bought, implements utensils, even entire ships in which he hoped to engage in th sandalwood trade on his own account, he also bought large quantitie of luxuries and useless knick-knacks which simply accumulated in his warehouses.

Kamehameha nevertheless had sought with some success to harness trade for the benefit of his people. He understood that relations with Europeans had to be controlled if the Hawai'ian peopl and their culture were to survive and he had the power to ensur that his wishes prevailed. In the other island groups where cen tralization had not been achieved, or where it was not accompanied by the same wisdom and power, potential wealth was squandered and assets dissipated by rival chiefs in competition, so that degeneration and exploitation followed. This, unhappily, was to be Hawai'i's fate also, after Kamehameha's death in 1819.

Foreign trade in these larger Pacific island groups was to lead ultimately to the chiefs becoming heavily indebted to foreigners. This in turn led to political embarrassment and humiliation, and contributed to the eventual loss of political independence. By 1820, however, only the remarkably prescient could have understood that, and by 1820 the opportunities presented by sandalwood in three island groups had all but gone; the pork trade in Tahiti was in decline, and but for the post-war revival of the whaling industry with its insatiable appetite for food, water and entertainment, the Pacific islands would have lapsed back into their former condition, disturbed rarely by entrepreneurs from beyond.

Trade of all kinds was the mechanism of change in Polynesian society, and the whaling trade, because of its comparative longevity and the great scale of its operation, was the most potent instrument of them all. The whaling industry was to become for about forty years the mainstay of the new Pacific economies. Like sandalwood and other extractive trades, it was to be ephemeral, for it would last only as long as the Pacific whale populations could sustain the onslaught being made on them. Not all island groups were exposed equally to the visits of whalers: the major grounds were arranged more or less symmetrically in the four quarters of the ocean, with smaller grounds on the margins of the continent and near the major island groups; those islands nearest the whaling grounds or the connecting routes were visited frequently, while others were all but ignored.

The usual pattern of voyaging was to leave the north Atlantic in summer to enter the Pacific via Cape Horn early in the southern summer, and then to spend a few months patrolling the 'off-shore ground' in the south-eastern Pacific. Thereafter, a vessel would follow one of two routes: either travel via the Marquesas and the equator to the Marshall Islands to circle the north Pacific via Japan and the north-west American coast to Hawai'i, planning to be in the 'off-shore' ground again in November; or sail north directly to Hawai'i for the months February to April, cruise the north-west Pacific and return to Hawai'i in October. Ships which were late leaving the north Atlantic often sailed via the Cape of Good Hope, reaching New Zealand by March, and then patrolled either the south-west Pacific, or made for the 'off-shore' ground by November.

During the whaling boom ships came in great numbers. After

about 1820 the industry was dominated by Americans: 200 vessels in the Pacific in 1828, 256 by 1835, 571 by 1844. The average crew size was thirty-three men, and by the 1840s voyages lasted about three and a half years. These figures are for American ships only—British, colonial and French interests dwindled as the American fleet increased, their ships numbering only dozens by the 1840s.

Refreshment of crews and refitting of ships kept the whalers in island harbours for periods ranging from a few days to a month or more, during which brisk trade was kept up, triggering various changes to island society. (These changes, while significant, were neither uniformly distributed nor necessarily permanent.) Internal patterns of distribution were radically altered: large numbers of people were attracted to the harbours, women usually for prostitution, and young men to ship as sailors, the latter often never to return. The gardeners concentrated less on cultivating for their communities' needs, and more on supplying the passing trade with the food crops most in demand, especially the white potato.

Structures of authority also changed: chiefs used their authority to become merchants, abused the *tapu* and exploited the labour of their people for commercial purposes. Young men and women were encouraged to become more individualistic, and seek their own futures rather than continue the traditional ways of life of their people. The genetic heritage of Polynesia became more mixed, and the size of the population went into a rapid decline as a result of the emigration of young men, and the introduction of diseases of infertility and death.

Whalers visited, but did not frequent the Melanesian islands to anything like the same extent; Polynesia on the whole was milder and more hospitable by virtue of both climate and social mores. Fiji, that border-land between Melanesia and Polynesia, was avoided by whalers because of the intricate dangers of its reefs and the cannibalism of its people, and the trade was diverted to the smaller islands nearby. Even small Rotuma and Wallis Island in the 1830s harboured so many whalers that some knowledge of the English language was widespread.

Fiji, instead of becoming immersed in the provisioning trade, became the locus of a new extractive trade, beginning about a decade after the end of the sandalwood: this was the *bêche-de-mer* trade (see glossary). Early attempts at collecting *bêche-de-mer* began in 1822, but did not become a regular trade until 1828. A boom lasted from then until 1835, with a second, smaller boom from about 1842 to 1850, after which the trade never recovered.

The traders coming to Fiji were coming to an island group which was almost beyond comparison with Hawai'i or Tahiti. Fiji, more than any other part of the Pacific, constituted the 'cannibal isles' which terrified and fascinated the European imagination. From the beginning of the century until 1854, a series of civil wars raged. Alliances were formed and changed, expeditions of war and vengeance sailed across Fijian seas, and public affairs were marked by human sacrifice and ostentatious cannibalism. The long struggle for ascendancy had been reduced to a contest principally between Bau and Rewa, but sideshows continued. War had become endemic to the extent that it seemed to the visitors of the early nineteenth century to be an indispensable part of Fijian life and custom.

The *bêche-de-mer* trade, even more than the earlier sandalwood trade, required protracted, sustained contact. *Bêche-de-mer* exposed a new generation of Fijians to sustained contact with comparatively small numbers of Europeans in circumstances which preserved for Fijians considerable power. This was in contrast to the provisioning trade elsewhere which, because it tended to introduce large numbers, caused greater distortions in island society.

The *bêche-de-mer* had to be collected from the reefs at low tide. Since time was limited and the work laborious, it needed a large labour force which could only be secured by negotiation with a chief. After collection, the creatures had to be dried, requiring long fire trenches and drying sheds with tiers of racks for the 'fish'. Fires were kept burning twenty-four hours a day, consuming enormous quantities of timber which had to be cut and transported sometimes great distances. All this work required Fijian labour, and while the chiefs agreed to it and were paid for it, the labourers did not relish the work. Fijian resentment and the uncertainty of Fijian politics (indeed, the uncertainty of a bargain) made the enterprise extremely hazardous. Fires sometimes consumed the drying sheds and not always by accident; the ships themselves were sometimes attacked, a risk which could be averted only by constant vigilance; and loss of life on both sides was an ever-present part of the trade.

The necessity for large quantities of *bêche-de-mer*, and for drying the cargo before shipping it, meant that this trade more than any other, was in the hands of the chiefs. The commodities they sought—like island traders elsewhere in the Pacific—included hardware, cloth and trinkets, and muskets. Between 1828 and 1850, perhaps five thousand muskets were sold in Fiji. The major chiefs thus had huge arsenals of firearms and powder, and the means for casting musket balls.

The risks were high, but so were the profits. John H. Eagleston, the doyen among the traders, made three voyages over a period of ten years, each involving two or three visits to Fiji, and was able to retire as a rich man after the third voyage. His wealth was dearly bought at the price of hardship, stress and risk to both life and capital, and his success was not typical. His rivals did not do so well, nor did his crews, and the Fijians, enthusiastic as they were for the trade, were bent on their wars, and bought only the means of destruction. When the second boom tapered off in the late 1840s, the Fijians again faced an economic crisis. Their demand for manufactured goods and iron had been awakened and fed but the means of satisfying that demand was again slipping from them.

Throughout this phase of island trade (that is, the sandalwood, provisioning and *bêche-de-mer* trades) commerce was mainly between a ship master who was a small capitalist (trading on his own account) and the indigenous population of the islands (usually through a chief, but often with a lesser person conducting his own trade to satisfy his own wants). At this stage there was no corporate capital involved, nor were there merchant middlemen. Instead, there were mediators who lubricated the cogs of commerce but were not themselves part of it. These men were often called 'beachcombers'.

The beachcombers were men who, cut off from their home societies, found themselves dependent on their Polynesian hosts for survival. Many of them were victims of shipwreck, or of ruthless captains unwilling to pay wages; most were simply deserters taking the easiest (indeed, the only) way to change vessels in mid-voyage. The vast majority wanted to sample island life for a holiday, so to speak, before returning to their old ways and haunts; some were escaped convicts from New South Wales; a few were romantics with idealized visions of a tropical paradise and free love, usually doomed to disappointment. Most stayed with their Polynesian hosts for only a few weeks or months; some stayed for years, and a small minority lived out a long life-time as 'naturalized' Polynesians.

Survival for these stray Europeans depended on conforming to the ways of their hosts and making themselves useful. After the few months usually necessary to learn enough of the language to do basic interpreting, these beachcombers were useful intermediaries between chief and captain, to the advantage of both parties. Others made themselves useful practising their own skills, carpentry, blacksmithing and musket maintenance being the most common. Some, like the famous Isaac Davis and John Young in Hawai'i, achieved prominence as chiefs, being among those selected by Kamehameha to be his lieutenants and administrators in preference to traditional chiefs. About thirty of these men wrote narratives of their island experiences some of which are valuable sources of information about traditional Polynesian society. Amongst the most valuable are those by William Mariner, the clerk captured by Tongans in 1806 and saved from the massacre of his shipmates, James Morrison of the *Bounty*, who lived for two years on Tahiti after the famous mutiny, and Edward Robarts, a deserter in the Marquesas.

The beachcomber phase passed when economic, social and political changes altered the conditions of culture contact. Replacing it was a new development occurring when the sustained nature of the provisioning trade eventually created opportunities for ship-chandlers to establish themselves in Honolulu, Apia (Samoa) and Pape'ete (Tahiti). Whereas the beachcombers lived in island society on their hosts' terms, the new class of resident traders were to set themselves apart to pursue characteristically Western goals, becoming middle-men in general provisioning. This role, together with property acquisition, gave them influence with chiefs and often political power as well. Meanwhile, these men and the islanders themselves, the latter guided by missionary advisers, sought a more permanent, reliable basis for trade. The only possibilities seemed to involve European settlement and land alienation on a larger scale, and consequently dealing not with individual merchants but with companies.

Chapter Five

POLYNESIA: MISSIONARIES AND KINGDOMS

When the stream of foreigners first began to flow into the Pacific changes in island cultures and politics became inevitable. The acquisition of new weapons of war, new tools, new foodstuffs and new microbes was bound to have irreversible effects which would be catastrophic for some, and unsettling for all. The process and its impact was essentially uncontrolled and unplanned, as individuals of both races pursued their best interests according to their own values and preferences—peaceful or warlike, immoral or righteous, prudent or reckless.

One group sought to introduce order and control into the chaos of *laissez-faire* contact, and were motivated by the desire to do good for others, especially for the islanders. These were the missionaries who, whatever their personal shortcomings, had a goal which placed them apart from all other strangers.

The first wave of missionaries—and by far the most influential—were Protestants and were known as Evangelicals. Their theology was of the Reformation and the eighteenth century Wesleyan revival. They believed in the inherent sinfulness of humanity, the constancy and urgency of the contest between good and evil, and in the pressing need for all people to seek the salvation of the soul. Their conscience was the conscience of emergency, their perception was of a world of permanent disaster. Their ethics were of the Ten Commandments and St. Paul and they understood the scriptures as literally true and unalterable in every detail. European civilization, however imperfect, was also Christian civilization, and they understood Christian faith and practice to survive best in the context of European habits of settlement, work and social life.

In this last respect at least, there were points of comparison between themselves and the Polynesians: for both, religious ideas and observances pervaded life, and daily boons and misfortunes were likely to be understood within a framework of ideas of the supernatural. Moreover, in their desire to civilize as well as to

Christianize, the missionaries' plans overlapped with Polynesians' desires for European tools and skills to supplement or replace their own. In practice, the conjunction of interests and outlook was much harder to establish than these superficial similarities might imply, and the first missions were to face long years of frustration, heart-ache and failure.

The conversion of Oceania had been among the plans of the Spanish colonizing expeditions of 1567, 1596 and 1606. With the failure of those expeditions, nothing further was attempted until the Spaniards heard of the English and French discoveries of Tahiti. To assert Spanish claims to Pacific dominion, priests were sent there in 1772 and 1774. Nothing was achieved by these visits except perhaps a realization by the Spaniards of the difficulty of the task.

In 1795 a group of English Evangelicals, with the South Pacific particularly in mind, formed the Missionary Society, which promptly fitted out an expedition of twenty-five 'godly mechanics' and four ordained clergymen, together with the wives of six of the party and three children, who all arrived at Tahiti on 6 March 1797. About half the party was to be stationed on Tahiti, and the remainder divided between the Marquesas and Tonga.

This first Protestant attempt to introduce Christianity was a costly failure. Within a year the Marquesas mission was abandoned, and all but one missionary had withdrawn from Tahiti; within two years Tonga was abandoned after the murder of three men and the out-break of civil war. Of those missionaries who had left Tahiti, several soon returned, and were joined by reinforcements in 1801 to resume the mission, impoverished and neglected, and despised by European visitors and Tahitians alike for many years.

It was not until 1809, after years of widespread distress into which Tahiti had been plunged by its contact with Europeans, during which civil war and virtual anarchy had prevailed, and the population declined dramatically in number and condition, that a handful of low-born people would give the missionaries any serious atten-tion. Two more years were to pass before men of note showed interest in the new teaching. After that success and recognition came quickly; the numbers of adherents rapidly rose, and after the end of the civil wars in 1815, mass conversions of a people not closely instructed in Christianity posed new problems. With the establishment of settled government the devout but ill-educated missionaries found themselves called upon to advise on constitution and law-making, and to try to explain to a puzzled king that church affairs and matters of government should be kept separate.

At the same time as the Tahitian mission was scenting the prospect of success, the Anglican Church with its own Church Missionary

Society began the work of evangelizing New Zealand. Like their colleagues in Tahiti, these missionaries found the people disinclined to listen to their teaching, however much they appreciated their presence in other ways. The first missionaries landed in 1814, and twenty years were to pass before conversions began to occur; after 1835 the missionaries were embarrassed by the numbers wishing to join the new church.

While the London Missionary Society, thriving on its success in Tahiti, was beginning to spread the Word to eager audiences in the Tuamotu Islands to the east and the Leeward and Cook Islands to the west, an American counterpart was being formed: the American Board of Commissioners for Foreign Missions (A.B.C.F.M.). The Americans, in theology, morality and method, are scarcely to be distinguished from the English, and chose as their field of labour the Hawai'ian Islands.

Their first contingent arrived via the brig *Thaddeus* in 1820. For their purposes, the time could not have been better chosen. There had been a generation of peaceful, stable government since Kamehameha's great victory in 1796; trade and acculturation had progressed beyond the point (unlike Tonga or Tahiti) that the missionaries would be looked on mainly as a source of material goods; and finally, a religious and political revolution had already taken place in the overthrowing of the old gods with their demands and restrictions.

Initial suspicion of the missionaries' motives (allegations had been made that they were coming to take over the islands—which they were, although not in the sense intended by their accusers) was soon overcome; within two years a printing press was producing teaching material in the Hawai'ian language; and within four years—in 1826—the most powerful chiefs chose Christianity as their personal religion. By the 1830s Hawai'i was virtually a Christian nation. The success had been dramatic and sweeping despite misgivings about possibly shallow or short-lived conversions.

The A.B.C.F.M. then—in the early 1830s—turned its attention to the Marquesas, perhaps the most intransigent objective in Pacific mission history. Notwithstanding their success in Hawai'i, here their work was as fruitless as that of the London Missionary Society, which before it finally abandoned the place in 1842, made at least three beginnings there.

The Wesleyans, feeling the need for a society distinct from the interdenominational L.M.S., had formed their own Wesleyan Missionary Society in 1817 and sent their first missionaries to New Zealand and Tonga in 1822. New Zealand was big enough to accommodate rival missions (although jealousies and competition developed nevertheless) and Tonga had been untended since the L.M.S. debacle in 1799. This second start in Tonga was also short-lived, and a third unpromising start was made in 1826. The two men sent in 1826 were ill-prepared, did not get on well together, and did not attract the respect of the Tongans. Two years of strain, anxiety, hostility and fear passed slowly, aggravated by the tension between the two missionaries. Discouraged, and on the point of abandoning the mission, the two were reinforced in 1828. Among the newcomers was an older and experienced man, Nathaniel Turner, who saved the mission. Within a year the remarkable and rapid conversion of Tonga had made its tentative beginnings.

Not the least remarkable aspect of it was the achievement of the unpromising beginner of 1826—John Thomas, the man who (if any one may be singled out) was most responsible for the religious transformation of Tonga. He worked there for thirty years. The kindest thing the visiting mission supervisor could find to say of him in 1837 was that he was 'plodding and laborious'. Yet John Thomas surpassed them all—an exemplar of the fidelity and sincerity of one who gave his life to his cause. Thomas had been a blacksmith, converted in early manhood to the emotional Wesleyanism of his time; he served his evangelistic apprenticeship as a lay-preacher and class-leader in England. Feeling a call from God to become a missionary, he left his job, farewelled his family, married a woman several years his senior who was as dedicated as he was to the work of God, and sought ordination. Ordination was delayed—the mission board had doubts about this uncultivated working man, with his unimpressive manner and rudimentary literacy. Thomas might have been a caricaturist's evangelist, typical of the poor material from which the protestant missions had to choose. But this was the man who, forty years later, was reverently referred to as 'Father' Thomas, the self-educated translator of much of the Bible into Tongan. Just as Thomas transformed Tonga, so did Tonga transform Thomas. Uncouth and semi-literate when he began, he worked indefatigably day and night for the Tongans; travelling, preaching, urging, arguing, healing and teaching, sitting at his desk for long nights after a long day's work, studying, translating and praying, subjecting himself to a truly arduous regime which would have killed most men. His notes on Tongan traditions and the manuscript history of Tonga which he left, together with his detailed diaries in a prose which became increasingly graceful, are the main source for Tongan history before 1860—a monument to the remarkable life of a great but humble man.

Tonga, Tahiti and Hawai'i were to become the centres from which Christianity spread to other island groups. Initially the news and some rudiments of the new teaching were spread by pupils and new converts, leading to requests from island communities for European missionaries to be sent. This demand of course, could not be met; but increasingly, indigenous converts were trained as lay-teachers and sent out. Thus, the first teachers of Christianity in Fiji were Tahitians who made a short visit in 1827.

In 1830 the voyaging missionary John Williams, nominally stationed in Ra'iatea, took teachers from the Society Islands to Samoa. On this journey he discussed with the Wesleyans in Tonga a possible arrangement whereby Samoa be considered L.M.S. territory and Fiji be reserved for the W.M.S. in order to avoid wasteful duplication and competition. Williams later claimed to have made a formal agreement with the Wesleyans on this matter; the Wesleyans denied it. After waiting some years for European missionaries from the L.M.S, however, the Samoan chiefs repeatedly petitioned the Tongan mission, with the result that the very situation which Williams had tried to avoid, happened. In 1835 the Reverend Peter Turner went to Samoa to meet the urgent demand, and then in 1836 a party of L.M.S. missionaries arrived; both parties stayed (Turner was withdrawn in 1839), but with little cordiality between them. At the same time various Fijian chiefs were making the same requests of the Wesleyans in Tonga, promising protection and attention to the new teachings. In response, David Cargill and William Cross, together with their families, arrived on Lakeba island in Fiji in 1835. The acceptance of Christianity from both L.M.S. and W.M.S. teachers in Samoa was rapid; in Fiji, as in Tahiti a generation earlier, substantial progress had to await the end of protracted and destructive inter-tribal warfare almost twenty years later.

Across Polynesia therefore, the 1830s was a decade of wonderful optimism for missions. The field of labour was large, the work demanding, the challenge growing as the increasing visits of whaling ships throughout the Pacific presented more dilemmas of morality and good order, but at the same time success could be seen, felt and built on. Large numbers were filling the new churches in dozens of islands, the converts were being numbered in thousands and the prestige and influence of the missionaries stood high. Small wonder that the Reverend John Waterhouse on a tour of inspection of Wesleyan missions in 1837 wrote that he wished to be young again, that he might be able to share the labour of gathering in such a harvest.

After this first flush of enthusiasm, however, not many years were to pass before backsliding, disillusionment and hypocrisy were to become the subject of complaint. The work came to be seen as more arduous and less rewarding; in England during the late 1840s, the collection of monies for the support of missions and the recruitment of men to become missionaries became increasingly difficult. The new island churches settled into a state of uncomfortable complacency with a native clergy under white leadership, while the Polynesian congregations accommodated themselves to the different demands which Christianity made of them, and adjusted Christianity to suit the patterns of thought and habits of life which they preserved from their pre-Christian past.

The success of the missionaries in converting the populations of Polynesia may be attributed to a combination of various causes. First, when a major chief converted, his people had little option but to follow his lead; in this way, many conversions were undoubtedly insincere or short-lived. Second, there was a considerable popular movement in favour of Christianity similar to mass-movements of revival elsewhere. Third, the people were willing to listen to the missionaries' message of salvation and reform because of the acute stresses caused by the changes to which they were being exposed.

These changes had three major causes, hardship, disease and population imbalance. Hardship and distress were characteristic of the early contact period during which civil wars were waged with a frequency, ferocity and mortality not previously known. Introduced diseases—elephantiasis, measles, whooping cough, tuberculosis, influenza and venereal diseases—swept most islands in repeated waves. Furthermore, large numbers of young men were eager to ship with the whalers to see the world; many of them never returned, others were absent for years at a time, upsetting the patterns of community work and food production as well as marriage and reproductive patterns.

The people's work and food supplies were further disturbed by the new commerce: producing food for sale rather than consumption, and producing goods (cargoes of sandalwood or *bêche-de-mer*) which were not related at all to the traditional, subsistence economy. The stresses of these changes led to demoralization, which in turn encouraged some to listen sympathetically to missionaries, just as it encouraged others to an exasperated demand for salvation and relief in the present.

Moreover, this same distress, especially if accompanied by military defeat and political disadvantage, was a clear proof of the decay of the community's *mana* and that of its chief. If the traditional ceremonial and political remedies (that is, a change of leadership) failed to rectify matters it could easily be concluded that the gods had abandoned their people. Hints of agnosticism among the chiefs, neglect of ceremonies and sacred places, and in Hawai'i the abolition of the *tapu* and overthrowing of the idols, are all indicative of this frame of mind. This might lead people to a permanent state of agnosticism, but with the presence of missionaries among a people with a strong religious tradition it is more likely that the people should come to believe the new teaching which seemed so much to be addressed to their present condition.

Throughout Polynesia, the missionaries found that they were required to play a wider role than merely spreading the Gospel. Their own definition of their task included teaching, for Christianity was the religion of 'the book'. As heirs of the Reformation they believed firmly that the Bible was the only reliable guide to God's teachings and will, and that it was imperative that every seeker after truth be able to read and search God's will himself. Private study and contemplation were daily practices of the missionaries which they also vigorously commended to their audiences. This was one of the distinguishing features of Protestantism: that every believer could come to know personally the perfect sources of Christian doctrine and not have to depend on any imperfect human agency. In this way, holding classes in reading and writing for adults as well as children was one of the first tasks the missionaries set themselves.

This, however, presupposed a knowledge in each island group of the local language, and the existence of an orthography. To the missionaries is due the credit for reducing the languages of the Pacific to written form by classifying the sound system and fitting it to a modified alphabet, and thus preserving the linguistic heritage of the people. This task initially was more difficult than anyone imagined. The Church Missionary Society in New Zealand enlisted in 1818 the assistance of Samuel Lee, an authority on linguistics at the University of Cambridge (and subsequently Professor of Arabic and Professor of Hebrew), but the missionaries on Tahiti worked unaided in isolation and laid the foundation for all subsequent language work throughout Polynesia. Years of work were necessary before they could preach in Tahitian and begin the slow and laborious work of translating the scriptures. Once translated, the manuscripts had to be sent to New South Wales or England for printing; eventually the missions acquired their own presses and became printers and publishers as well.

While doing all this, the missionaries were also called on to attend the sick with such rudimentary medicines and amateurish medical skills as they had. This work, sometimes successful and continually in demand, not only helped to establish relations of friendship and obligation between missionaries and people, but was occasionally instrumental in making converts.

This work of teaching, healing and preaching, and especially the message of ethical conduct and sincerity, conveyed to the Polynesians an impression of good-will and disinterested goodness. Accordingly, the missionaries everywhere were consulted for advice on the ticklish political problems which were inevitable in the 1820s and later.

These problems emerged from the ever-changing relations between Europeans and islanders during a period when Europeans were becoming less inclined to acknowledge indigenous authority. Out of the chaos of the rapid political changes of the late eighteenth century, and the radical social changes of the early nineteenth, new political forms began to emerge in Polynesia.

Tahiti

Between 1767 and the 1790s in Tahiti, the Pomare family, which had been pursuing the traditional goals of titles and honorific insignia, had been saved from a decline into political obscurity by the patronage of a succession of explorers and other visitors. With these revived fortunes and by adroit political manoeuvring in the early years of the new century, the family was able to advance its position further with the acquisition of several important titles attached to the person of Pomare II (ca. 1782-1821). By 1808, however, the jealousies of other noble families combined with resentment at Pomare's pretensions to govern Tahiti led to his military defeat and retreat to the nearby island of Eimeo (later called Mo'orea). In defeat, Pomare paid closer attention to the teachings of the missionaries, concerned perhaps at the apparent decay in his own *mana* and the loss of the favour of 'Oro demonstrated by his own fall. At the same time, he called for reinforcements from his kinsmen in the Leeward Islands (Ra'iatea, Bora Bora and Huahine) where he also held titles. As years passed, Pomare was able to return to Tahiti to fulfil his ceremonial functions, but not to rule. In 1815, however, he was there with a large body of armed supporters when his rivals and enemies decided that he needed to be checked again, along with the Christian teaching with which he and his party were now identified.

The resulting Battle of Feipi on 12 November 1815 was an overwhelming victory for Pomare. The greater marvel, however, was the restraint of the victors: there followed no pursuit of the defeated, no massacre, no pillage nor any destruction of property. Pomare's victory seemed indeed to be a victory for Christian ethics. Pomare, however, was determined to *rule*. He set his own nominees over the tribes of Tahiti, and with the abolition of traditional gods and social controls, looked for a new basis for government and good order. He turned to the missionaries: there was no-one else, and these were the men who in good faith had spent twenty years teaching, exhorting and praying for the spiritual and temporal good of his people; since God gave laws for human conduct, the missionaries could advise on laws for Tahiti.

This request was certainly more than the missionaries had expected when they set out. They had not then seen themselves as potential constitutional advisers, and did not now consider themselves able to advise. Several times during 1816, 1817 and 1818, Pomare asked for advice, or asked for comment on his own ideas; the missionaries would give nothing more than advice and opinions and insisted that the King make his own laws. He did indeed reject some of the opinions of the missionaries, for example that he should have a council of senior chiefs to discuss and approve any proposed laws.

At last, in September 1819, Pomare announced his laws to the people. They were few and simple: injunctions for the protection of life and property, observance of the Sabbath, the sanctity of marriage and the provision of courts and judges to enforce and uphold the laws. The missionaries were disappointed with the limited scope of the laws, but nevertheless the code, though a modest achievement, was a notable one. For the first time in Polynesia there was a written code of law: justice was set apart from whim, the poor were protected and the mighty restrained, and the idea of the rule of law established. That at least was the achievement in theory: breaking the habits of authority and the habits of mind which this revolution necessitated was to be a slow, erratic and painful process, which would not be finished before the Tahitians lost their political independence. Pomare himself did not live long enough to guide this tentative political experiment, and his death on 7 December 1821 brought the missionaries into greater political prominence as the educators and unofficial regents for his infant son, who was crowned three years later as Pomare III.

Meanwhile, in 1820 and 1822 respectively, Ra'iatea and Huahine, while vaguely recognizing the leadership of Pomare, had introduced law codes of their own, including among other things checks on the power of the king, trial by jury, and a regular system of taxation to replace the former capricious levies. In 1824, these codes provided a basis for the new Tahitian constitution which provided for a parliament elected by manhood suffrage. In that respect at least, the Society Islands were rivalled in liberalism only by the United States of America.

Visitors to Tahiti in the 1820s and 1830s, dismayed at the new morality which was then enforced, were apt to see Tahiti as a theocracy and to attribute to the missionaries an authority and intolerance which made Tahiti sound like a priest-ridden, Calvinist despotism. The missionaries, for their part, were anxious to have no such power, but were dismayed that the king, regent and queen successively, took their advice so little, and that the judges and chiefs were so merciless and inflexible in their interpretation and enforcement of law. After the death of the child-king Pomare III in 1827, the missionaries lamented even more the lightness of their impact. Pomare III was succeeded by his seventeen year-old sister, 'Aimata, who took the name Pomare IV. The queen, mainly under the malign influence of her great-aunt, remained for some years deaf to the missionaries, neglected the government, and tried to revive pagan ceremonies, thereby provoking vigorous opposition from the great chiefs.

The resulting misgovernment, erratic law enforcement and increasing discontent of both Tahitians and the small but growing number of European residents, made reform necessary to avoid a crisis. Such a crisis was postponed, however, because of the assistance of a new missionary, the charming and energetic George Pritchard, who became the queen's confidant and adviser after 1831. She needed him, for over the next ten years her own modest gifts of intellect and resolution were not equal to the difficulties posed by chiefs who resented her authority, and by traders and a consul who sought to embarrass her for their own political or commercial gain. A succession of crises in the late 'thirties over law enforcement, land ownership, trade regulations, and the residence of Catholic priests, finally brought a confrontation with the government of France in which neither the advice of missionaries, nor the structure of government inherited from Pomare II were of any use. In 1842 Tahiti became in name a French protectorate, in practice a French possession.

Hawai'i

In Hawai'i, meanwhile, a similar pattern of events was unfolding. A strong, single government had been established there by Kamehameha long before the missionaries of the A.B.C.F.M. arrived. He had been succeeded in 1819 by his son, Liholiho, who under the formidable and irresistible influence of Kamehameha's favourite wife, Ka'ahumanu, had abolished religion and *tapu*, and was ruling as best he could over restless chiefs and oppressed people with only the inherited authority of an *ali'i-nui* (paramount chief). The situation could not last long. With the abolition of religion the regime had no continuing legitimacy other than the inheritance of Kamehameha's victories and the willingness of some subjects to subdue those who wished to rebel.

Liholiho died in 1824 on a visit to England where he had hoped to cement earlier promises of English protection and benevolence. The accession of his younger brother, Kauikeaouli, who was only about twelve years of age, meant several years of regency under the aegis of the still-powerful Ka'ahumanu. It was a dangerous time in the history of a nation with tremendous social changes taking place, and a growing foreign population inclined to be contemptuous of native claims to nationhood.

In 1822 notices were printed in Hawai'i prohibiting the boisterous conduct of visiting sailors. These, in a sense, were the first laws. Knowing that these laws were manifestly inadequate, the recently-converted chiefs asked the missionaries for advice. As in Tahiti, the chiefs got advice, not legal draughtmanship; they had asked the missionaries if the Ten Commandments were a suitable basis for law, and accordingly compiled in 1824 a list of injunctions modelled on them. Over the next few years piecemeal laws were added, but there was no constitution to prescribe how or by whom laws were to be made, or what principle made a pronouncement law. A succession of visiting naval officers, English, American and French, prompted by incidents or legal defects, gave the Hawai'ian government advice about laws and law making, and although constant adjustments were made, including a new code of law in 1835, no comprehensive system existed which would satisfy the turbulent foreign residents or the quarrelsome consuls or the pedantic and protocol-sensitive naval commanders. Nor were the missionaries wholly satisfied as they responded to appeals for advice which was then only partly accepted.

By the mid-1830s, the king and ruling chiefs were becoming increasingly harassed by opinionated foreigners who claimed exemption from the laws of the land. At the centre of this harassment were the questions of land tenure (because traders and investors felt insecure with only a traditional Polynesian tenure), and law enforcement; consequently in 1836, the chiefs requested the missionaries to find a teacher of government who could instruct them in constitutional and legal matters.

After almost two years of frustration and disappointment in trying to find such a person, one of the missionaries, the Reverend William Richards, agreed to do the job, and resigned from the mission in 1838. The result of his lectures was a Declaration of Rights and Code of Civil Law in 1839 to supplement the existing criminal provisions, and in 1840 a constitution: the first formal definition of the form of government, providing for a house of representatives, a supreme court, definition of the roles of officials, procedures for constitutional amendment and the rights of the people.

These reforms were drafted by mission-educated Hawai'ians and were polished with the advice of the missionaries. Foreigners for the most part were not pleased: they saw in the laws indirect government by priests, or at best such an ascendancy of missionary views in the minds of the Hawai'ians that it amounted to the same thing. What the foreigners wanted, however, was no native government at all; or if there must be one, it should be one in which their own interests were paramount. There was therefore no-one else but the missionaries to give the king and his chiefs the advice they sought; given the needs of the Hawai'ians at that time and in the future, and given the moral and intellectual context of the early nineteenth century, the missionaries' influence was timely and appropriate.

Their role as political advisers was not finished with the constitution of 1840. The next objective of the government was to secure international recognition, and in this and other tasks for many years into the future, ex-missionaries and other Europeans were appointed as cabinet ministers, ambassadors and public servants, some of them serving comparatively selflessly and with distinction.

Tonga

The island group which appeared to be most under missionary domination was neither Hawai'i nor the Society Islands, but Tonga, where the comparative absence of European settlers during the formative years of government meant that they exerted little influence. In the absence of settlers and bullying consuls, and the absence of any cause for 'gunboat diplomacy', the only model provided for the Tongans in nation-building was that provided by the missionaries.

The revolution among the aristocracy in the late eighteenth century had seen a Tu'i Tonga humiliated, a woman seize the office of Tu'i Kanokupolu, the title of Tu'i Ha'atakalaua left unclaimed for years and finally the murder in 1799 of the Tu'i Kanokupolu, Tuku'aho. Subsequently, a white pig was installed as Tu'i Kanokupolu by Finau 'Ulukalala, demonstrating this powerful chief's contempt for the old order which was now clearly defunct. Various men held the office of Tu'i Kanokupolu over the next quarter of a century, all of them without commensurate authority, and for half that time the title was not claimed at all. Meanwhile there was no Tu'i Ha'atakalaua, and the Tu'i Tonga was not formally installed. By

1820 the fighting had ceased, and the Tongan kingdom became a collection of independent tribes, with no chief willing and able to establish a universal authority.

During this process, there were no missionaries in Tonga; by 1827, however, the Wesleyan missionaries were beginning to influence Aleamotu'a who in that year was installed as Tu'i Kanokupolu. Aleamotu'a, or Josiah as he became after his baptism the following year, was a weak candidate with a fair genealogical claim as Tuku'aho's brother, but could command no great authority. His possession of the title, combined with his own weakness, provided an opportunity later for his nephew Taufa'ahau to claim the right to govern a re-united Tonga. At this time, however, he had only recently accomplished the conquest of the central part of Tonga, and had become Tu'i Ha'apai. On his uncle's advice he listened to mission teachings and accepted a Tongan convert, Pita Vi, to teach him. By 1831 he had been baptised, had become a class leader and lay preacher, and an instrument in the rapid conversion of his people, and those of the northern group, Vava'u.

Two years later in 1833, the death of 'Ulukalala, the Christian chief of Vava'u, gave Taufa'ahau an opportunity to further expand his power; he had been nominated by 'Ulukalala as his successor, and he backed his claim with a large show of force. Taufa'ahau thus became Tu'i Vava'u. Tonga was now close to re-unification, but the most powerful and most independent chiefs were those of Tongatapu where Taufa'ahau's uncle, the Tu'i Kanokupolu, was virtually powerless. These chiefs, however, were careful to give Taufa'ahau, or King George as he was now called, few excuses to interfere in their affairs.

Intent though he was on conquest and reunification, George nevertheless was a pious and conscientious king faced with the same dilemma that the Pomares and Kamehamehas had already confronted. He needed a new legitimacy for government and new instruments for its conduct. Like his counterparts elsewhere, he turned for advice to the Word of God and its teachers. The result was a code of laws for Vava'u, enforced during 1838, but not formally promulgated for a year. Like its counterparts elsewhere, it was modelled on biblical injunctions, but was more explicit than the first steps elsewhere in limiting the power of the chiefs. The chiefs were subject to court and judge in the same manner as commoners and only the judges had the prerogative of passing judgment and sentence. Most of the laws in the eight-item code may be called morality laws; they sought to remove the cause of quarrels and more serious crimes, and by requiring all to work, struck at the idleness which missionaries condemned as the root of mischief.

Between the promulgation of this code and its successor in 1850, King George waged war on Tongatapu in 1840 to curb the restless independence of the heathen chiefs there, and in 1845 succeeded his uncle as Tu'i Kanokupolu. War and inheritance thus made him king of a re-united Tonga. Before long he was asking the missionaries for advice on an improved law code. Aware of their own shortcomings, they advised him to seek advice in another quarter; so with their help he wrote to the Chief Justice of New Zealand, and was referred to the Society Islands codes of the 1820s. After further consultations with various chiefs, George issued a new code in 1850 which clarified and expanded the previous one. Under it, the king remained supreme—the only form of government and source of law. Challenges to his authority, however, had not yet finished, and a further civil war on Tongatapu was waged in 1852.

After suppressing this last outbreak, George then turned to the problem of securing international recognition, as his Hawai'ian counterpart had done after issuing the constitution of 1840. He knew well enough the fate of the Tahitian kingdom in 1842, and had recently had encounters with the French navy himself over the same issue—the treatment of Roman Catholic priests. Future constitutional development therefore was a response both to his desire for good government, and the need to win the respect of nations and thus preserve Tonga's independence. The new law code of 1862 should be seen against this diplomatic background.

For the 1862 law code, George was determined to obtain wider advice than the missionaries could give him. He corresponded with various authorities, including Sir George Grey, Governor of New Zealand, and travelled to Australia in 1853. George's constitutional experiments had to be made slowly and cautiously for not only had he become estranged from the older generation of missionaries, but he also faced resistance from the chiefs as he strove to shift their opinions his way. At this time, moreover, he was being harassed by Roman Catholic priests and their allies of the French Navy. The new code confirmed much of the old, including the absolute supremacy of the king, but introduced some important innovations: the emancipation of the people from serfdom, compulsory education of children, regular taxation, and new principles of land distribution. Delayed though it was, it was a bold step.

Elsewhere in Polynesia kingdoms under missionary influence did not evolve at this time. In Samoa and Fiji (the political culture of which was Polynesian rather than Melanesian), political unification was not so readily established and had to await a further stage in European penetration. The Marquesas, annexed by the

French in 1842, had been prevented by geographical fragmentation and pronounced tribal jealousies from even attempting unification. In New Zealand the wars of the two great chiefs, Te Rauparaha and Hongi Hika, fought in the 1820s and 1830s, brought only chaos, and provided no basis for extra-tribal developments in government. Conversion to Christianity began to sweep the country in the 1830s, and although a powerless British official, James Busby, tried to establish a confederation of northern tribes, a stable and larger political unit was created only by British annexation in 1840. Disunity drained possible power from Maori hands, and New Zealand became a settlers' country.

In the Cook Islands the various islands were each brought under a single ruler, but there was no attempt to unite them. The islanders' enthusiastic embrace of Christianity in the 1820s was soon reflected in law codes similar to those developed elsewhere in Polynesia. Further influences of change were retarded by prohibitions on land alienation and inter-racial marriage. For a generation, the Cook Islanders were ruled by a strict code vigorously enforced by their own chiefs, before the whaling industry eroded their isolation.

Through most of Polynesia, the islanders had managed to continue their existing political traditions, but the momentum of change had been redirected and accelerated. The unification of Tonga, Tahiti and Hawai'i would probably not have occurred without European contact, although such unification was not planned by any influential European. The missionaries so far served their people well: ill-educated and poor, they had nevertheless by their teaching and advice promoted peace and good order. Their medicines and the knowledge of writing which they brought were of incalculable benefit to the Polynesians during a period of severe stress. Their partnership with the Polynesians earned them much contemporary enmity and subsequent criticism but for the most part they were men for, as well as of, their times.

Chapter Six

POLYNESIA: EUROPEAN SETTLEMENT AND THE LATER KINGDOMS

The establishment of the Polynesian kingdoms was the culmination of pre-European stresses in island society, in conjunction with the needs and opportunities presented by contact with Europeans. Political centralization satisfied individual ambitions but also simplified the developing relationship with Europeans, both visitors and settlers.

This relationship increasingly needed to be brought under control. For the first few decades of contact the main regulating principle was self-interest; in every island group the pursuit of self-interest had led to incidents of plunder and massacre, the blame sometimes resting with the islanders, sometimes with the ship-people. Occasionally, especially in New Zealand and Hawai'i, the ship-people became involved in island wars as the allies or accessories of one faction or another. In addition there were petty incidents of violence which were the result of fear, ignorance, misunderstanding or carelessness. For the most part, however, the desire for trade enforced peace and tolerably fair dealing, which carried over and continued to prevail when ship-people became shore dwellers.

By the 1820s with the increasing volume of shipping throughout Polynesia, various anchorages became favoured places of resort. To these places gravitated beachcombers with varying motives, including escaping from their tarnished island paradises, seeking news of 'home', or obtaining supplies of European goods. Sailors wishing to leave ship life behind them increased with the numbers of ships, and added their numbers to the settlements which grew along the beach of the most hospitable anchorage in each island group.

Circumstances of indigenous politics, island geography and European commerce determined that several of these communities would achieve greater prominence: Honolulu in Hawai'i, Pape'ete in Tahiti, Levuka in Fiji, Kororareka in New Zealand, and almost two decades behind the others, Apia in Samoa.

In the early years dependence on Polynesian chiefs for protection, and on popular acceptance for most other needs of life, was a guarantee of peaceful and trouble free residence. Over a period of two or three decades, these communities of Europeans rose in population from a handful to several dozens, and in the case of Honolulu quickly mounted into the hundreds. Initially these men were not colonists and did not consider themselves such. They were not the bringers of civilization nor the founders of overseas empire; they merely eked out a living in the fringe area between ships and villages as occasionally-employed pilots, blacksmiths, interpreters, carriers, carpenters, boat-builders, coopers, or at any other trade for which there might be call. Unlike the earlier beachcombers who became assimilated Polynesians, these men spent most of their time in idleness, and that often meant drinking.

As shipping and settlement grew, so did commercial opportunities. Merchants arrived, trading on their own account or representing established firms from the cities of eastern North America or western South America, to facilitate the extraction of island products or to re-supply ships with imported supplies of iron, cordage or canvas. As commerce grew, so did the means of social differentiation within the settler communities; leaders in community wealth and property emerged, and became leaders in community opinion, and began to perceive (perhaps for the first time) that their interests and those of native chiefs did not perfectly coincide. Indeed, they might be quite opposed.

The first issue on which this opposition became apparent concerned the security of property, as might be expected of representatives of a materialistic civilization. The right of land-ownership, the security of movable property against theft or damage, and the obligations of debt-ridden chiefs provided incentives and opportunities to challenge the authority of chiefs and the powers of the inchoate governments which they were attempting to establish.

In Honolulu the two consuls, John C. Jones for the United States and Richard Charlton for Britain, led the assault in the 1820s and '30s. Both were merchants, neither had any respect for the Hawai'ian rulers and both were concerned above all for their own dignities and material well-being. Charlton in particular was a coarse, choleric, intemperate, violent fellow, obsessed with litigation, alternately plaintiff and respondent in a succession of cases involving violence and slander. On three notorious occasions, 1829, 1836 and 1843, his conduct invited foreign intervention in Hawai'ian affairs. The second occasion led Hawai'i into a disadvantageous treaty with Britain, and the third, sparked by an acrimonious law suit over land, led to the attempted but unratified annexation of Hawai'i to Britain by an English naval officer, Lord George Paulet.

Contemporary with Charlton in Honolulu, a Belgian, Jacques-Antoine Moerenhout, successful merchant and principal of a modest trade-empire in the south-east Pacific, was in turn United States and French consul in Tahiti. Possessed of the charm which Charlton lacked, Moerenhout was equally ruthless and far more dangerous. Exploiting a clumsy Tahitian attempt to refuse residence to French Catholic priests, he urged official French intervention and assisted the high-handed actions of the French Admiral Abel Du Petit-Thouars in demanding reparations, imposing an unequal treaty and finally in 1842, imposing an unwanted protectorate status on Tahiti.

In the 1850s an American consul in Fiji, John Brown Williams, employed a similar strategy, inflating claims for alleged property damage into massive debts which pliable naval captains, in particular Commander E.B. Boutwell in 1855, were persuaded to attach to the pretended authority of Cakobau as the paramount chief of Fiji, in order to claim damages from him. This preposterous debt was subsequently to become one of the considerations leading the Fijian chiefs to cede Fiji to Britain, first in 1858, and again in 1874.

These notorious and conspicuous examples of challenges to indigenous authority and independence were symptomatic of growing settler confidence and impatience with the uncertainties and irregularities of the early island governments. Settlers with property demanded a structure of laws to define and secure their wealth and the means of increasing it. Its absence, and the transparent failings of the governors of the largest island nations brought those authorities into contempt. Hence the settlers sought and welcomed both the naval intervention and the succession of dictated, unequal treaties of the age. As they watched these tragi-comedies unfold, they became emboldened to make further demands and to elevate their own pretensions.

These swelling ambitions were measured and advertised by symbols of civilization which turned the settlements into colonial outposts: the importation of white women as wives to replace native liaisons, the emergence of social stratification among the settlers, the introduction of formal courtesies such as visiting cards, the use of silver dinner services, the advertising of changing European fashions in clothing, imported furniture, grand houses of weatherboard with corrugated iron roofs; all marked a new social self-sufficiency in the settler communities and a growing gulf of identity and interest between them and the host Polynesian societies. Segregated bathing areas, the formal Victorian picnic, and the public amenities of paved roads, bridges and jetties, of public libraries, cultural organizations and social clubs showed that these settlers were now the evangelists of civilization and white supremacy, and no longer merely its fringe-dwellers.

Hawai'i

In Hawai'i where a single unified government had been established on native initiative, the community of settlers was eager to influence the government in its own interests. Elsewhere, the settlers felt that they had to take the initiative in creating stable government—again, in their own interests. Regular laws and the consistent application of them was the first requirement. That came in Hawai'i in 1840 with a constitution, followed quickly by attempts to standardize land leases, and a code of civil law. As the trade boom generated by the whaling industry rose to a short-lived peak, accompanied by an increasing emigration of young Hawai'ian men (several thousand are estimated to have left the country in the late 1840s, and five hundred a year in the 1850s), investors in Hawai'i became as worried about a labour supply as they were about land. The native Hawai'ian population was declining steadily and epidemics in the late 1840s seemed to confirm a trend. Moreover, the native Hawai'ians were seen by would-be plantation-proprietors as unwilling or unsuitable for plantation work. Extensive reforms were called for, and the Hawai'ian government, seeing that economic development in the hands of Europeans represented its best chance for prosperity and political survival, took the necessary steps. Importation of foreign labour was authorized in a tentative beginning, and in 1848 native land holdings were individualized.

This last measure was truly revolutionary. It was the first step in 'The Great Mahele' whereby traditional communal rights to land were abolished, breaking the old feudal, serf-like relationship of commoner to chief and land. The native Hawai'ian now might claim his own block of land to sell if he wished or to hold if he could, and no longer owed labour to his chief; as a potentially landless peasant, he then became a potential labourer on a European-managed plantation. Despite this often tragic consequence, the Great Mahele was not quite the act of national betrayal which it might seem: national survival and economic development demanded land; the native population had declined to a mere fraction of its former numbers and much land was locked up in unproductive, inaccessible idleness. Twentieth-century development experts have since recommended similar reforms in Melanesia. It was a choice between preserving native culture and national survival; since the first seemed doomed anyway, there was no real choice; the land was unlocked.

The path of economic development was even then not smoothed. Later steps included allowing fee-simple ownership of land for foreigners. When this was implemented in 1852, the speculator and investor alike could be more optimistic. With imported labour, a Masters and Servants Act, and a free land market, Hawai'ian economic development still lacked two other necessary things: capital and markets. Without the latter, the first would stay scarce. The gold rush in California in 1849 served to cushion the onset of the depression which was to accompany the decline of the whaling trade, but large scale access to American markets was restricted by American tariff policies. Two solutions presented themselves: a trade reciprocity treaty with the United States, or annexation to the United States; the first was achieved after a quarter of a century of trial and disappointment; the second suggestion was floated as regularly as economic difficulty and native Hawai'ian assertiveness in politics commended it to the mainly American settlers.

Much of Hawai'ian politics in the second half of the nineteenth century was concerned with these same basic issues in greater complexity: how to make Hawai'i attractive to foreign investment and especially to planter interests; how to maintain the supply of labour without provoking racial animosities or social evils; how to secure and ensure continued access to American markets; and finally, how to maintain the pride and dignity of a native monarchy which too easily became the object of settler ridicule or hostility. In trying to satisfy these requirements, King Kamehameha III worked and worried himself to death in 1854; his successors Kamehameha IV (Alexander) and Kamehameha V (Lot) conducted ambivalent and vacillating reigns of about a decade each; Lunalilo, a notorious drinker, survived less than a year. Kalakaua, the most flamboyant monarch, reigned from 1873 to 1891 through a period of growing national indebtedness and threatened revolution from both white 'reformers' and Hawai'ian conservatives. His world tour, lavish coronation and monumental building programme gave his regime style, but could not over-awe the inflated vanity of the planter society which was increasingly infected by the European mood of racial superiority and the American imperialist mood of manifest destiny. When he died in 1891 he bequeathed to his sister Liliuokalani a troubled kingdom and an unsteady throne, neither of which lasted long. Within two years, Liliuokalani had been overthrown, the victim of a conspiracy of a handful of fire-brand whites, who were encouraged by the U.S. consul and abetted by a U.S. naval captain. A republic was established and Sanford J. Dole, an eminent planter and son of a missionary, the most moderate of the very conservative revolutionaries, became the nation's president.

The kingdom established by Kamehameha the Conqueror had lasted almost one hundred years. That it should have survived for so long in the age of European expansion owed much to great power rivalries and the fact that it had been well-served by its missionary advisers; but in the last analysis its survival depended on its fostering the development which would ultimately cause its downfall.

Tonga

The only other Polynesian kingdom to retain both its political integrity and its independence till the end of the century was Tonga, which (perhaps it is no coincidence) was the only other highly stratified Polynesian society. Unlike Hawai'i, Tonga had little to attract European settlement and so was not subject to such destabilizing influences. Like Hawai'i, the kingdom was established by a man who lived to a great age, and was able to provide effective government through successive crises. If Kamehameha III who died in his early forties had been as long lived as his father, the Hawai'ian government might have been better able to deal with the crises of the second half of the century. Tonga had only three monarchs in a period of 120 years, from 1845 to 1965. Taufa'ahau or King George, born in the year 1798, personally dominated Tongan politics from the 1830s until his death at the age of 95 in 1893. This longevity was a powerful factor in ensuring Tonga's successful adaptation to modernity. And like Hawai'i again, Tonga was the beneficiary of great-power jealousies.

In the 1850s, fresh from his final conquest of the independently-minded Tongatapu chiefs, King George could turn from the problem of national unity to the problem of independence. By weakening the power of the chiefs, the constitution of 1862 further guaranteed internal stability; it was hoped that its other provisions would command international respect and obtain recognition. International respect was denied rather than admitted in the unequal treaty forced on him by the French in 1855; a fairer treaty with another power was still a long way off.

Until the early 1850s, George had frequently consulted the Wesleyan missionaries when he felt he needed advice, but during that decade he became increasingly detached from them in political matters. This growing distance was bridged between 1860 and 1862 by the Reverend Shirley Baker, a new, young missionary who despite his humble origins and lack of education was to become the king's partner for nearly thirty years.

The reforms contained in the 1862 constitution stimulated Tongan cash cropping, and also attracted merchants. The resulting development coupled with the old concerns moved the king to seek a new constitution. For this, he consulted Baker who helped him to frame the new constitution, promulgated in 1875. This constitution, comparatively liberal for its time, established a legislative assembly with twenty of its forty members popularly elected, and was one of three measures which Baker and the king devised to give the Tongan kingdom a more secure political and economic footing. The second measure attempted to establish an independent Tongan church to supersede the Wesleyan mission; this was not achieved at this time, but a large measure of autonomy was granted which satisfied Tongan nationalism and reduced the amount of money being sent out of the kingdom in mission contributions. The third measure was a treaty of friendship with the German empire.

Germans were late comers in the Pacific, but since the middle 'fifties vigour and commercial boldness led by the Godeffroy company of Hamburg had given them a major share in the commercial development of the central Pacific area. The coconut oil trade, and the copra trade which was replacing it, were largely in the hands of Godeffroys. German settlers were developing plantations in Fiji and Samoa, and a handful of traders and would-be planters had become established in Tonga as well. After the unification of Germany had been completed in 1871, and the new state had assumed the dignity of empire, vessels of the German navy joined those of other nations in patrolling the Pacific and supporting the ambitions of their own nationals. German ambition made a useful counterpoise for Baker and King George to weigh against the belligerence of France and the casual indifference of Britain to which the mission-influenced Polynesians looked (usually in vain) for protection and patronage. A Tongan-German treaty of friendship was concluded in 1876, granting Germany the use of the Tongan harbour at Vava'u for a coaling station in exchange for recognition of Tongan nationhood.

Tonga's twin aims were realized: not only was recognition by a great power thus secured, but the British government was now obliged to seek a treaty on similar terms. This treaty was ratified in 1879.

Baker's service to Tonga, however satisfactory it was to the king, antagonized both his mission colleagues and the small community of European settlers, including the British consular agent to whom Baker seemed a vehicle of German influence. The mission decided that an inquiry and disciplinary action were called for, and despite Baker's impenetrable defence he was recalled from Tonga in 1879. King George, however, was not to be deprived so easily of so useful a servant, and in 1880, when Baker reappeared in Tonga escorting the body of the king's son who had died in Auckland, George appointed him Prime Minister. For all the political influence commonly and popularly ascribed to missionaries in the new states of Polynesia in the nineteenth century, this was the only case outside Hawai'i where a missionary (or ex-missionary as Baker had now become) possessed real power.

Baker proved an energetic and resourceful prime minister: taxes were regularised, increased and collected, government schools were established, and land was apportioned more equitably. Baker's policy, like that of the king, was 'Tonga for the Tongans', and he did not please the small settler community. Many of the chiefs objected to his democratic reforms, and the commoners also felt the pinch of his sumptuary laws and morality laws.

Baker was also the man to do for Tonga as prime minister what he had failed to achieve as a missionary in 1874. In 1885 the Free Church of Tonga was proclaimed, and severed from the Wesleyan mission. This was a political move, not a theological or doctrinal issue, and was important to the Tongan government sensitive about its independence. This step proved to be the turning point in Baker's career: a significant minority of Tongans insisted that they remain members of the Wesleyan Church. Since the matter was one of politics and obedience to the king rather than a matter of doctrine and private conscience, the government was willing to use force. Dissidents in public office were dismissed, land-holders dispossessed, citizens flogged or harassed in other ways.

The persecution lasted only a few months before the king put a stop to it, but it was followed several months later by an attempted assassination of Baker. The attempt probably had nothing to do directly with the Free Church affair, but it led to another burst of anti-Wesleyan brutality which observers called religious persecution. Baker meanwhile became uncharacteristically careless and intemperate in the aftermath, eventually accusing the British consul of complicity in the attempted murder.

Baker had never been popular with British officials and the High Commissioner for the Western Pacific, Sir John Thurston, was glad of the opportunity thus presented to intervene. With superficial regard for Tongan sovereignty, he persuaded King George that Baker had exceeded reasonable limits of conduct; Baker was dismissed, and Thurston had him removed from the kingdom.

With this ignominious end to a distinguished career of service, Baker sank into obscurity, but his long partnership with the long-lived king had ensured Tongan independence. By the time he left Tonga in 1890, new reforms in both law and administration were necessary, thus opening the door for official British intervention in Tongan politics. The end result was a protectorate under a new Treaty of Friendship with Britain in 1900, in a deal between the imperialist powers which divided the Pacific into several spheres of interest.

Economic development and settler agitation had undermined Hawai'ian independence; Tonga had been spared the worst of these pressures; Fiji and Samoa lacked Tonga's advantages, and so shared Hawai'i's fate.

Fiji

Fiji in the years of the *bêche-de-mer* trade (1828-35 and 1842-50) became increasingly enmeshed in warfare between the great *matanitu* or kingdoms. Bau strove to extend and reinforce its influence over the islands in and around the Koro Sea; Rewa maintained its hegemony over eastern Viti Levu; and the northern states of Bua and Macuata tried to assert their independence. Into this complicated and confusing chaos of warfare and political manoeuvring came missionaries in 1835, the response of the Wesleyan mission in Tonga to requests from various Fijian chiefs. The Fijians and the missionaries evidently had contrasting understandings of what was involved, for it was to be many years before Fiji was both Christian and at peace. No Fijian chief converted until 1845, and none of any importance until the Tui Nayau in 1849 whose conversion proved to be an event of considerable importance.

Whereas the Wesleyan mission in Fiji was uncompromisingly pacifist, unconverted Fijian warrior-chiefs were devoted more to war than they were to life itself and killing and cannibalism were enthusiastically undertaken. Moreover, the political issues currently being contested were seriously regarded. Since the Tui Nayau was the paramount chief of the Lau islands (that eastern fringe of atoll lands which forms the eastern side of the Fiji group—see Map 5), he was subordinate to Cakobau of Bau who had already been enraged and had his military strength weakened by the conversion of some of his people. The conversion of Lau was too much: Cakobau let it be known that Lau would be brought back into line by war.

War was averted, however, by the presence of a large and martial body of Tongans at Lakeba. Tongans had for generations been accustomed to voyaging to Fiji. They imported pottery and bought the large *vesi* tree trunks necessary for their great twin-hulled canoes, their own islets not supporting such timber. At the same time they practised their military prowess in the service of one Fijian chief or another and perhaps sometimes on their own account. The Tongans thus had a reputation in Fiji for turbulence and belligerence, and their influence had been inadvertently extended by the practice of the Wesleyan mission in sending Tongan converts as mission teachers.

Therefore when Cakobau threatened war on Christian Lau in 1849, he backed down when he realized that by the presence of the Tongans, he had no assurance of success. It was a decision which possibly changed Fijian history because defeat for Cakobau at that time would probably have meant the end of Bau as the hegemon of Fiji. As things were, his failure to subdue the Tongans at that time allowed them to become within a decade his most formidable rivals under the leadership of the Tongan chief, Ma'afu.

Ma'afu was the son of Josiah Aleamotu'a, the late Tu'i Kanokupolu of Tonga who had died in 1845, and was thus a cousin of King George, Josiah's successor. Ma'afu himself had come to Fiji in 1847, although he was probably still unknown to Cakobau in 1849. In 1853 George appointed him to govern the Tongans in Fiji, a charge which Ma'afu exploited to emerge soon after as Cakobau's most dangerous rival. Thus the mission had a powerful (if sometimes embarrassing) ally, and Ma'afu the chief had a network of subtle and effective agents in the mission teachers and their converts.

Shortly after the conversion of the Tui Nayau, war broke out instead between Bau and Rewa again, and Bau's decline as a power in Fiji became a public spectacle. Its forces suffered defeat, Bau itself was blockaded, and when Cakobau levied his tributaries for *bêche-de-mer* to pay for his vain and foolish purchase of two schooners, he met passive resistance and humiliation. Finally, within his own domain, there was rebellion. As the Tongan king warned him after visiting him on his way to Sydney in 1853, 'It will be well for you, Cakobau, to think wisely in these days.' Conversion to Christianity was one of the things the beleaguered chief was urged to think about, and in April 1854, with his fortunes at their ebb, he made his decision to convert. Some months later Rewa, leaderless and war-weary, made peace, but the Bauan rebels stood firm and recalcitrant until the Tongan warriors of King George who had come to mediate, crushed them at the Battle of Kaba in February, 1855.

Cakobau's situation had now dramatically been reversed. He was again paramount on the western side of the Koro Sea, but over most of Viti Levu he had no real authority, while his benefactor's cousin and subject, Ma'afu, was paramount on the eastern side of the group, and was rapidly extending his influence more by statecraft than war in the great northern island of Vanua Levu. Cakobau at this point may have been content to preserve the status quo, but two things happened which would disturb his peace of mind for nearly another twenty years: the growth of European settlement, and the so-called 'American debt'.

The increasing European population congregated at Levuka on the island of Ovalau, and followed in its development the pattern set by the settlers in Hawai'i. Without a centralized government, however, these settlers were more able to buy land from the Fijian chiefs for the plantations of cotton and coconuts which they hoped to establish. This population was still small and had scarcely begun to disperse when the American debt crisis arose.

The American consul ('commercial agent' officially) in Fiji, John Brown Williams, was the same petulant, belligerent, self-seeking type of man as the early consuls in Hawai'i. He had arrived in Fiji in 1846 and almost immediately held Cakobau responsible for the looting of the *Elizabeth* which had caught fire and run aground. Three years later, his house caught fire through his own folly (during 4 July celebrations) and was looted; two years later, in July 1851, when an American ship-of-war at last called, Williams submitted a claim for $5,000 compensation, for himself and on behalf of the owners of the *Elizabeth*. By 1855 the compensation claim against various chiefs on behalf of several American citizens had swollen to $43,686, of which Williams's personal claim came to $18,331. Commander Boutwell of the U.S.S. *John Adams*, held Cakobau responsible as Tui Viti ('King of Fiji'), and required him to pay three instalments, each of $15,000, in 12, 18, and 24 months. Cakobau immediately sent a letter of protest to the U.S. Consul in Sydney (of higher rank than Williams), but to no avail. From then on, Williams obsessively pursued the alleged debt.

In 1858 another U.S. officer, Commander Sinclair, of the U.S.S. *Vandalia*, reiterated the demands and in desperation Cakobau turned to the new (and first) British consul, W.T. Pritchard, offering a conditional cession of Fiji to Britain in return for payment of the American debt.

Cakobau might have had another motive in taking this step; during the war with Rewa and since, Ma'afu had gradually been extending his power with the expansion of Christianity in northern Fiji; Cakobau knew by 1858 if he had not known it earlier that he was no match for Ma'afu in either war or diplomacy, but if Britain accepted the sovereignty of Fiji and allowed him certain powers and dignities such as Tui Viti, then Ma'afu would be checkmated.

Between the offer of cession in 1858, and its refusal in 1862, the government of Fiji was virtually in the hands of two men, Ma'afu and Pritchard. Pritchard, acting far beyond his consular authority, established order and justice for the Europeans, stability in relations between settlers and Fijians, and fairness and accurate records in land transactions. Ma'afu in his half of Fiji, similarly provided good order and stability from his headquarters at Lomaloma, encouraging

European trade and settlement and maintaining peace with a very firm personal control of his domains. This stability in Fijian affairs came to an end in 1862 when Britain declined Cakobau's offer as being beyond his authority to give, and Pritchard was dismissed.

Now Cakobau had little of either power or statesmanship (Pritchard, whatever his other failings, had had both), and a power vacuum was about to develop. The missionaries and a new consul, Jones, stepped in and under their guidance a confederation of the Fijian *matanitu* or states was organised in 1865. It was a modest enough experiment in government: an attempt to present a unitary state to governments and foreign residents (rapidly becoming more numerous), while still leaving local administration in traditional hands. The experiment failed. Ma'afu felt restricted without receiving any compensating advantage; he withdrew in 1867 and organized his own confederacy of Northern and Eastern Fiji. It was not destined to last long because of continuing provincial jealousies; Ma'afu finally renounced his willingness to involve himself in wider Fijian affairs, and organized a new chiefdom of Lau with a European secretary and advisers, incorporating a streamlined structure for law making, law enforcement, tax-collection and economic development.

Meanwhile, further trouble was to arise from Cakobau's failure to match Ma'afu's skill in government. When the confederation broke up in 1867, it was replaced by a settler-dominated government, with Cakobau (now crowned king) as its nominal head, and an expensive, cumbersome and ineffective white legislature and public service, distinguished for its cheap-land policy, and pro-settler labour laws. The government simply did not work: its authority was ignored by settlers, Fijians and the British Consul. In the midst of this bizarre farce came the U.S. navy again, demanding settlement of the claims last raised nine years before. Cakobau was in a quandary.

To his aid came a delegation of Melbourne capitalists with whom he speedily made a deal: payment of the American debt and a handsome annuity for himself in return for 200,000 acres of Fijian land and the right to govern and develop Fiji in the manner of the old seventeenth century mercantilist monopolies like the great East India Company. The Polynesia Company deal caused a rush of immigration and a land boom. Disorder, disputation and anarchy took hold, the quality of race relations sank to a new low, and the settlers clamoured for law and order as they eagerly exploited its absence. Cakobau, goaded or urged by a handful of Levuka residents, dusted off the old 1867 constitution and proclaimed a new government; Ma'afu was persuaded to lend his nominal allegiance, but many of the settlers refrained.

Meanwhile, the misgovernment of Fiji and the alternatives were being discussed in the Australian colonies; annexation was talked of. In Britain, officials continued the old practice of trying to find a form of words for legislation which would control the behaviour of British subjects without incurring any expense or responsibility. The question of Fiji was rapidly becoming both complicated and contentious: labourers were being recruited from elsewhere to work in Fiji, and the Cakobau government staggered impotently from crisis to crisis in a climate of no-confidence on a path of near-bankruptcy and increasing racial violence. The fiction of native government, and the destabilizing proclivities of the settlers were exposed, and at last early in 1874, Cakobau offered Fiji again to the British government. The negotiations were long and complicated but eventually Fiji became a British possession in October 1874.

Ma'afu was thus robbed of his Fijian ambitions by Cakobau's ineptitude: seldom can defeat have been more bitter for a statesman than to have lost his goal in such circumstances. Ma'afu had had to perform a delicate balancing act: if he had been recognized as all-powerful in Fiji, foreign governments might have undermined him; without such recognition he could not quite outmanoeuvre Cakobau. He had needed a few more years, and the settlers came in a little too fast for him.

The case of Fiji is instructive: in essence the Fijians were so bent on pursuing their traditional interests and rivalries that foreign domination in the climate of nineteenth century affairs was scarcely avoidable. But if Cakobau had not had second thoughts back in 1849 over the conversion of the Tui Nayau, Fiji would have become a Tongan kingdom.

Samoa

Samoan affairs at the same time were infinitely more complex, but can be reduced to a similar, simple formula: white settlement created the need for government, the Samoans dissipated their strength on concerns of the past; so the settlers with some foreign official encouragement provided government themselves, and in due course Samoa joined the list of territories which became some-one else's colonial possession.

Samoan traditional politics were conducted rather differently from politics in other parts of Polynesia. Samoan society was not organized on the pyramidal descent-group which was generally typical of Polynesia and so lacked the tribal cohesion visible elsewhere. Nevertheless, there was a system of titles for which well-born men might compete on their basis of their personal prowess, conduct of warfare, and the oratory and wisdom of their *tulafale* or talking-chiefs. The most important titles which were won by accumulating lesser, local titles, were four in number: Tui Atua, Tui A'ana, Gatoaitele and Tamasoali'i. A chief who acquired all four became Tafa'ifa. Possession of the title of Tafa'ifa did not bring king-ship in the European sense: it conferred status, prestige and enormous influence, but not sovereign authority or government. That sort of authority was wielded only in the man's home territory, which might be quite small.

In the early 1830s when the remarkable voyaging missionary, John Williams, visited Samoa, the Tafa'ifa had become vacant through the murder of the last holder, Tamafaiga, who had somehow acquired the titles without meeting the usual requirements of eligibility: he had won them by force and he exercised a reputedly brutal and ruthless authority by the same means.

His murder meant war, both for revenge and to begin again the competition for titles. The leading candidate was Malietoa Vai'inupo of Tuamasaga, the middle part of the large island of Upolu. Malietoa presently became Tafa'ifa and having converted to Christianity, with mission patronage and the only good harbour in Samoa in his territory, he was well placed to emulate Pomare II of Tahiti and establish a new set of rules for Samoan politics. Malietoa, however, was a traditionalist and was disinclined to make any changes of this kind; before the settler population of Apia became large enough to stimulate him to political experimentation, he died. On his death-bed in 1841, he dispersed by his own wish the four titles so that the competition might begin again.

Events were to prove, however, that there would not be another Tafa'ifa, even though a brother succeeded him to the important title of Malietoa. This unsettled state of affairs was partly the reason for the recurrence of inconclusive wars from 1848 to 1856, fought between the major districts which were arranged by alliances into two large factions. The main effect of this contest was to pre-occupy Samoans during a critical period in the development of the settler community and in the development of commerce. During that time there were several attempts by settlers and by the captains of English and American ships of war to establish (with or without Samoan co-operation) some sort of ground-rules for the conduct of affairs, but the absence of a clearly identified paramount chief to deal with was, in European eyes, a grave defect in Samoan society.

Increasing unruliness at Apia, the European settlement, gave the place a 'wild west frontier' character and it quickly became known as 'the Hell of the Pacific'. Apia and Samoa were in need of government more than any other settler community in the Pacific. A hint of change in the pattern of events came with the establishment in Apia in 1857 of a new trading company: Godeffroy und Sohn of Hamburg. The Germans proved to be formidably efficient, as were those who followed them into various ventures in the Fiji-Tonga-Samoa area.

Godeffroys transformed the economic history of the Pacific islands. Hitherto, commerce had been a fitful thing, spectacular but transitory, dependent on exhaustible resources, and conducted by individual entrepreneurs. The transformation effected by Godeffroys was two-fold; first, it marked the beginning of the dominance of corporate capital as against the individual merchant; and second, it developed sustainable, permanent trade in a humble commodity which made trade available at the lowest levels of society. This commodity was coconut oil which could be produced and sold by almost any member of practically any village on any island, large or small, and it gave practical economic expression to the small, personal wants of innumerable people across the Pacific.

Coconut oil had been a small item of trade early in the century. After 1840, when the process of refining it for use in soap and candles had been perfected, European and American demand increased rapidly. For a time, the trade continued to be merely a sideline, as it was not an attractive commodity of commerce. Godeffroys changed that by recruiting agents who quickly superseded the independent traders, and the company made its Apia headquarters an entrepôt where the oil was collected and consolidated for shipment.

The company had even larger plans; profit and reliability of supply could both be improved if Godeffroys owned the coconut trees and if the work was done by hired labour rather than by native entrepreneurs. This plan required land and the authority of a master-servant relationship, and these requirements in turn implied government—preferably a pliable one. The Samoans, however, were anything but pliable. They would not at this stage form a government; they could not be induced to sell land; nor did they see any merit in becoming wage-labourers. So for a time the small settler community dwelt on the fringe of Samoa, causing difficulties and embarrassements from time to time, but also serving the useful function of funnelling foreign, manufactured goods into Samoan society.

Godeffroy's Apia manager, August Unshelm, however, was not content with a fringe-dweller existence. He was a shrewd businessman, a gifted administrator and a talented political perturbator, and found a way of exploiting Samoan divisions with a plan which depended on the co-operation of the French navy, but Unshelm perished at sea in 1864 before this scheme could be put into effect. His place was taken by a young man of twenty, Theodor Weber, whose talents matched those of Unshelm. Under Weber's shrewd management, the firm penetrated the Samoan resistance to land sales, buying several thousand acres in 1864, and planted them with cotton and coconuts with labour from other island groups to the north and west. Within the next few years, he tightened his grip even further by phasing out the extraction of oil and henceforth bought copra (the dried flesh of the coconut) from which oil could be extracted more efficiently by mechanical presses in Europe, without the handling difficulties posed by heavy, leaking casks of rancid oil.

While Godeffroys flourished, the Samoans continued to pursue their traditional political goals. The European settlers in the 1850s and '60s governed themselves and settled inter-racial difficulties by negotiation with the local chiefs; it was an arrangement which evolved out of the situation. Meanwhile, the Samoans continued to be distracted by issues which came out of the past; no successor to Malietoa Vai'inupo as Tafa'ifa had emerged (partly because European peacemaking efforts had prevented a conclusive outcome to the war of 1848-1856), but the title of Malietoa was the one on which for the time being, the major contest pivoted.

A new Malietoa (the chief Moli) had been appointed in 1858, but he died in 1860. Two claimants contested the succession, Laupepa and Talavou, both of them being installed by their respective supporters, a rivalry which effectively destroyed settler proposals for a joint settler-Samoan government. For the rest of the decade, therefore, the settlers governed themselves under their own *ad hoc* institutions, while relations between the two races gradually declined with the increasing commercial penetration of Samoan life.

By 1870 the settlers were relying increasingly on visits by the ships of various navies to regulate their relations with the Samoans. Relations between the two Malietoas had reached the point of war in 1869, just at the time when the settlers' cotton boom had burst and Samoan subsistence agriculture was recovering from the effects of drought and storms. The war of 1869 to 1873 became a watershed in the history of Samoa: as before, European attempts at mediation and peacemaking rendered the outcome inconclusive in Samoan eyes, so that the resulting political solution was almost bound to be impermanent. After this war, moreover, Europeans became so deeply involved in Samoan politics that it was no longer possible to distinguish the politics of the settler community from the politics of the Samoans. One reason for this new relationship was that the war had been of such importance in the eyes of the Samoans that it had broken their resistance to selling land on a far greater scale than the combined effect of Weber's intrigues and drought had done after 1864. The land sales of the early 1870s were conducted with such recklessness on both sides, that the subsequent claims amounted to two and a half times the total land area of Samoa. To the extent that these sales were valid they gave the settlers a permanent stake in Samoan affairs; because many of the sales were suspect, the settlers had an interest in establishing a government which would uphold them.

Consequently, from 1873 till the mid 1890s, Samoan politics were a confusing and chaotic process as settlers of different nationalities vied for pre-eminence, as appeals to naval captains were made for justice or leverage, and as a succession of governments were formed from temporary alliances of Samoan chiefs, foreign consuls, and influential foreign residents.

The most successful attempt to form a multi-racial government was that by a mysterious American adventurer, Colonel Albert B. Steinberger, the basis of whose success was his plausibility. First, he hinted that he was the personal envoy of the American president, Ulysses S. Grant, whatever quasi-official status he may have had; second, he had a gift for negotiation, and brought about peace between the two rival Malietoa; and third, he had the ability to perceive other peoples' expectations, combined with an ingratiating manner. In order to win the confidence of so many factions, he made contradictory promises; in particular, he had made such generous concessions to Godeffroys in matters of land and labour policy, that he could not possibly have satisfied the expectations of either the settlers or the Samoans. Moreover, his apparent alliance with the Germans so alienated the British and American consuls, as well as many of the settlers, that when it finally became known that he had misrepresented his standing with the American government, confidence in him vanished, and he was deposed and deported.

From 1876 to 1889 there were at least seven attempts to establish governments, there was a major civil war, and two smaller rebellions. Each government fell in turn to the unsettled rivalries of claimants to Samoan titles or to the unsettled jealousies of the foreign residents who, as time passed, became more and more conscious of the national identities which divided them, while they hoped and schemed for the active intervention of their home governments.

Treaties with Britain, Germany and the United States deprived any Samoan government after 1879 of the power which was necessary to curb the foreign residents. The inevitable impermanence of every attempted solution led foreign statesmen to the conclusion that Samoa could be governed only by international agreement, and therefore a series of conferences was held between 1885 and 1889 to try to work out a formula. Finally in 1889, it was agreed (although the Samoans were not party to the agreement), that Samoa should be a single, independent kingdom, with a chief justice and prime minister to be selected by the uninvolved King of Sweden, and the conference chose as king the ineffectual Malietoa Laupepa.

Samoa thus remained independent for a time, but not because of any political genius of the Samoans. Their own refusal to acknowledge the importance of the European invasion inevitably involved the home governments of the turbulent and disunited settlers. The great powers' failure to agree on any other solution created a government which although nominally independent, remained subordinate to the decisions of foreign statesmen, a solution which turned out to be only a short-lived expedient.

The Polynesian response to European penetration, therefore, shows no perfect duplication from place to place, but there is a consistent pattern. Everywhere, the failure to sink traditional jealousies and meet the demands for modern government inevitably brought humiliation and dependency, the consequence of a commercial penetration which was an anonymous and often shapeless force. In Polynesia this humiliation and dependence was caused in part by the citizens and governments of the west, but was as much a product of the decisions made by the Polynesians themselves.

Chapter Seven

MELANESIA: SANDALWOOD AND 'BLACKBIRDING'

The common means of change in both Melanesia and Polynesia was commerce initiated and conducted by Europeans, but between the two regions there was a major difference. Whereas in Polynesia the process of religious conversion and political centralization overlapped and was entangled with commercial penetration, in Melanesia in the nineteenth century, missionaries were conspicuously less successful, and there were no significant indigenous attempts at political centralization. European trade therefore dominated events, and two trades in particular became synonymous with European civilization: the sandalwood trade in the 1840s and '50s; and the recruitment of labour ('blackbirding') for overseas employment from the 1860s to the end of the century.

Melanesian participation in these two trades ranged from enthusiastic willingness, through deliberate and selective co-operation, to uncompromising hostility. Nowhere else in the Pacific were relations between the races so marked by violence and danger, and nowhere else did the believers in racial inequality find so much support for the myths of innate inferiority of an entire race.

The pattern of Melanesian life had been little disturbed before 1840. The ubiquitous whaling ships had found a few harbours where their visits were welcomed and where refreshment could be had as long as both parties were careful and vigilant; the Roviana lagoon in the western Solomons was particularly favoured (see Map 6). Lesser trades were also conducted in a desultory way, *bêche-de-mer* and tortoise-shell being good and lucrative sidelines for Pacific traders, without either of them attracting the 'rush' which *bêche-de-mer* had brought to Fiji in 1830s and '40s.

As long as trade remained on a small scale it could be conducted with reasonable safety and without severe disruption to Melanesian life; but as the supply of muskets, steel-axes, knives and ironware became more reliable and began to filter more extensively into village

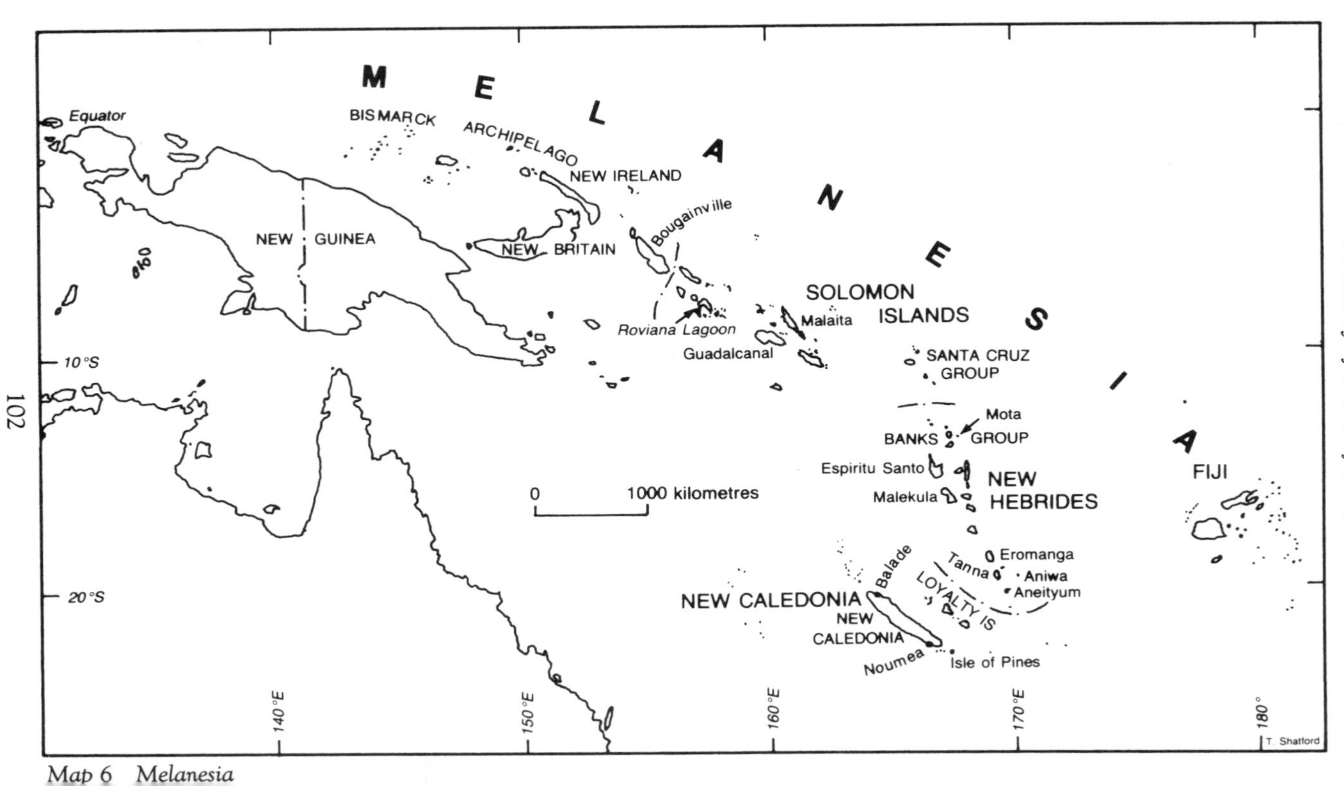

Map 6 Melanesia

life, so the old rhythms and restraints of Melanesian life began to change.

The changes must have begun first with food and craft production as metal tools increased productivity. Perceptibly less time needed to be spent in gardens or hewing wood or in the major communal activities of house-building and canoe construction. But it is unlikely that this increased efficiency allowed greater leisure: Melanesian competitiveness and devotion to display, to demonstrating success and *mana*, more likely led to increased production and accelerated rivalry. The ability to achieve more, whether in yam production or head-collection, probably spurred greater efforts in all things. Head-hunting certainly became bolder in some places, and as the behaviour of some became more extravagant, the old restraints became diminished and an accelerated and intensified cycle of competition and warfare developed.

Besides acquiring muskets and axes, the people became subject to new diseases: venereal, tubercular, and the sweeping bacterial epidemics. The effect on some communities was no doubt devastating, and realignments of power and territory surely followed. Disease and other misfortunes were interpreted by Melanesians as the work of offended spirits or of antagonistic, ill-disposed sorcerers. For offended spirits placatory ceremonies and offerings had to be found; for sorcerers, the remedy was further sorcery, simple murder or inter-tribal warfare.

One way or another life became less secure, and the equanimity of men and women was disturbed. The white men and their technology alone were a challenge to the Melanesian world view; these subsequent trials and disasters were traumatic. The only remedy for social dislocation was further disturbance and Melanesia embarked on a spiral of volatile disintegration.

This process was, however, a slow one. In few places can the full sequence have unfolded before the mature observation of an adult, so an appreciation of the nature of the changes might not have been realized. Moreover, the changes filtered only slowly through the islands and from coast to bush, so that a century after the changes began, there were still communities not directly acquainted with Europeans, and not much affected by the events which their coming had set in motion.

The changes, nevertheless, were greatly accelerated by the increased scale of contact brought by the trade in sandalwood. This fragrant timber had been first reported growing in the New Hebrides in 1825, at a time when the Hawai'ian sandalwood trade was entering its last stage. Apart from a few small cargoes taken in the next few years, the find was not followed up. One of the early attempts was organized and led by a Hawai'ian chief, Boki, in 1829. Boki, the governor of the Hawai'ian island of Oahu, was the man primarily responsible for raising the money to pay the Hawai'ian debts to sandalwood traders, and he saw here an opportunity to restore Hawai'ian (and his own) fortunes. Boki was lost at sea, together with his ship, but his consort-vessel returned to Hawai'i, its crew having been reduced to a fraction of its original number by fighting with the New Hebrideans and by disease. Boki's was not the first Hawai'ian attempt to adopt the European role in commerce but it was the most conspicuously disastrous. It was to be many years before Pacific islanders were to take a similar initiative again. In the same year another expedition involving Polynesians was made. Captain Henry, son of a missionary in Tahiti, led an expedition of over one hundred Tongans, whose time and energies were divided between cutting timber and defending themselves from the hostile people of Eromanga.

Indeed, there were several simultaneous attempts in 1829-30 to harvest the timber of Eromanga, each with its own Polynesian labour force. On the whole, they did not succeed. Their lack of success was due partly to mismanagement, and partly to a failure to maintain good relations with the native people. But it was typical of Melanesia that where good relations were established with one group, the enmity of neighbours and traditional enemies automatically ensued. There were other difficulties as well, including low prices in China, and consequently a regular trade with Melanesia could not be established at this time.

The trade began in earnest in 1841. The London Missionary Society, working its way progressively westward from its beginnings in Tahiti in 1797, had now turned its attention to Melanesia. In 1839, the voyaging missionary, John Williams, bringing Rarotongan and Samoan teachers to Eromanga to begin the work, had been murdered on the beach at Dillon's Bay. The mission, inspired rather than discouraged by martyr's blood (its first), continued with its programme. This renewed contact with Melanesia reawakened knowledge of the lucrative sandalwood, and a rush began: seven vessels joined the trade in a few months at the end of 1841, setting a race which was to continue throughout the '40s. The volume diminished during the 1850s and tapered off to extinction in the early 1860s. The locations of good stands of timber were quickly established, and suddenly the inhabitants of parts of New Caledonia, of the Loyalty Islands, and the Southern New Hebrides found themselves presented with unprecedented opportunities to obtain the wonderful wares of Europe.

Like the Polynesians before them, the Melanesians quickly

recognized the merits of iron, glass and cloth, and willingly joined in the trade. Willingness, however, did not necessarily smooth the path of the traders, for covetousness could be satisfied by theft, murder or fraud, as well as by honest trade, and the sandalwood business quickly won a reputation for danger and depravity.

Initially, the trade was conducted by buying directly from the islanders who cut the wood, brought it to the shore, floated it to the ship and were there paid for it; the work was not only laborious for the natives but it also provided tempting opportunities, and ships were attacked during this process. That was one drawback with this method of trade: allowing islanders on board or around the ship was dangerous. Another drawback was that other village activities might take precedence over supplying wood, causing an expensive ship (probably chartered for several hundred dollars a month) and her crew to be kept idle while war, agriculture or ceremony engaged the energies of the local people.

There were two ways around this difficulty. One was for the ship's crew to cut and transport the wood itself, but this was slow as well as dangerous, and was often frustrated by the theft of tools. While the timber was being brought, often from many miles inland, the ship was idle and undermanned, vulnerable and costing money. The better solution was to maintain a shore station where sandalwood might be stockpiled, and from where the ship could simply collect a cargo, thus ensuring a rapid turn-around and less risk to ship and crew.

That was a good plan from a ship-master's point of view, but what about the shore party? Who would take a risk with Melanesians and malarial mosquitoes? The Melanesians, for the most part, were not averse to having a resident white-man nearby; through him trade goods could be channelled, and over him (because he was a resident) they could exercise some control, usually by supplying him with a female companion and thus tying him to the kinship web of Melanesian society. But a permanent party of European sandalwooders was a less attractive idea: white men were expensive and hard to control, and this solution could be worse than the original problem. Andrew Cheyne, one of the stayers in the sandalwood trade had tried this course in 1841, right at the beginning of the trade. The risks, the difficulties of maintaining good relations with the host people, the strain, and finally the failure to procure a cargo were too much. The answer was to use a Melanesian work force, recruited from another island; such men would not have traditional enemies nearby to harass them, nor would they have kin to make awkward demands. There would be no traditional obligations to interrupt the work; they could be paid in goods a fraction of the value of a white man's wage; and when a labourer died from disease or misadventure, there were no awkward questions to answer nor any inconvenient paperwork.

From comparatively few such stations in the 1840s, this method of trading eventually became the accepted and only satisfactory way to conduct business. During the 1850s, most sandalwood islands had at least one station, and large islands like Espiritu Santo could support many, although many of these were short lived. These stations might each employ a few dozen labourers at any time, usually engaged for a period of several months, to be returned to their homes during the wet, stormy summer months which were unfavourable for shipping. At the same time, it became increasingly common for Melanesians, like their Polynesian relations in preceding decades, to ship as sailors in this and other trades, to the point where there was often only a skeleton crew of Europeans to direct a predominantly Melanesian ship's company.

The practice of employing Melanesian migrant labourers, as well as the accumulation on both sides of experience in the trade, resulted in less violence during the later years. As traders in Polynesia had found before, the logic of commerce and mutual dependence were the surest regulators of conduct on both sides.

The most conspicuous shore-station operator was James Paddon. Not an employee but a modest-sized capitalist, he preferred to conduct his business from an island base, whereas most of his rivals managed their affairs from Sydney. Formerly a captain, Paddon established himself on Aneityum in 1844, evidently with a more ambitious settlement in mind than a mere sandalwood entrepôt; he had a large party (including, later, women and children), livestock, and a huge range of equipment both for a settlement and for meeting the needs of passing shipping. It was a farsighted, bold move which with luck, might have made Aneityum the South Pacific counterpart of Honolulu. Paddon's determination and persistence, however, could not offset his shortage of capital, and his project was in difficulties from the start. Sandalwood profits which were to have carried him through the foundation years were disappointingly small, and the competition from larger capitalists such as Robert Towns, was sharp. Paddon made his settlement the base for a network of shore stations scattered through the southern New Hebrides, the Loyalty Islands and the adjacent parts of New Caledonia.

Paddon's settlement survived for nearly a decade, but prosperity eluded him and in 1848 he had to face competition of a new kind, from a man as persistent, stubborn, single-minded and resourceful as himself, but with whom he could not agree. This man was the Presbyterian missionary, John Geddie. Geddie was not opposed to commerce as such, but he did have strong views on commercial ethics and on the personal morals of the settlers, whose example to the Aneityumese was the contrary of what he was trying to teach. Inevitably, the two men quarrelled and almost as inevitably, opposing groups of islanders were drawn to each.

In 1850, for reasons which are obscure, most of the Aneityumese opted for Geddie and Christianity. One last great feast was held under the auspices of the old gods and then they were abandoned. Paddon gave up; because of the conversion of the people there would undoubtedly be obstacles in his future dealings with them; the native population was much depleted by now from the effects of disease; and the sandalwood of Aneityum was exhausted. Paddon, hoping that his diverse interests would be better served elsewhere, moved to Tanna which was only about sixty kilometres to the north-west.

Despite the change of location, Paddon continued his business as before: out-stations strategically placed, relying mainly on sandalwood. When France annexed New Caledonia in 1853, he turned his mind again to schemes of colonization, with the result that the early colonial economy of New Caledonia owed much to his enterprise and resourcefulness, which had still not been exhausted when he died in 1861, aged about fifty.

Paddon had enjoyed a reputation unusual for a Pacific trader: he was a hard man (how else could one survive in those times?) but fair and well-liked by people of both races; and widely known throughout southern Melanesia. His residence there almost perfectly spanned the years of the sandalwood trade, and bridged the years from when trade was a dangerous occupation carried out between strangers with no common language and with mutual suspicion, through the period of regular but cautious commerce, to the beginning of permanent European settlement. By the time of his death, most of the coastal peoples of New Caledonia and New Hebrides were acquainted with the Europeans, understood something of their customs, and could deal with them in mutually satisfactory ways.

To generalize about the character of the trade is hazardous. Extremes of conduct by both Europeans and Melanesians recalled tales of piracy in the Caribbean in the seventeenth century, with their atrocities and disregard for human life. Nevertheless, the trade extended to many islands and scores of tribes, and lasted two decades—a youth at the beginning of the trade was by Melanesian standards an old man at its end. The trade changed; so did the people in it; generalizations, therefore, should all be considered as qualified.

First, sandalwood was the most violence-ridden of Pacific trades. According to the historian of the trade, Dorothy Shineberg, perhaps one hundred and thirty members of ships crews were killed, and about two hundred islanders; boats were attacked on perhaps twenty occasions, four ships were captured, and as many more attacked. These are figures based on reliable evidence; hearsay and anecdote would swell the number enormously, and there must have been other incidents of which nothing is known at all. These estimates take no account of clashes involving shore stations.

About three quarters of the losses of life occurred in the 1840s; the 1850s was a more peaceful time. Nevertheless, considering the evil reputation of the trade and the real dangers, and the fact that the number of voyages over twenty years amounted to over two hundred, these figures should not be considered high. They certainly did not prevent the trade from continuing, or other forms of commerce developing.

Second, the trade was commonly believed to be lucrative, as is supposed of all trades in luxury goods. 'What will man not do for money?' asked the Rev. George Turner, describing with both astonishment and disapproval the work of a sandalwooder. To the discomfort of the traders, however, the trade was not a wonderful money-spinner; although sandalwood voyages could sometimes turn a handsome profit, those who made money out of Pacific islands commerce generally did it comparatively slowly, dealing in mundane, humble commodities like pearl-shell and coconut oil. For the large capitalists, of whom the best example is Robert Towns, the boom voyages balanced the failures and returned a good income for many years. This income, however, required a large investment and was not really an attractive rate of return, while for the smaller operators, the trade could be ruinous.

The price of sandalwood in China reared and plunged unpredictably: at times it fetched £50 per ton, but it could be as low as £12. The costs to the trader varied widely, depending on the following questions: was a cargo procured quickly or slowly; did he make a fast or slow voyage; what labour was he employing; was he trading on borrowed capital, and at what rate of interest; did his wood sell quickly in China? The costs established by the answers to these questions generally amounted to between £20 and £30 per ton. The successful trader therefore needed both good management and luck on his side; for Robert Towns, the doyen of sandalwood merchants, the profits were maintained by transferring to others the risks (and thus the losses). The possibilities are summed up in two extreme cases of Towns': one voyage made

£2000, another lost £1300. His other interests needed to be more lucrative and less volatile.

The nineteenth century traders were commonly believed to be exchanging junk for treasure, exploiting the ignorance and innocence of the islanders to get something of great value at no great cost to themselves. Every merchant, of course, aspires to such a position and so did the Melanesians. They must have marvelled at the Europeans trading the wonderful hoop iron and glass beads for unusable wood which did not even burn well. But soon the Melanesians realized that Europe had better things to offer than hoop-iron and glass beads; the price of their worthless yellow wood rose to include good quality axes, fish-hooks, knives, scissors, adzes, iron pots, cloth and fire-arms. Native demand was continually responding to new knowledge and new opportunities, so that a trader might find himself facing ruin if he did not have the right brand, right style, right quality or right commodity that the islanders wanted to buy.

It is often argued on the basis of such observations that the islanders entered knowingly and intelligently into the trade; that commerce was based on the participants coming to mutually satisfactory terms; and that consequently the idea of exploitation is irrelevant.

Appealing as this idea might be to those who believe that true values and equality are to be found in the market place, commerce between the races was not on equal terms. The trader was buying potential wealth at the risk of going bankrupt, with a chance of death or injury along the way. The islanders were buying leisure, greater ease of life and work, greater status in their own competitive economic game, also with the means of death and injury for themselves and others from the fire-arms, axes and tobacco which were traded in huge quantities. The exchange meant, however, social dislocation and decay, and devastating diseases from the moment of contact—these were the commodities which accompanied the beads and calico.

The commerce was unequal in another sense; the Melanesians were dealing with the unknown to a far greater extent than were the Europeans; the Melanesians did not understand the likely consequences to their own lives. Furthermore, only tiny fragments of Europe (or Australia or America) were coming into contact with Melanesia; but entire communities of Melanesians were being contacted. This inequality of scale gave the Melanesians a tactical advantage of numbers and position, but it was a strategic weakness because it threatened the survival of their communities and the preservation of their cultures.

While the sandalwood trade was dying in the early 1860s, Robert Towns was expanding his economic interests in Australia. By now an old man of seventy, wealthy, influential, a member of the New South Wales Legislative Council, he was still vigorously forming and pursuing new commercial opportunities and was about to launch cotton planting as his next project. Actuated by the same considerations as those settlers in Fiji and Samoa who were hoping to take advantage of the high prices caused by the American Civil War, Towns concluded that Queensland had good plantation possibilities. He planted cotton near Brisbane in 1863, and since the work was arduous and monotonous in an unpleasantly hot and humid climate, he had his employees recruit a party of men from Tanna to work for him there for twelve months.

Towns was pleased with the venture. He had employed Melanesians before on his ships and on his sandalwood shore stations; so had James Paddon, and most of the other sandalwood traders. Labour migration, therefore, was not a novelty, and the traders knew that Melanesians could work hard and well, and were good value as employees. British settlements elsewhere had made extensive use of labour imported from Africa and India, and the old slave trade notwithstanding, traffic in labour had a long and well-established history; consequently, Towns anticipated no serious difficulties or objections in bringing coloured labour to Australia's northern, humid colony.

Despite the expression of strident and intemperate objections from various quarters, Towns, pleased with his Melanesians, immediately recruited more of them, using as his agent Ross Lewin, a man of ambiguous reputation who was to play an important part in the subsequent development of the trade. Other capitalists with plantation ambitions copied Towns' lead, and there were several ship-masters willing to emulate Lewin. By 1865, there were several ships bringing Pacific islanders to Queensland and it was found that there was a strong demand for this new island commodity.

The islands which first bore the brunt of this new commerce were the southern islands of New Hebrides, in particular, Eromanga and Tanna. New Caledonia was more or less closed to outside recruiters, having been annexed by France in 1853, but by 1864, France had decided that New Caledonia should become a convict settlement. The people of New Caledonia were going to be required for the European economic development of that country, and were therefore unavailable for the Queensland trade.

It was the New Hebrideans, with their long experience of trade with white men, and their experience in being recruited to work on other islands, who were looked to for the supply of labour to Queensland. Meanwhile, other potential employers were thinking about employing Pacific islands labour; the planters in Fiji had found local labour difficult to manage for the same reason that the sandalwooders had been driven to hiring migrant labour—local obligations to chiefs, family and village, and the ease of absconding made local workers expensive and unproductive. Imported labour was entirely dependent on the employer, had no conflict of interest, no refuge, and no local sympathisers; while labour from elsewhere within Fiji was satisfactory, totally alien labour was far better for an employer's purposes. The same observations were true of Samoa, where plantation development was in its very beginnings, and where the principal developer, Godeffroys, was in the market for labourers.

Unconnected with Melanesian migrant labour, was another sinister attempt at labour recruitment, the so-called 'Peruvian slave trade'. For several months during 1862 and 1863, vessels sailed from Peru to all the island groups of the South Pacific as far west as the Gilberts to engage labourers to work in Peru. Almost three and a half thousand Polynesians are known to have been removed from their islands, and according to available data, about 70 percent of them by violence or deceit. Most of the islands affected were small, with populations numbering only hundreds: most lost more than a quarter of their populations, many lost over half, and in one case the loss was 80 percent. Of the 3500 recruited, only 257 were still alive in 1866; those who were returned directly to their own homes numbered only 37. To complete the balance sheet of death, almost as many (about 3000) died in epidemics introduced by the recruiters as were taken away. The inhumanity of the recruiters and the tyranny and cruelty experienced by the Polynesians in Peru gave that country an evil name. Reports which filtered into the English-language presses of the Pacific region coloured the perceptions of those interested in the labour traffic which was soon to follow in Melanesia.

The Melanesian traffic seemed at first as if it would replicate the horrors of the Polynesian-Peruvian affair, but there were a number of things preventing it. The population of Melanesia was larger than that of the islands raided by Peruvian ships, and the separateness of the many Melanesian communities made wholesale fraud and kidnapping impossible. Moreover, the trade in Melanesia was begun by ship-masters already well-known in those islands, while missionaries were present in many places to warn the islanders about the labour recruiters. Finally, patrols by the British navy, and public pressure in the Australian colonies kept the recruiters on the defensive.

During the 1860s, nevertheless, the trade quickly acquired an unpleasant reputation. The reason can perhaps be narrowed to the exploits of a few men, and especially of Ross Lewin, who, by all accounts, was a hard, ruthless and unscrupulous man. In 1863, and for four years after, Lewin was Towns' agent; after that, he began recruiting on his own account, placing the recruits with whomever would take them. His success spurred others; in 1867, over 1200 Melanesians were brought to Queensland, whereas the annual total in previous years had been well under two hundred.

Bad publicity came almost immediately. The *Syren* in 1868 arrived in Queensland with a cargo of sick and dying men, and tales of death and mistreatment: at about the same time, the *Young Australian*, which had apparently been kidnapping, had had fighting on board between traditional enemies. Injuries had been inflicted, and to stop the fighting, three men had been shot and thrown overboard. The scandal added weight to the criticisms already in currency, and the Queensland government hastily brought in legislation, the Polynesian Labourers Act. It was intended to control the trade by providing for supervision on ships and in port, to remove the scope for fraud, violence and inhuman conditions, and to ensure full documentation so that recruits could be eventually returned to their proper homes.

This Act was only partially effective, and was of course irrelevant to those vessels recruiting for Fiji and Samoa. Abuses continued: the *Daphne* was arrested on suspicion of fraud, overloading and coercion in 1869, and the worst case of all occurred in 1871. The ship *Carl*, under control of the totally irresponsible and amoral Dr. James Murray, acquired 180 recruits mostly by kidnapping. As with the *Young Australian*, the crowded confinement below decks of men who were probably traditional enemies led to fighting, and in a bid to quell it, Murray and his crew fired indiscriminately into the hold for hours with the result that over one hundred of the passengers were killed.

This was by far the worst case of its kind, and it justified the long delayed action of the British government in passing the Pacific Islanders Protection Act in 1872. This act attempted to police British recruiters throughout the south-west Pacific by prescribing similar provisions as those implemented by Queensland in 1868. For all its limitations it succeeded in suppressing incidents of extreme exploitation, but the trade continued to be tough and dangerous; vigilance and caution were necessary on both sides for the next thirty years.

As with the sandalwood trade, the Melanesians did not behave as if they thought they were being exploited. On the contrary, once each community had had some experience of the business, had seen men go away and most of them return about three years later, a supply of young men became available on a fairly steady basis. In the course of time, as former labourers told of and compared their experiences, people became knowledgeable about destinations and conditions, and would favour particular destinations and even particular employers. Recruiting levels also reflected changing conditions in the Melanesian homeland: warfare or famine could increase recruiting numbers; a labour shortage in the villages would reduce it. Moreover, if the trade goods which a recruiter had to offer were of a type not wanted, recruiting would be difficult. If a chief, or a recruit's family objected, he might not be able to go, or might have to arrange an escape and surreptitious meeting with his recruiter-accomplice. Surreptitious recruiting indeed was often a welcome escape for men (and women) who had something to run away from: a crime, illicit love-affair, sorcery, fear, a *tapu* or even the unwelcome teaching of a missionary.

The labour trade thus became an institution of Melanesian life. A young recruit of the 1860s could have lived to see his sons and grandsons follow his path to Queensland or elsewhere: over the decades, it became part of the process of growing up, something young men were expected to do. They gained experience and prestige by recruiting, they acquired trade goods which were of value to their family and village, and they earned a bride-price with which to get married on their return.

The attitude of Melanesians to the trade can be conveyed with two illustrations. In 1878, Queensland prohibited the trading of firearms and ammunition to Pacific islanders; the resulting resistance was so strong that the regulations could not be enforced. In 1883, when the regulations were re-imposed, recruiting numbers fell to record low levels, and the government again had to back down. Then in 1885, responding to growing opposition in Queensland, the government gave five years' notice that the trade would cease. Consequently, in the last few months of 1890, record numbers of Melanesians recruited, taking advantage of this 'last chance'. In fact, the trade was resumed in 1893, but when it finally came to an end another decade later, it did so amid resentment and bitterness.

As the business developed and demand for labour rose, the sources of labour changed so that for northern and western Melanesia this was the commerce responsible for bringing large populations within the purview of Europeans. In the 1860s, labour was supplied mainly by New Hebrideans; in the early 1870s, recruiters wanting less sophisticated, cheaper and more plentiful recruits looked to the Solomons. By the mid '80s, especially during the short-lived firearms ban, recruiters looked for new recruiting areas in New Guinea and the adjacent islands. Each time new territory was 'broken-in', the early pattern of deceit, kidnapping, and reciprocal violence re-emerged until experience and mutual knowledge made milder methods effective. After the brief New Guinea interlude by English-speaking recruiters, the northern Solomons and north-eastern New Guinea became a German preserve by agreement between the great powers. The German plantations in Samoa and New Guinea made heavy demands for labour, which was necessitated in part by their comparatively high mortality rates.

An interesting development, especially in the mid-'80s during the firearms ban, was the emergence of indigenous entrepreneurs. There had probably always been a minority of recruits who had been taken captive in war, perhaps specifically for the purpose of selling them to a recruiter, and such a fate was preferable to that usually met by the defeated in Melanesia. Later, people of the inland, who were usually denied direct access to the trade goods monopolized by the coastal tribes, could be funnelled through a coastal chief or 'big man' who made a handsome profit on the transaction.

Perhaps the most conspicuous of these Melanesian middlemen was a man of Malaita, called Kwaisulia. Kwaisulia was born with no special advantages: not only was his parentage undistinguished but his father was a man of the bush, not of the coast, among a coastal people. These were not usual times, however; Melanesia was under strain, old precedents could be challenged and new ones set. In 1875, Kwaisulia went to Queensland, one of the first of his people to do so, and worked for two three-year terms. Within a short time of his returning home, he had established himself as a man of authority and power on a stage, which though small, he did his best to enlarge beyond all local precedent. In a tacit commercial alliance with the traders ('a friend of the white man'), his influence extended, and with the help of firearms, his power spread likewise. This wider authority naturally made his stretch of coastline attractive to visitors and as success bred new opportunities and more success, Kwaisulia became a great and wealthy man in Melanesian style, surpassing all others. What gave him the greatest notice in European eyes was his ability to provide labourers, mainly from inland. It is unlikely that he was the only one of his kind: all trades create opportunities for middlemen, and when such opportunities can also be converted into political power, important changes may follow: such changes were part of the impact of the labour trade on Melanesia.

The importance of the labour trade can hardly be overstated. It deepened and widened the distribution of the social changes put in train by the sandalwood trade. It rescued the Melanesians from what would in any case have been a temporary abandonment by traders after the decline of sandalwood. More importantly, it gave perhaps 100,000 Melanesians direct, personal experience of life in European frontier-settlements: perhaps half of them in Queensland, about 20,000 in Fiji, and the remainder recruited by French and German agents for work in New Caledonia, Samoa and New Guinea. It provided a channel for vast quantities of arms, edge-tools and other manufactures which included large quantities of liquor and tobacco. It provided an alternative life (permanently for many) for those Melanesians who wanted to escape the sometimes appalling conditions in their homeland.

Politically, the labour trade created the need for regulation of European activity in Melanesia. Some form of law besides that of capricious force became necessary, and the Western Pacific High Commission and eventually British and German government of the Solomons were direct results. The development of a *lingua franca* for Melanesia was another important result which facilitated further European penetration (and subsequently a common language for new nations) in the form of 'pidgin-English'. Several varieties of this form of speech (modified-English vocabulary, modified-Melanesian grammar) developed from the time of the sandalwooders and before. The labour trade made it almost ubiquitous, an innovation which, since the transformation of Melanesia had become inevitable and irreversible, has been a major blessing.

Importance does not mean beneficence. Melanesia might, arguably, have been better off without the sandalwood and labour trades, but to the Melanesians at the time the benefits as they understood them outweighed the understood disadvantages. The ethics of contact, indeed of the spread of European civilization at all, have been often called in question, or condemned outright. These two trades have perhaps more to answer for than other forms of contact between black and white, but when the nineteenth century ended, and direct colonial rule brought new ways to labour recruitment and migration, it was found that a vacuum developed in Melanesian life. The vacuum was to be filled partly by what came to be called 'native policy', and partly by the Christian missions. The missionaries had been there at the beginning and throughout; they were there at the end, when at last, the islanders turned to them with new interest.

Chapter Eight

MELANESIA: MISSIONARIES AND COLONISTS

By the mid-1830s, all the major groups of Polynesia had been introduced to Christianity, although not all were yet converted. Protestant missionaries, impelled by a sense of urgency for the souls daily being lost and the miseries daily being endured, hastened to new islands as soon as progress elsewhere freed resources for redeployment. The most ardent 'exporter' of evangelism was the Reverend John Williams. Originally sent in 1817 to the Leeward Islands, west of Tahiti, his restlessness and energy led him to the Cook Islands where he introduced Christianity; then in 1830, he travelled to Samoa and Tonga where he discussed a territorial demarcation with the Wesleyans. He visited Samoa several times in the 1830s, and in 1839 approached his next goal, the New Hebrides, which was the next major group in the east to west progression of Christianity. Williams had, however, run his course: he chose Eromanga for his first Melanesian landing, and was there struck down and killed on the beach. This first Protestant martyrdom, if martyrdom it was, was a valuable fillip to the Protestant cause: Melanesia was to provide many more 'martyrs' over the coming decades; indeed, Melanesia was to be a heart-breaking challenge.

Missionary attention in the late 1830s had re-awakened commercial interest in these western islands, and the sandalwooders were soon swarming around the coasts. Despite the dangers of the trade, it was clear from the beginning that they were having more success than were the missionaries. The missionaries were inclined to blame the traders for the slow progress of evangelism and in a sense they were right. The missionaries alleged that the sandalwooders by their corruption, immorality and criminality were confirming the depravity of the islanders. The truth of that is doubtful but the sandalwooders impeded the missions just the same, in that they provided access to the goods of the west without at the same time providing an edifying example of the Christian life in action. The same, of course, had been true in Polynesia, but in Melanesia there were other factors to retard further the spread of Christianity.

Foremost among these difficulties was the nature of Melanesian religion with its absence of the powerful, 'departmental', sky-gods of Polynesia; conveying the Christian idea of God was more difficult because the Melanesians with their hosts of spirits and ghosts did not have an existing mental category into which the introduced God could be fitted. In Polynesia, missionaries had been able to seize on the word *Atua* to express the name and idea of God (not without some misunderstanding); in Melanesia, they generally found no equivalent word.

Language also presented a new difficulty. Whereas in Polynesia a single language of perhaps two or three closely-related dialects had to be mastered and used for scriptural translation for an entire island group (a labour which could occupy a mission for a generation), in Melanesia the task was magnified by extreme cultural fragmentation: a small island might be home to several languages, with no *lingua franca* until 'pidgin' English developed.

Third, there was the absence of any prospect of indigenous political unification. No great chiefs with sufficient *mana* could lend their prestige, influence or authority to the new doctrine, so that the acceleration of conversions evident in Tahiti after 1815, for example, was not possible.

Thus, even on small islands where a missionary might have been thought able to convey his message to the whole population, the mission societies were disappointed. Compared with Polynesia, Melanesia needed even greater resources, but by the 1840s the mission societies were over-extended. Because the enthusiasm for revival in Britain and America had passed, funds and volunteers were in short supply. Partly for this reason the burden of evangelizing Melanesia was very heavily shared by Polynesians: pastors from the Cook Islands and Samoa in particular came forward from the training institutes established by the L.M.S. on Rarotonga in 1839, and in Samoa in 1844. By 1850, forty of these teachers or members of their families had lost their lives in Melanesian mission work. While Melanesians accorded them less prestige than they did Europeans, some of them nevertheless achieved extraordinary successes, especially in the Loyalty Islands (between the New Hebrides and New Caledonia) which were almost totally converted by 1860.

In 1848, after a decade of frustration, two new developments occurred which were eventually to have profound effects: a Nova

Scotian Presbyterian and an Anglican bishop both turned their attention to the south-west Pacific.

The Presbyterian was Paddon's adversary, John Geddie, who with his wife and an assistant, Isaac Archibald, went to Aneityum in the southern New Hebrides in 1848. Geddie was an extreme example of the missionary who was faithful to God and his calling to the point of folly; in the critical eyes of a later generation he would be called a bigot. Zealous he was; narrow-minded, arrogant and belligerent he was not. Refusing to compromise on any detail of his belief or mission he survived mortal danger from the islanders and met the redoubtable James Paddon head on, and in two short years the issue had been decided—the Aneityumese turned *en masse* to Geddie and Christianity, the change having been made possible by Aneityum having only a single language. By 1852, the conversion was virtually complete, and another transformation begun. Roads, schools and chapels were built, settlements laid out anew, and the people clothed. The population, previously troubled by an acute imbalance of sexes, by a decline in numbers and harassed by sorcery and warfare, began to recover. If Geddie did not build a paradise on his island, he certainly saved it from being a hell on earth, as Aneityum had fallen into a desperate state since the first coming of foreigners.

Geddie was the spearhead of a more ambitious Presbyterian thrust from remote Nova Scotia. Others followed during the 1850s: the Gordon brothers (both to die violently), and John Paton, later a figure of controversy for his condemnation of the labour trade and his role in reprisals by the Royal Navy for losses of European life and property. None of them, however, duplicated Geddie's success on Aneityum. It was as if southern Melanesia had dug in its metaphysical toes: further advances were to come slowly, in the 1870s and later.

In the same year that Geddie established his mission on Aneityum, a reconnaissance voyage was being made by Bishop George Augustus Selwyn, first Bishop of New Zealand, sailing as chaplain on a warship on a tour of inspection. Selwyn's reconnaissance took advantage of a clerical loophole: the northern limits of his diocese had been defined at 34° 30' north latitude instead of south, and Selwyn rejoiced at the error for the opportunity it gave him. Several years' experience in New Zealand, and his observations on this voyage, led him to formulate an audacious and novel plan; instead of sending priests and teachers to the islands, he would organize a 'fifth column' in the islands, so that the conversion of Melanesia would start with a Melanesian priesthood rather than finish with one.

The idea was to bring boys from their island homes to New

Zealand, and there educate them and train them in evangelism, so that when they returned home they could introduce Christianity to their people. There were difficulties of course, and Selwyn was not naive. A young man could not be kept in New Zealand for the years necessary for his training or else he would return home a stranger, perhaps having even forgotten his own language. Moreover, the protracted absence from home would be cruel. It was better therefore, for a trainee to divide each year between his home and the seminary in New Zealand. This expedient, of course, created other difficulties: constant travelling with its inconvenience and expense, the slower and shallower progress of interrupted training, the risk of boys not returning for subsequent terms in the seminary, and the risk of back-sliding for a young convert alone among his heathen family and villagers.

The advantage of the scheme, if it could be made to work, was that it relieved the mission of the burden of mastering scores of new languages. Each trainee would learn, and be taught in, English, and would have less difficulty than an English missionary in translating the new doctrine into a Melanesian language. The idea was as bold as it was novel, but it required the linguistic aptitude, the showmanship and tact of Selwyn himself to make even the first part of it work. Trust had to be won from people who were extremely suspicious of strangers of all kinds.

Selwyn made his first recruiting voyage in 1849 to the southern islands of Melanesia and took five boys from various islands back to Auckland. In the next few years he ventured further north; by 1853 he had scholars who between them spoke ten distinct languages. Selwyn and his schooner, the *Southern Cross*, soon became widely recognized, and his visits welcomed for the trade goods that he brought.

Results were not expected early, but even Selwyn must have been disappointed at the inability of his system to influence Melanesian life throughout the 1850s. Out of 152 boys brought to Auckland during the decade only thirty-nine had come more than once. Nevertheless, the foundations for later achievements had been laid: the visits of the mission ship were well and widely known and persistence would eventually pay dividends. Towards the end of this decade, Selwyn had gradually handed the management of the mission project over to a younger man of like mind; this was John Coleridge Patteson who in 1861 became the first Bishop of Melanesia. Patteson now modified Selwyn's strategy, seeking to overcome its greatest difficulties by having some missionaries resident in the islands and having them select promising boys for training in Auckland. The first island base was Mota, to the north of the New Hebrides, a strategically sound choice. The old recruiting strategy was continued and priests were enlisted to visit islands on a more regular and sustained basis, giving missionaries and Melanesians a much more comprehensive exposure to each other. In 1865, the mission headquarters and school were moved from Auckland to Norfolk Island, again a more convenient location, and at about the same time, Patteson discarded English as the mission's *lingua franca* in favour of Mota. Selwyn's original choice of English had been sound for his time but now the scope of the mission's work had a clearer focus. Patteson (a linguist of near-genius) and his assistants had mastered Mota which, being a Melanesian language, would be easier for recruits to learn than the alien English tongue. By the late 1860s, the mission came closer to its first goal, a Melanesian priesthood, when it ordained its first Melanesian deacon. Progress from then on was steady and encouraging to the mission, but it was not fast. Striking progress did not come until the 1890s and later, when the establishment of a British protectorate in the Solomons and the winding down of labour migration to Queensland gave missionaries a more prominent profile in Melanesian life.

Patteson himself did not survive the pioneering stage. In 1871, in a characteristically courageous but dangerous visit to Nukapu, an island between the Solomons and the New Hebrides groups, the bishop was murdered in retaliation for the kidnapping of some youths by a labour recruiter a few days earlier.

Patteson's death (in the same year as the *Carl* atrocity) focused attention on both the labour trade and Christian missions. Long overdue regulatory legislation for the former was hurriedly passed and mission sympathisers were spurred to increased effort. The dead bishop, following the lead of his patron Selwyn, had given intelligent and articulate expression to a philosophy of missions which showed a subtle shift from that of the earliest missionaries in the Pacific, and which distinguished the Anglican mission from its Nonconformist colleagues to the south. Patteson had argued that a total cultural change for Melanesia was neither possible nor desirable: the fundamental teachings of the scriptures did not depend on European cultural characteristics. Without compromising Christian teaching, Patteson and his mission strove to change as little as possible of Melanesian life, believing that if Christianity was to prosper in Melanesia it had to be able to address the people as Melanesians, not as imitation Europeans; this outlook was one of Patteson's legacies to the Melanesian church.

Selwyn's plan for a 'fifth column' to infiltrate Melanesian society had been a good one. If it had not had dramatic and rapid results, it had at least succeeded as well as the Presbyterians and London

Missionary Society further south. Forty years after Selwyn's first arrival in New Zealand, and about ten years after Patteson's death, another 'fifth column' had its beginnings, not with an intellectual patrician like Selwyn, but with a humble young woman of small education yet powerful faith, named Florence Young.

In the early 1880s, Florence Young became acquainted with Melanesian labourers on Queensland plantations, who having been brought to Queensland to work, were left in their heathen condition. This troubled Florence Young, and she had the leisure, wealth and Christian resolve to do something about it. She began by taking Sunday classes on her brothers' estate; the work spread to neighbouring plantations, where instruction was enthusiastically received by the labourers, and conversions in the confined environment of the plantations were numerous. Within a few years this work had become formally organised and was named the Queensland Kanaka Mission.

When the labourers returned to their island homes, many of them found, as had Selwyn's younger and less thoroughly-Christianized recruits, that maintaining the faith in isolation, perhaps even amid hostility, was difficult. Many of them lapsed, but others had been so thoroughly converted that they tried to introduce Christianity to their homes. Some such men in the 1890s appealed to the Queensland Kanaka Mission to extend its work to the islands, but a decade was to pass before it would do so. Not until recruiting had ceased and the labourers had been repatriated, was the Mission willing to follow its people to Melanesia. After two visits to the Solomons by Miss Young and other members of the mission in 1904 and 1905, the Queensland Kanaka Mission was dissolved, and re-established as the South Seas Evangelical Mission. The wide distribution of its former pupils ensured that the mission had many potential outposts; and with these men as its agents, the mission did not have to rely entirely on expatriate, European missionaries.

The South Seas Evangelical Mission was characterized by several distinctive features. It was founded and staffed mainly by women, whereas in all other Christian missions, women had been merely missionary wives, long-suffering and hard-working, in both mission and their own domestic roles. Second, it held that any community of believers was a *church*, which ran its own affairs and supported its own clergy, like those of the earliest Christians. Finally, it accentuated the distinction between pagan and Christian to the extent of insisting on separate Christian settlements where Christians could encourage each other and where converts were cut-off from the rival spiritual claims of another system of belief with all its cultural associations. This mission, a fundamentalist late-comer to the Pacific islands, thus became more characteristic of twentieth century Melanesia than its predecessors.

The evangelizing of Melanesia by these three missions, and by the Roman Catholics in the French colony of New Caledonia, is both complicated and obscure. There were many hundreds of communities to be contacted separately, each with its own needs; the previous experience of Europeans varied widely amongst Melanesians, and accordingly, the degree of acculturation also varied greatly from village to village, with the result that the missionaries worked in greater isolation and greater danger than their counterparts in Polynesia.

Resident traders and settlers were less attracted to Melanesia than to Polynesia, and nowhere was there a 'settler-rush' the way there had been to Samoa and Fiji in the 1860s. The Melanesian environment was hostile to the individual settler of private means, but by the 1880s, there seemed to be sufficient potential to attract both French and British company-colonization schemes.

In 1845, a French territorial interest in Melanesia began with the placing of several Roman Catholic missions of the Marist order. All proved short-lived except the one at Balade in New Caledonia. As in eastern Polynesia, Catholic missions proved to be the forerunner of French annexation, which was undertaken in 1853. Since it was intended by the French that New Caledonia should become a colony of settlement, a generous land grants policy was adopted, ignoring the prior claims of the Melanesian inhabitants. It was not till the 1860s that the decision to make New Caledonia a convict colony, together with the discovery of gold there, attracted a significant number of settlers, British as well as French. The convicts, like those in Australia two generations earlier, were required to be useful developing the colony, and were set to work for both government and free settlers.

Although New Caledonia was capable of absorbing more immigrants than France could send, its progress as a colony inevitably directed attention towards the adjacent islands from a variety of groups. Official French attention was aroused by the rivalry between Catholic and Protestant missions in the Loyalty Islands with the result that the governor of New Caledonia annexed the group in 1864. During the 1860s, a handful of mainly British settlers made private arrangements with New Hebridean communities to settle and begin plantations. As elsewhere, the incentives were high cotton prices and a buoyant copra market, but by the late 1870s, most were not doing well, owing to the shortage of labour and a fall in prices. By 1880 informal colonization was in retreat.

During the 1880s, many of the surviving settlers were pleased at the opportunity to sell out. Their benefactor was an Irishman, John Higginson, who had settled in New Caledonia and taken French citizenship, and since the early 1870s, had been interested in the potential of the New Hebrides as a French colony. Higginson was an ardent advocate of French expansion as well as a shrewd and successful businessman, and in 1882 after years of unsuccessful agitation for official French action, he established a company, the Compagnie Calédonienne des Nouvelles-Hébrides (C.C.N.H.) which vigorously pursued a policy of buying out British settlers. By this means Higginson planned to strengthen French interests in the group and thus force French annexation which would in turn facilitate his further commercial aims. In his first goal he was largely successful; in his second he failed. His success in promoting French interest alarmed the Presbyterian missionaries in the New Hebrides and their Australian sympathizers. Their pressure on the Australian colonial governments and on the British government deterred the French from ratifying a protectorate variously secured between 1882 and 1884, and eventually in 1887, an Anglo-French agreement was signed, repudiating any territorial claims and establishing a joint naval commission to regulate settlers' affairs in the group. Higginson, disappointed but undeterred, continued with his own company-colonization activity. His Australian opponents, also knowing that the matter would not rest, saw that they must adopt Higginson's tactics, and in 1889 established a company to compete with the C.C.N.H.: the Australian New Hebrides Company (A.N.H.C.).

For a few years the A.N.H.C. proved a successful rival to the growing French interest: its trading operations did well, it bought land in large quantities which it made available to new settlers; but by the mid-1890s, both companies were in financial difficulties, and both had to be thoroughly reorganized. In 1894, the C.C.N.H. became the Société Française des Nouvelles-Hébrides, with a French government subsidy; the A.N.H.C., having at least averted the worst fears of its founders, and having seen British settlement successfully re-established, was taken over by the future giant of Pacific commerce, Burns, Philp and Co. in 1897. Both companies continued to promote the European settlement and development of the New Hebrides, and each prevented the other from securing the predominance which would have urged outright annexation by either Britain or France. Without this rivalry, however, it is unlikely that European settlement would have become established at that time, nor would it have been so extensive. No company nor settler could make up for the natural obstacles of climate and isolation which impeded prosperous European economic development in the islands.

This rule was to be further exemplified elsewhere in Melanesia: the Solomon Islands were to remain a fringe area for western commerce with little to attract settlement (though gold prospectors were another matter) even after a colonial government was established, and Papua New Guinea also demonstrated the same inexorable economic laws, but with some important differences of method.

As both missions and traders moved their operations northward during the 1870s, imperialist passions in the Australian colonies were rising. Just as anxiety was provoked by French enterprise in southern Melanesia, so was it aroused by the conspicuous success of German commerce in northern Melanesia.

The main focus of this competition was the large island of New Guinea and its smaller adjacent islands, which were well-populated and mountainous, promising abundant resources and potential wealth to the imaginative and adventurous. New Guinea was the subject of perhaps more visionary schemes and colonialist follies than any other part of the Pacific, and the participants ranged from charlatans to shrewd, practical businessmen and developers, and even to some missionaries and scientists of great force of character.

New Guinea had been frequented by traders and whalers on a small scale since the 1820s; the Dutch had annexed the western half in two stages, in 1828 and 1848; British naval surveyors had been busy in the 1840s and 1850s; and from 1847 to 1855, a French Catholic mission had been struggling to survive on Woodlark Island in the Solomon Sea. By the 1870s, the progress of missions and commerce had both reached the point at which New Guinea must inevitably be brought into the mainstream of European activity. After such long neglect, events now happened quickly. Beginning in 1871, the London Missionary Society placed several Polynesian and European missionaries on the south coast of New Guinea, and in 1875, the Methodist Missionary Society began its activity on the shores of the strait between New Britain and New Ireland. At the same time, a new influx of traders arrived to reinforce and supplant those few who had remained there from an earlier time. The new traders, although not all German, mainly represented two German firms, Godeffroys and Hernsheim, both of which were already well established in the Pacific. Godeffroys in particular had plans to expand its operations, and accordingly in 1878 its manager, Theodor Weber, already famous for his work in Samoa, bought land and harbours in New Guinea and elsewhere.

Individual adventurers, many from Australia, were being attracted to the south coast, and in 1877 when gold was discovered in the hinterland of Port Moresby, more prospectors came. Enough news of New Guinea was now being disseminated to fire the imaginations of visionaries and speculators and a number of associations were formed: in 1872, a prospecting association in Sydney; in 1875, a New Guinea Colonizing Association; in 1878, the Australian Colonization Company; and a few years later, the New Guinea Exploring Company. All these groups had grand plans, none achieved anything. They did evince, however, a growing Australian interest, and they accompanied official and unofficial urgings in Australia that New Guinea be annexed as a natural extension for Australian enterprise and settlement. More quixotic was the real colonizing expedition of the French Marquis de Rays in 1880, which attempted to form a settlement on the southern tip of New Ireland, an appallingly incompetent scheme which cost much in the lives of the colonists who were gulled into joining the scheme. Such was the accelerating pace of private colonization that in 1878 the Western Pacific High Commission appointed a deputy Commissioner to supervise British subjects, and the Queensland government went so far as to send a magistrate to Port Moresby.

So far, the activities of Australian traders and prospectors on the south coast, and of German traders on the north coast and nearby islands suggested no conflict of interest. Rivalry, when it came in 1882, was brought by Queensland labour recruiters working in the area where the Germans were recruiting for their Samoan plantations. In this way the informal colonization of trade and settlement was brought to the attention of the British and German governments. If that was not sufficient, Sir Thomas McIlwraith, premier of Queensland, made a more noticeable demonstration when he purported in 1883 to annex all of eastern New Guinea and its adjacent islands. McIlwraith knew that he could not thus legally commit the imperial government, but he hoped to force the British government to action. Protracted negotiations followed on the terms of acquisition and colonial cost-sharing; Anglo-German negotiations were initiated because of Germany's obvious interest in the matter. Towards the end of 1884, New Guinea was partitioned, and the boundary was settled by agreement in April 1885.

In British New Guinea there had been sporadic contact along the coasts and up some of the major river valleys, but the impact on native life at this stage was slight, and it would be many years before it would increase or penetrate far inland. Despite the ambitions of company promoters, New Guinea was not inviting; the climate, the diseases, the isolation, the risks of every kind, deterred the cautious, and the illusory promise of fortune could not attract even the optimistic. In German New Guinea it was a little different: the extensive operations of two well organised companies, Deutsche Handels-und Plantagen-Gesellschaft (the successor of Godeffroys) and Robertson & Hernsheim were well known along the coasts for their trading and labour recruiting; trade was well established, and if it had not penetrated far inland, it foreshadowed more intense contact. Now that annexation had cleared the way, contact on a massively disruptive scale was soon to be prosecuted by a company-colonization scheme which dwarfed any previously suggested elsewhere in Melanesia.

Situated between the New Hebrides and New Guinea, and largely neglected by the formulators of colonizing schemes, lay the Solomon Islands, as daunting in the 1870s as they had been in previous decades, where a handful of traders did no more than attach themselves to the outer fringes of the group for a precarious and dangerous livelihood. The volume of contact increased during the 1870s as labour recruiters came north looking for ever larger and less wary populations. As a mission field, the Solomons remained a preserve of the Anglicans' Melanesian Mission until 1898, when the Marists returned after a fifty-year absence, and converts of Florence Young's Queensland Kanaka Mission returned to their homes.

The Western Pacific High Commission, authorised to exercise jurisdiction over British subjects, took an earnest but ineffective interest in the group; and the Royal Navy's Australia Station sent regular patrols which from time to time inquired into clashes between islanders and traders, exacting reprisals when in the judgement of the young officers on the spot, they seemed both justified and likely to be efficacious.

For the Melanesian Mission, the Solomons was a stony field: it was dangerous, and its people ranged in manner from hostile to unyielding. In the 1880s, signs of change came with steady conversions on the island of Florida, but progress elsewhere was painfully slow: mission personnel were accepted and heard, and became part of the island scene, but the real objective, conversion, was rarely attained.

The Solomons were also affected by the political re-classification of New Guinea in 1884. Britain and Germany, in demarcating their spheres of influence, partitioned the group, but only Germany (in 1886) formally took possession. British action was deferred until 1893, when the revival of the labour trade by the Queensland government revived the old problem of policing a territory which had no settled government, and Britain therefore declared a protectorate over its part of the group. It was merely an exercise in tidiness: European residents numbered only a few dozen; there was no settlement as such, no settlers as such, no investment, no contest between nationalities—only Melanesians still very much in possession and control of their territories, but with changes beginning to appear in their traditional ways of life. The influence of Europe on the indigenous population and its culture had been uneven, and the new protectorate would have only a small impact for many years.

So far, missionaries, traders and settlers had changed Melanesia, though they had not yet transformed it. Melanesia was proving a much less pliable, less malleable subject for cultural experimentation than Polynesia, and as the colonial era dawned, it still presented a forbidding and hostile image.

Chapter Nine

MICRONESIA: INFORMAL COLONIZATION

Micronesia, the world of small islands, has for long been the forgotten zone of the Pacific. More remote than other island groups, and containing no large land areas, it has been studied less than other regions in the Pacific, and for much of its history has been less frequently visited.

In pre-European times it was, however, the most closely integrated of the Oceanic culture areas. Despite its being a collection of four or five separate archipelagoes, scattered across nearly eight million square kilometres of ocean, Micronesia was better known to its native navigators than Polynesia and Melanesia were respectively to theirs. As European contact developed, Micronesia was subject to the same influences as the other regions, but a major source of difference was its extreme resource-poverty. It had little to attract either the settler or the investor, and of the succession of traders who visited the region, most failed to find the visits worthwhile.

Sustained contact with Europeans did not come to most of Micronesia until the 1850s, although Spanish voyaging between America and the Philippines had located a great many of the islands in the sixteenth century. Guam and the Mariana group of islands in the west were discovered by Magellan in 1521; the Marshall group in the east was sighted by Saavedra in 1529; and in 1564 several discoveries were made in the Carolines. Few of these sightings changed the course of history: it was not until 1565 that Spain claimed Guam and the Philippines as its own, while the other Spanish discoveries were forgotten; and a century was to pass before Spanish Jesuit missionaries in 1668 moved from the Philippines to Guam and northwards into the rest of the chain, now renamed the Mariana islands (Magellan had called them Los Ladrones—the thieves). Mass baptisms quickly took place, and were followed almost immediately by vigorous, violent resistance to colonization. The resistance had to be subdued by Spanish soldiers, a process which was not finally completed until 1695, when the survivors were resettled on Guam

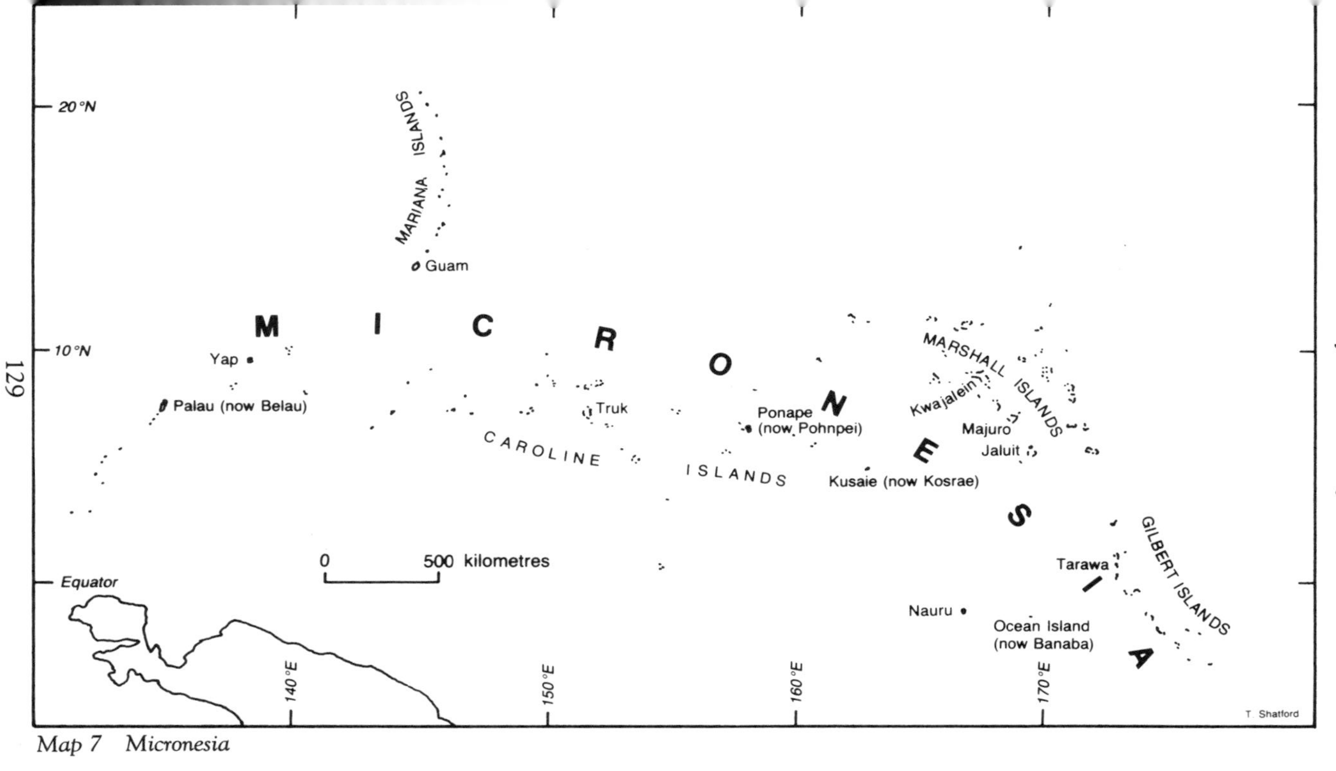

Map 7 Micronesia

to become a peonized peasantry, working under the centuries-long somnolence of Spanish colonial rule. Early in the eighteenth century, the Jesuits placed missionaries on Palau and Ulithi in the Carolines, where most of them were murdered, thereby causing the plans to be discontinued. It was not until the end of the eighteenth century that Micronesia was again disturbed, but this time by a different influence.

Ships of the British East India Company, sailing between India and China passed through the western Carolines; one such ship, the *Antelope*, was wrecked on Palau, where its crew spent several months living with the Palauans while building a small vessel, and as a result the East India Company surveyed Palau in 1791. At about the same time, the eastern side of Micronesia was placed on the map by two East India Company captains who, having transported convicts to help establish the British colony of New South Wales in 1788, sailed from there to China to collect a return cargo, and consequently discovered and named after themselves the Gilbert and Marshall groups.

The North American fur seal trade, which brought Hawai'i into the orbit of European trade, led to further occasional sightings and desultory attempts at casual trade. Ships sailing between Hawai'i and Canton passed through Micronesia, but there was little to attract them to stop. Some Carolinian communities, acquainted with European goods, took the initiative in maintaining access to them by making regular canoe voyages over long ocean distances to Guam.

The sustained, large-scale contact history of Micronesia (apart from Guam and the rest of the Marianas) began, like so much else in Pacific history, with the whaling industry and its need for refreshment places handy to the principal whaling grounds. Micronesia offered two such resorts: Kusaie (now called Kosrae) and Ponape (now Pohnpei). By the 1830s, both places were well-known; they were not only frequently-visited resorts, but were also refuges for escaped convicts from New South Wales as well as for deserters from whaling ships. The usual contact vices of arms sales, drunkenness and prostitution were rapidly established, and introduced diseases worked their inevitable damage. During the 1840s, both places were being visited annually by perhaps fifty whaling vessels, which, being concentrated in a seasonal pattern, were more than sufficient to effect great damage. Populations declined, 'key' people (chiefs and experts in traditional lore) whose numbers were small at the best of times, were lost; the result was social and cultural degradation, and ultimately anarchy.

While this was happening on these two large islands, the rest of Micronesia was having incidental, sporadic contact with whalers or traders; for the most part, the Micronesians acquired a reputation for savagery and treachery, which is to say that Europeans usually came off badly in the violent encounters which characterized these occasional visits.

Thus, Kusaie and Ponape, which from the 1830s onwards were both better known to Europeans, were in greater need of a benign influence. By the 1850s, the American missionaries of the American Board of Commissioners for Foreign Missions (A.B.C.F.M.) in Hawai'i, disenchanted with the Marquesas (which were in any case under French control) and victorious in Hawai'i, now looked to Micronesia. In 1852, European missionaries supported by Hawai'ian teachers were introduced to Ponape and Kusaie, where they were received with interest and courtesy, and found ready listeners not only among the chiefs and people but among the resident beachcombers as well. As in Polynesia, the missionaries were made secure by the patronage of chiefs, which helped to guarantee them a congregation. But the decadent state of both communities was the missionaries' greatest asset, for they preached a message of relief and salvation, and inveighed against prostitution, drunkenness and disorder. The doctrine they taught provided both the opportunity and the impetus for the Ponapeans and Kusaieans to begin their recovery from the disasters of twenty years of close contact, with the result that both islands were substantially converted by the early 1860s.

Not long after they began their activities in these two islands, the A.B.C.F.M. placed missionaries elsewhere in eastern Micronesia. They sent to the Gilberts in 1857 the Rev. Hiram Bingham Jr., the son of the pioneer missionary of the same name in Hawai'i; and in the same year the Marshall Islands mission began on the island of Ebon, an important centre of political power and trade in the traditional order. There, and in the Gilberts, the events followed the pattern of Kusaie and Ponape: the missionaries seemed to be meeting a need which the islanders themselves perceived. Conversions came quickly, to be followed after a few years by the challenge of a heathen revival which was often the result of a change of chieftainship.

As in Polynesia and Melanesia, the acceptance of the missionaries and their doctrines accompanied the acceptance of the medicines and schools with which they were closely identified. Out of the schools came native teachers who in their turn spread the Christian teaching further. In 1869, a training school was established on Ebon specifically for potential mission teachers, and thus by the 1870s, the affairs of these new churches and their continued evangelism were very largely in indigenous hands.

In the 1870s, a new phase of expansion began with the placement of native teachers in those islands in the eastern Carolines still awaiting missionary presence, namely Mokil, Pingelap, the Mortlocks and finally in 1879, the large island of Truk. By the end of the 1870s, in the space of a quarter of a century, fourteen strong churches had been established in the eastern Carolines.

The missionaries, like the Micronesians themselves, did not compartmentalize religion—to the thoroughly converted, religion is all of life and the pursuit of holiness embraces all relationships. Consequently, the missionaries and the converted chiefs attempted to make appropriate reforms in Micronesian society: internal migration sometimes occurred so that separated Christians might enjoy solidarity; settlement patterns were modified as full Christian living was perceived to imply villages and nuclear-family households; land-tenure reform was attempted, and—especially on Ponape—changes in the political system towards democratic ideals were attempted. These reforms, where they were attempted, were generally short-lived. The American Puritans found that the policy of the Anglicans in Melanesia was best: Christianity was most acceptable when it changed only the bare essentials of heathen life; beyond that, Christianity was bound to be 'indigenized', with whatever compromises in doctrine and practice native Christians deemed appropriate.

The concern of the missionaries for the whole life of the people gave them an ambiguous relationship with the prophets of commerce. Unlike the contemporary Melanesian situation where missionaries and traders seemed to have incompatible interests, there was considerable mutual acceptance, the cause of which was the result of a different attitude on the part of the traders, rather than the result of greater tolerance by the missionaries.

The tolerance of the traders was due fundamentally to one thing: missionaries and missions were good for business. During half a century of occasional contact most Micronesian communities lost their reputations for friendliness and hospitality, and were generally feared. Until missionaries showed the way, no resident trader settled in the Marshall Islands, nor in Truk, nor in the lesser islands of the eastern Carolines, nor in the Gilberts. The missionaries either made those places safe for Europeans, or showed that former fears were not justified. In the western Carolines, the traders Cheyne and Tetens and a few others preceded missionaries but did not prosper; Cheyne, indeed, a veteran of the Melanesian sandalwood trade, was killed on Palau in 1866 after a decade of failed commercial undertakings. Moreover, although the missionaries preached vigorously against prostitution, and the selling of alcohol, firearms and tobacco, Micronesian Christians were good customers in other commodities. They dealt honestly if honestly dealt with, eagerly buying cloth and clothing, utensils and tools, and exotic food like rice and salt meat; material civilization and Christianity seemed to go together, as the first missionaries in the 1790s had believed. But it was not a case of one being dependent on the other: acquaintance with European products was sufficient to engender an insatiable demand for them, which Christianity redirected to those which were less obviously harmful and which fitted a European sense of propriety.

The Micronesians, of course, had to have a commodity to sell, and their islands had none of the resources of the larger islands of Polynesia or Melanesia. The labour trade reached some parts (mainly the Gilberts) in the 1870s, but could never be a large scale trade; there was no sandalwood; *bêche-de-mer* and shell, though tried, could not sustain a steady trade. Trade of any kind would not flourish in Micronesia in the hands of the small independent merchants who had pioneered Polynesia and Micronesia. Micronesian trade was delayed until the age of the merchant companies with capital to invest in plant, and organizational expertise to consolidate stocks, find viable markets and balance losses with profits. Whereas the early luxury trader depended on a volatile Chinese market, the merchant companies dealt in the humble copra for European and American industrial markets.

The first large-scale trader was Adolph Capelle who, from small beginnings in the Marshall Islands in the 1860s, built up a business using several schooners and employing resident agents scattered throughout the Marshalls and eastern Carolines. At the same time the German firm Godeffroy und Sohn of Hamburg spread into the region from its base in Apia where it had become established in 1857. Other companies joined the competition in the 1870s, notably the German firm of Hernsheim and Co. (later Robertson and Hernsheim), and the New Zealand firm of Henderson and MacFarlane.

Other competitors tried to enter the field, but had fleeting success or none at all; while frauds, notably Ben Pease and Bully Hayes, had Micronesia as the main scene of their unsavoury operations. The greatest challenge to the big companies came from a castaway who established himself not in Eastern Micronesia, but in the west where so far no one had succeeded. This was D.D. O'Keefe, an almost legendary figure, who after being washed ashore on Yap half-drowned in 1871, built up such an extensive trade network through imagination, integrity and sensitivity to the societies within which he worked, that when he died in 1903, his fortune was estimated at half a million American dollars.

The trading companies did well enough during the early Christian era and while the islands were still independent, but the margin for competition was slender because of the limited resources of Micronesia and the distance to foreign markets—the aggregate size of the Marshall, Caroline (including Palau) and Gilbert Islands is only about 1,700 square kilometres. By 1885, Micronesia was exporting only four thousand tons of copra per year, worth only $US250,000. While these figures might represent comparatively high productivity for the islands, it was not a speculator's return on investment and the resulting sense of insecurity was probably the main reason for the traders turning towards political intervention.

As elsewhere in the Pacific, contact was bound to lead to a conflict of interest, or to misunderstanding, or to plain false dealing. British ships from the Royal Navy's China Station made periodic patrols and looked into allegations of mistreatment of British subjects. Occasional tours were made by U.S. ships, and after about 1870, by ships of the German Imperial Navy as well. Cheyne's murder in 1866 was promptly avenged by the British navy; in 1870, the U.S. navy imposed a typically unequal treaty on the chiefs of Ponape which severely restricted their freedoms; and in 1878, the German navy supported some unjust claims of Hernsheim against the chief of Kusaie. A controlled commercial environment which pre-empted interventions such as these promised larger profits—perhaps even monopoly. In contrast with the pattern in Polynesia, native Micronesian politics were too finely balanced for indigenous movements towards political centralization to occur (although there was the appearance of an attempt at such in the Gilbert Islands); missionaries, content with the existing local chieftaincies, did not attempt to set up Polynesian-style kingdoms; and there were no large settler populations to advance their own pretensions to state-formation.

Thus, if the trading companies wanted the advantages of sympathetic government they had to look to external sources for it, and their first response came from the German navy in 1878, which secured special privileges for the traders in a one-sided treaty with a puppet king of the Ralik Islands (part of the Marshall group). Similar treaties were made the same year with chiefs in the Ellice Islands, the Gilbert Islands and in New Britain. In effect, these treaties deprived island chiefs of any authority which they might have pretended to exercise over German citizens, and laid the foundation for more direct intervention later when such treaties were inevitably violated.

In the early 1880s, foreign interests in the islands were pressing more stridently for intervention, and the mood for annexation was stronger in European politics. Germany, whose citizens by now far overshadowed the British and Americans in Micronesia, was seriously contemplating action; at the same time, Spain revived its ancient claim to the Carolines, having first attempted to do this in 1874. The basis for its claim was three-fold: the right of discovery, the ancient Papal division of the world, and its unsuccessful missionary activity of one hundred and fifty years earlier. In 1885, a compromise was reached: while Germany annexed the Marshalls without opposition, Spain's annexation of the Carolines proceeded at the cost of making concesssions—trading rights and naval stations—which amply satisfied German ambitions. German trading interests in the Marshalls then coalesced in the formation of the Jaluit Company which in 1887 took over the tasks of government in the new colony. Nothing could have been more agreeable to the traders, except perhaps a pliable government from which they could dissociate themselves. By 1885, the only islands outside European control were the Gilberts where the trading interests were mainly British, and the British government, true to its behaviour in Melanesia, preferred not to emulate the Germans.

By this time, further social changes had accompanied these political adjustments: there were now fewer Micronesians than there had been half a century before. The Marshallese population, for example, had declined from an estimated 15,000 to about 10,000, and the Kusaieans from 3000 to 300; overall, the loss throughout Micronesia had been perhaps as high as fifty percent. Introduced disease was the main agent of depopulation, but demoralization resulting from loss of traditions and powerlessness in the face of externally-induced change was an indispensable, if immeasurable component.

Micronesian history up to this point is therefore a variation on a theme: the same sequence of events unfolded, and the same procession of foreign interests came and acted out the familiar roles. Nevertheless, there are distinctive features in the Micronesian response resulting from the particular circumstances of geography and culture which weave a subtle pattern of variations.

Chapter Ten

THE POLITICS OF ANNEXATION

By 1900, all Pacific islands had fallen under the authority of foreign powers. This experience links the history of the Pacific islands with the history of Asia, Africa and the Americas, and there may therefore seem to be an inevitability of design about the outcome. Contemporaries certainly thought so; by the second half of the nineteenth century, Europeans at home and overseas, and those in the derivative states of America and Australasia, were intoxicated with sentiments of racial supremacy, and had devised crude philosophies to justify the political and material ascendancy to which they had risen. In the resulting atmosphere of imperialism, and particularly during the 1870s and 1880s, the major powers of Europe had assumed sovereignty over most of the peoples inhabiting the tropical parts of the world.

In the Pacific, this apparent 'rush' for colonies was slightly delayed, occurring for the most part in the 1880s and 1890s, giving the appearance of being the final stages in a grand design; but in fact the Pacific islands did not become incorporated in the European empires as part of any grand design to partition the world, nor simply to give expression to an irrational European fantasy of racial superiority. There was a multiplicity of motives and a diversity of circumstances, with ample testimony, as usual, to both the noble and despicable characteristics of humanity, and the process extended fitfully not over two decades, but over six. In most cases it resulted from actual or threatened chaos occasioned by the uncontrolled, self-interested contact between foreigners and islanders.

New Zealand was the first island-group to fall to an extra-regional empire, annexed by Britain in 1840. Unlike Tahiti and Hawai'i, there had been no indigenous trend towards political centralization in New Zealand. The wars of the 1820s and 1830s were purely destructive, pursued for the traditional concerns of prestige and revenge. Defeat of an enemy, while it led to the territorial dispossession of the defeated in some cases, was not followed by any consolidation of power or attempt to create a new dominance by one tribe, or of any supra-tribal polity. Consequently, the challenges posed by increasing European trade and settlement in the 1830s had to be met by Maori clans or tribes acting individually with neither common policy nor mutual support. This naturally made European penetration much easier than it might have been. When to that is added the mutual jealousies and hostilities of Maori communities, and the absence of law among the Europeans, it can be readily understood that New Zealand should be perceived as being in a state of anarchy. European whalers and timber cutters and, by the late 1830s, settlers intending to farm were bound to come in increasing numbers, and it was in the interests of neither race that there should be no regulation of how that contact should be conducted or how the inevitable conflicts of interest should be resolved.

Successive governors of New South Wales had long recognized that this could be a problem: as early as 1814, in a vain and useless measure, the missionary Thomas Kendall had been appointed as Justice of the Peace for New Zealand; then came a British Act of 1817 which attempted to give British courts cognizance of crimes committed in New Zealand and other Pacific islands as if they had been committed on the high seas. Recognizing the ineffectiveness of both of these measures, but hesitating to take the only realistic steps to meet the needs of the situation, the British government accepted a moral responsibility for the actions of its subjects in New Zealand, attempting, however, to meet that responsibility by mere moral suasion.

In 1832 a British Resident was appointed to New Zealand. His job was to represent British law and thus to restrain the behaviour of British subjects. The Resident, James Busby, was in an invidious position: by no means all of the foreigners in New Zealand were British, he had no force to support his authority, and there was no single native authority with which he could treat. Clearly, as Busby perceived, the only solution to the problem was the establishment of a government of New Zealand. Doubtless he knew something of the modestly successful Polynesian kingdoms of Tahiti and Hawai'i, and he therefore tried to establish a tribal confederacy in New Zealand in 1835. The attempt received cautious but ineffectual support from the British government, but in New Zealand itself the attempt was bound to fail, since it was too much at odds with Maori political ideas, and would in any case have had great difficulty in commanding the respect of an increasing foreign population.

At last in 1839, the British government, with no particular desire for further colonial obligations in the remote south, yielded to the inevitable, and appointed a naval officer, Captain William Hobson, as consul to the Maori chiefs and as lieutenant-governor over any British settlements in New Zealand, with authority to negotiate with Maori chiefs to establish British sovereignty over whole or part of New Zealand. Hobson's instructions must surely constitute the most diffident and self-effacing act of imperial expansion in human history, but the result was the Treaty of Waitangi and the annexation of New Zealand in 1840.

France, meanwhile, with a more strongly-felt need to declare its honour and glory as a world power, planned to plant its flag somewhere in the Pacific, but like Britain, found itself committed further than its official policy makers had intended. By the 1830s, French maritime trade had revived to a level commensurate with France's position in Europe: its whaling fleet in the Pacific, while much smaller than the American, rivalled the British, and its trading vessels had a large share of the trade of South America's western sea-board. Supplementing this presence were the voyages of several scientific expeditions in the 1820s and 1830s, namely those of Duperrey, Bougainville, and Dumont D'Urville; others were more frankly concerned to show the flag than add to science. Moreover, the Catholic church through its French branches showed in the 1830s a willingness to offer competition to the Protestant missions in the Pacific which had been undisturbed except by their own rivalries since 1797. The government of France focused a benevolent eye on the church's plans and in subsequent years gave proof of its willingness to support the church's instruments. Indeed, Catholic missions were to give France the opportunity for political intervention in various parts of the Pacific.

In the late 1830s, private adventurers and entrepreneurs in France, as in England, were looking to new fields for colonization, and by 1839 had persuaded their government to support such ventures. One was despatched to New Zealand in 1839, but was too late to influence the course of events there which were drawing New Zealand into the British empire.

Denied the acquisition of New Zealand, France still felt that it needed a base in the Pacific as a resort for its commerce and a base whence its interests could be protected. Admiral Du Petit-Thouars recommended the Marquesas far in the eastern Pacific, astride the route between Cape Horn and Hawai'i, and between South American ports and the western Pacific. The group was much frequented by whalers, and Marquesan society had proven impervious to Protestant missionaries. Du Petit-Thouars, sent back to the Pacific to carry out his own recommendations, annexed the various islands of the group in May and June 1842.

The annexation of the Marquesas was a calculated act of imperialism, the first seen so far by European powers in the Pacific. It was soon followed by a case of accidental imperialism. Du Petit-Thouars, convinced that his annexation of the Marquesas would smartly bring a retaliatory British annexation of Tahiti, hastened to that group. Britain in fact, had no such intention, but since 1838 there had been a series of crises in Tahiti involving French priests and French traders whose difficulties with the Tahitian monarchy had caused them to appeal several times for the support and protection of their government, which in practice meant the French navy in the Pacific. A succession of officers, Du Petit-Thouars among them, had bullied and threatened the Tahitian government, and by imposing repeated humiliations which the Tahitians were powerless to repel, encouraged further defiance by self-interested European settlers. Pomare IV, queen of Tahiti, was defended only by the British consul and former missionary, George Pritchard. Her only recourse, indeed, was to send repeated letters appealing for protection by the British government. The British government responded with nothing more tangible than sympathy and promises of moral support indicating in reality their utter indifference to Tahiti.

And so, acting on his own inclination, and guided by the prejudices and ambitions of the French consul, Moerenhout, Du Petit-Thouars extracted from suborned chiefs and helpless queen a dictated request for French protection. There was no other alternative to the ultimatum which the admiral had presented. In Paris the French government accepted the unlooked for and unexpected possession because it did not want to offend popular, nationalistic opinion, and it did not want to give British opinion the satisfaction of a French humiliation.

The questions of New Zealand, the Marquesas and Tahiti came before the British and French governments at about the same time, and the solution accepted in each case was all much of a piece. A further component (together with other issues in Europe and the Mediterranean) was the settlement of the Hawai'ian affair. The chiefs of Hawai'i since their dealings with Captain George Vancouver in 1794 had considered themselves under British protection in the common, simple sense of that word. It had suited successive British governments on the few occasions when Hawai'ian affairs had come to their attention, to leave the relationship vague.

During the 1820s, however, increasing European settlement and commerce (most of it concerning American citizens, not British), necessitated the appointment of consuls to mediate between the native authorities and the foreigners. Disputes over property and civil-versus-criminal jurisdiction were inevitable, the ill-chosen consuls themselves being leaders in the difficulties which developed. Consequently, from 1826 and continuing for the next twenty years, there was a succession of treaties, all of them putting the infant Hawai'ian state at an acute disadvantage in its dealings with the nationals of Britain, France and the United States. The first of these treaties was negotiated in 1826 by Captain Thomas Jones of the U.S. navy, and although one-sided and imposing obligations which it would be difficult for Hawai'i to perform, did not seriously restrict Hawai'ian sovereignty.

The implications of sovereignty, however, were things which headstrong consuls, bellicose naval officers, and self-seeking foreign residents were unwilling to accept, and during the 1830s there was a series of incidents involving claims to land and the scope of Hawai'ian jurisdiction, which came to a head in 1836. The immediate precipitant of the crisis was the attempt by the Hawai'ian government to exclude priests of the Catholic church from living and evangelizing in Hawai'i. This issue had first arisen in 1827, and had now festered. Unfortunately for the hapless Hawai'ian government, the priest at the centre of the controversy of 1836 was an Englishman, Father Walsh, to whose defence came an English ship of war and a French one. The English captain, Lord Edward Russell, dictated a one-sided treaty and bullied and threatened the Hawai'ian king into accepting it. The affair did not rest there, for the following year the two priests who had originally been expelled returned. The ensuing diplomatic farce reflected no credit on the diplomatic and naval representatives of either France or Britain. The Hawai'ian government was further humiliated, and Admiral Du Petit-Thouars obliged the Hawai'ians to accept a treaty similar in provisions to those already existing with Britain and the United States.

This time the French followed up their intervention in Hawai'ian affairs, with the likely intention of provoking a Hawai'ian reaction which would justify annexation. This after all was what the same officers were doing in Tahiti, with that very result in 1842 (although in that case the possession was called a protectorate). In July 1838, the French government, acting on the one-sided reports which it was receiving of events in Hawai'i, ordered Captain Laplace to exact reparation, and to make an unforgettable impression of French power and political morality. Arriving in Honolulu in July 1839 he issued an ultimatum demanding freedom of worship, land for a Catholic church, and a $20,000 bond on the threat of war. When these concessions were granted he insisted that the Hawai'ian king sign a treaty which contained two particularly objectionable articles: Frenchmen accused of crimes in Hawai'i were to be tried only before a jury of foreign residents nominated by the French consul and accepted by the Hawai'ian government, and no article of French produce was to be excluded from Hawai'ian trade, with the maximum duty set at only five percent.

Since all the previous treaties contained 'most favoured nation' clauses, these provisions immediately became applicable to the British and Americans as well; Hawai'i was thus at one stroke deprived of effective jurisdiction over foreign residents (given the unco-operative attitudes of the consuls), its liquor law was demolished, and its principal source of revenue (import duties) was strictly limited.

This was a situation intolerable for any nation. All the treaties except that of 1826 with the United States (and which America never ratified) had been extracted under duress by officers unauthorized to make treaties at all. The Hawai'ian government in 1840 therefore sent a mission to America and Europe to seek the revision of the treaties, and to have the independence of the Hawai'ian kingdom placed on a more secure footing. Annexation by one power or another had been a continual fear (though an unrealistic one) throughout the 1830s, and the present treaty situation made the preservation of independence a hopeless ambition.

In its main objectives, treaty revision, the mission to the powers was a failure: there is doubt that it was even considered seriously by Britain and France. While the mission was away, however, the very situation which it was intended to prevent came about. In February 1843, a British naval captain, Lord George Paulet, acting on the face-value of complaints by the litigious Consul Charlton and of his accomplice, Alexander Simpson, made several peremptory demands backed up by an ultimatum, aimed at overturning decisions of Hawai'ian courts and challenging Hawai'ian sovereignty. When these demands were met, more outrageous ones followed; whereupon the king of Hawai'i, Kamehameha III, in desperation took the only course remaining and ceded his small kingdom to Britain, placing it in Paulet's hands as Britain's representative. Paulet's superior officer, Admiral Richard Thomas, knowing that the acceptance of such an offer was contrary to his government's policy, hastened to Hawai'i to restore Hawai'ian independence, which he did after extracting a treaty similar to the French Laplace treaty of 1839.

Meanwhile, negotiations involving Britain, France and the United States over the issue resulted in an Anglo-French convention recognising Hawai'ian independence (in effect, a mutual 'hands-off' agreement) in 1843 and an American undertaking to the same purpose. Revised treaties followed in 1846 but modified only the most obnoxious of the articles. Another decade was to pass before there would be any alleviation of Hawai'i's diplomatic troubles. Meanwhile there were further crises with the French, provoked by intemperate consuls and exploited by a belligerent naval officer, de Tromelin in 1849. France, as before, was reluctant to make amends for the unauthorized extremism of its agents, so that finally, in 1849 the United States entered into a much fairer treaty which amounted to a guarantee of Hawai'ian independence, and issued stern protests to the other powers. Within a few years, Britain and France fell into line after Hawai'i had secured new treaties with other European nations.

The attitude of the great powers was thus made fairly clear. None of them was particularly anxious to acquire colonial possessions in the Pacific during the first half of the nineteenth century; they were willing to maintain the semi-fiction of recognizing Pacific polities as independent states, but were not generally willing to accord them equal status and equal rights with themselves; and above all, they were not prepared to see other nations gain political or strategic advantages, even in places where the stakes were small. National pride, racial pride, and national interest combined to engender in the relevant governments a 'dog in the manger' attitude. The years of the 1830s and the early 1840s were the time when social and economic changes in Polynesia evoked incidents which brought this 'policy' to consciousness.

After 1840, another generation was to pass before the Pacific again became the scene for international rivalry; in the meantime, naval ships of the three major nations continued to patrol the Pacific, performing police duties and periodically advising or intimidating island chiefs according to the situations and the inclinations of the officers concerned. The Americans threatened Cakobau of Fiji in the mid 1850s, but it was the French in particular who maintained a minatory stance. Not only was a suggested French protectorate over Wallis and Futuna islands (between Fiji and Samoa) aborted on British insistence in 1844, but there were also threats to Tonga in 1855. Two years earlier in 1853, France declared a protectorate over New Caledonia, having deferred its plans for a decade because of the events of the early forties; reasons for this action were mixed, involving the search for a penal colony, the needs of the Catholic mission in New Caledonia and a nationalistic wish to counter the almost inevitable tendency for the Pacific to become a British lake.

In the absence of serious international rivalry there were no challenges to the *status quo* in the Pacific before the late 1870s.

In 1874, Britain had annexed Fiji after lengthy inquiries and negotiations initiated by the government of the unfortunate Cakobau. As in the early cases, Britain's emissaries on the spot were more enthusiastic about the idea than was their government. Indeed, it seemed clear enough to all concerned that the Fijian government was in a chaotic state and that colonial status would probably be an improvement for everyone. It was less clear why Britain should accept the offer, but while inquiries were still in progress, an election in Britain brought to power a government which was more sympathetic to the idea of empire than its predecessor had been. The Australian and New Zealand colonies were vigorously in favour, and it could be plausibly argued that larger British interests were at stake. Moreover, there was the moral consideration: British subjects and British investment had changed Fiji and largely brought about the mess there, and British subjects were the people mainly involved in the recruitment and employment of Melanesian labour, that 'scandalous' trade in humanity which was so resistant to any form of regulation. Government action had brought some improvement to the Queensland end of the trade, and presumably nothing less than annexation could ameliorate the evils at the Fijian end.

In conjunction with the annexation of Fiji, additional measures would be required if the labour trade and related activities were to be cleaned up. The difficulty was that the areas of recruitment would remain outside the limits of colonial authority. Annexing the whole of Melanesia was out of the question, and so a device was sought which would give effective authority over the actions of British subjects although they were outside British territory. After a protracted delay while various government departments worried about legal implications and conflicts of responsibility, the Western Pacific High Commission was established in 1877 giving the Governor of Fiji as High Commissioner extra-territorial jurisdiction—essentially the same solution which the unsuccessful Act of 1817 had posed to the same problem. The details this time were different, and 'the problem of European lawlessness' could now be tackled more realistically, if not wholly successfully.

But once the British flag had been planted in Fiji, expectations and fears were aroused both among Pacific islanders and Europeans about what other imperialist moves might follow. Instability in Samoa invited intervention (indeed, formal invitations for intervention were periodically issued by Samoans to both Britain and the United States), and the astonishing acceleration of the German commercial and naval presence in the central Pacific seemed to suggest imperialistic opportunism was to become the new ethic of Pacific politics.

Tonga, nervous of its vulnerability since the unequal French treaty of 1855, was anxious to secure recognition from abroad. Britain, formerly perceived as a friend and protector, was now seen as a threat, but was in fact indifferent, and being indifferent, it showed no inclination to enter into the sort of treaty relationship which Tonga wanted. That disinclination seemed sinister, and thus when a German officer was willing to give Tonga the security that Prime Minister Baker asked for, a German-Tongan treaty was speedily concluded in 1876. Now it was the turn of Britain (or at least of Britain's colonial appendages in Australia and New Zealand) to become nervous, for amongst other things, the German-Tongan treaty allowed the German navy coaling rights at the very fine harbour in the northern group of Vava'u. The proximity to Fiji and to the trans-Pacific trade routes was uncomfortably strategic, and Britain therefore concluded a similar treaty with Tonga in 1879 to counterbalance the German initiative.

Meanwhile, the question of demarcating British and French interests had again arisen. In the New Hebrides, French expansion from New Caledonia and British expansion from Australia were rapidly bringing about a conflict of interest, in anticipation of which the French government had in 1878 proposed a joint undertaking that the independence of the New Hebrides be respected. The proposal came to nothing, but at the same time the growing German commercial presence in eastern Polynesia (the Leeward Islands in particular), was attracting periodical German naval patrols and German offers of treaties to the island authorities. France therefore sought a revision of the convention of 1847 whereby France and Britain had agreed to a 'hands off' policy there. Before the matter could be discussed, however, a French protectorate was established over Borabora, Huahine and Ra'iatea, followed in 1881 by a conversion of the protectorate over Tahiti into annexation.

The rivalry between French and English settlers in the New Hebrides was to be less easily resolved. Tension arose because of Higginson's machinations which, besides increasing French investment, had secured a number of native requests for French protection between 1882 and 1884. While he was trying to get France to act on them, the New Caledonian governor sent a peace-keeping force into the group in 1886. This action, together with Australian agitation, obliged the British government to take some notice, and resulted in a convention in 1887 establishing a Joint Naval Commission to provide some form of authority for the French and British subjects active in the group. This commission, however, was not government. Over the next few years measures were taken to restrain the trade in arms and liquor and to control labour recruiting for New Caledonia; but the increasing settlement under the auspices of the rival French and Australian companies, with their increasing land claims, provided the inevitable potential for racial hostility. Actual outbreaks of violence between settlers and Melanesians underlined the need for a form of closer supervision. In 1900, the French created their own equivalent of the Western Pacific High Commission, and both nations had resident commissioners in the group by 1902; but the increasingly unsatisfactory state of affairs led at last to a form of joint government. Under a convention signed in 1906, France and Britain undertook to share the government of the territory, the subjects of each nation being subject to their respective laws, and others having to choose between the two systems. The condominium, as the arrangement came to be called (or pandemonium as it was more facetiously and popularly called) solved the problem of national rivalries, and averted the problem of a large proportion of the European settlers having to accept alien rule. It did not, however, eliminate future rivalries or avert future anomalies, nor did it provide a very satisfactory basis for the government of the colonized native population.

As the end of the century approached, there was more imperialistic tidying-up to be done. The assumptions of governments had now changed, although the old principle that none should be allowed to gain an advantage over the others remained a guiding star. By now it was generally accepted that European settlement and investment had reached such a point, that in the interests of Europeans and islanders alike, restraint was no longer a feasible policy. There was, however, no 'scramble for the Pacific'. Neither the British government after 1840, nor the French government after 1853 showed any enthusiasm for taking on colonial responsibilities in the Pacific; both had plenty of subjects who thought otherwise, and tried like Higginson to force events. Germany, newly unified and newly powerful in the 1870s, was anxious to exert a comparable influence in world affairs, and after 1881, began a quest frankly to acquire overseas possessions.

With their convention of 1887, France and Britain had arranged their interests in the Pacific to avoid friction between their citizens and between their governments. Britain had by this time also come to an arrangement with Germany to the same purpose. Yet although Britain was the common factor in these arrangements, she seems more to have been reacting to events rather than initiating them.

Since the late 1870s, Theodor Weber of Godeffroys had been working with a succession of naval officers and consuls to strengthen

German influence in the Pacific at large. The Tongan treaty had come first in 1876; in 1878, Captain von Werner had toured the western islands where Godeffroys and other German firms had interests, and bought rights to various harbours in New Britain; in the same year, he made a treaty with the chief of Jaluit in the Marshall Islands; the following year, a new Samoan treaty was made, catching up, so to speak, with the recent American treaty. For the next few years, successive crises in Samoa dominated events; the German government became further involved with the necessity to reconstruct Godeffroys, whose Pacific interests passed to the Deutsche Handels-und Plantagen-Gesellschaft (D.H.P.G.), and the German colonial lobby looked to Samoa as the favoured object of its dreams.

In 1884, a German-dictated treaty initiated some years of chaos in Samoa, provoking such British and American official indignation that a three-nation conference was called to settle the matter in 1887. The conference lapsed with the matter unsettled, but was re-called again in 1889 by Germany. The German initiative of 1884, however, had coincided with a German determination for action in New Guinea, where German traders had been active on the north coast and northern islands for over a decade. Britain had hitherto shown indifference to the fate of New Guinea, confident that no other power was interested in that inhospitable place, and had recently disavowed the action of the Queensland government purporting to annex the whole of eastern New Guinea. Britain was then embarrassed to learn of German plans to secure its interests there, and while negotiations were in progress, Germany declared a protectorate over its sphere of interest. Britain reacted with a counter-declaration over the south coast, and after some mutual recriminations about bad faith, a border was settled. In 1886, a convention was signed defining spheres of interest which would thus do away with the uncertainties which had tainted Anglo-German relations of the previous few years. By the terms of this convention, the Marshalls, Carolines and Palau were defined as a German sphere, and the Gilbert and Ellice groups were to be considered British. The Solomon Islands were also divided, the northern islands (Buka, Bougainville, Choiseul and Ysabel) going to Germany.

Germany lost no time in establishing legal authority in its sphere: protectorates were established in all places except the Carolines and Palau, where Germany acceded to Spanish claims of prior rights, but on terms which gave it wide privileges but no responsibilities. Britain again took no action, being content with the knowledge that no other power could pre-empt her.

Back in eastern Polynesia, there were others who were less sure of their security. In 1885, the chiefs of Rarotonga, nervous of the French, petitioned for British protection; response to this was delayed while the New Hebrides issue was being settled, but eventually the protectorate was declared in 1888. Over the next few years, a succession of protectorates and annexations embraced the remainder of the Cook Islands, where tottering experiments in indigenous government were sponsored with such lack of success that in 1900, annexation and colonial rule was accepted as the only feasible option.

Germany, however, remained dissatisfied with the untidy state of affairs in the west, and particularly for its implications for labour recruitment. Britain's non-intervention policy was quite unsatisfactory; the Western Pacific High Commission had its defects as a device to control British subjects and left the wider problem of lawlessness unresolved. At last in 1891, Germany asked Britain to take action in its sphere of influence, and thus protectorates were established in 1892 over the Gilbert Islands and Ellice Islands, and in 1893 the Solomon Islands.

Little remained to complete the partition. The compromise in Samoa failed in 1898 on the death of the king, Malietoa Laupepa, and a new round of international conferences became necessary. Compromise was finally abandoned: in 1899 Germany annexed western Samoa and the United States eastern Samoa; in compensation, the German islands in the Solomons (except for Bougainville and Buka) were surrendered to Britain. In an unrelated but contemporary move, Britain made a treaty of friendship with Tonga which amounted to a protectorate. The United States in 1898 had finally acceded to the wishes of the revolutionary government of Hawai'i and its own bellicose citizens to annex those islands, and in the same year, having defeated Spain in war, took possession of Guam. The remainder of Spain's Pacific territories, the Marianas, Carolines and Palau, were bought from Spain by Germany.

The history of the partition of the Pacific islands does not fit very well the idea of predatory European imperialist nations grasping for every speck of available land. Certainly Germany seemed to be behaving like that: Samoa's independence lasted as long as it did only because Britain and the United States had interests there as well, while German activity in the other territories seemed to have as its ultimate design the establishment of formal empire. France, after indulging its imperialist ambitions on a limited scale in the 1840s and 1850s, was thereafter concerned mainly to avoid confrontation over such insignificant stakes. Britain remained till the end of the century wedded to the idea of native independence; but, in a series of *ad hoc* decisions, was obliged time after time by pressure from its own antipodean colonies, from its own officials, from its international peers, from its own adventurous citizens, and by its own declared altruistic concern for the 'defenceless islanders', to reverse its policy until it finished up in the Pacific with heavier colonial responsibilities (liabilities would not be too strong a word) than any other nation.

By the end of the century, Europeans generally had abandoned any idea that native self-government was a realistic aspiration in a world of increasing rivalries and tension between the great powers. The problems of good order had not been solved by indigenous governments on the whole; indigenous populations were declining everywhere, rapidly in some places; the world-wide experience of European expansion had seemed to confirm the belief in European racial superiority and a European destiny of world mastery. Absorption of the Pacific islands into the great empires was in fact if not intention the inevitable consequence of the extraordinary and unprecedented outpouring of people and capital from Europe. In the sequel, the government of islanders by Europeans was to reflect the circumstances of annexation.

Chapter Eleven

AFTER A CENTURY OF CONTACT

By the end of the nineteenth century, profound changes had occurred in all three culture areas of the Pacific, as old people with long memories knew. The passing visitor, however, might have been more impressed by the things which had not changed. For most Pacific islanders life was still governed by the exigencies of subsistence: cultivation of crops, fishing, and the production of a range of material goods by traditional methods. Almost everywhere, people still lived in houses made of local materials, derived mainly from the pandanus and the coconut palm. Food was still produced and prepared in traditional ways, although new food plants, imported food, and the practice of boiling food in iron pots had been introduced to most places. The daily routine was still ordered by the tasks of family life, under direction of the head of the family or of a larger local group. Village life and the web of kinship governed social life as well as work. Children were still reared to respect and obey their elders; older children still looked after the younger and became involved in work as well as play; traditional tales still told of folk heroes, the power of spirits, and the pragmatic ethics of the society. The same values as in former times permeated peoples' lives and relationships, and people continued to lead lives which spoke more of continuity than of change.

Foremost among the innovations which were being grafted on to this pattern of existence, were the use of iron and the practice of Christianity, with the latter still inseparable from literacy. Ironware in various forms had come to be regarded in many places as a necessity of life; in most other places it was at the very least a sign of status. In a few areas, especially the inland, mountainous regions of the large islands of Melanesia, the people remained innocent of Europeans and their culture; but in most islands, Protestant Christianity occupied a conspicuous place in public and private life.

Catholic missions had come comparatively lately to the Pacific, an early attempt having been made in 1826 with the introduction of two priests into Hawai'i, Fathers Bachelot and Short. In 1834, under a separate administrative structure, the Catholic church began systematic work in the Gambier islands, south-east of Tahiti. Attempts were made to spread Catholicism from there in 1837, but instead of tackling the unevangelized islands as had originally been planned, Bishop Pompallier, the man in charge, turned his efforts to challenging the dominance of the 'Protestant heresy' in the places where it had become established. Thus, in the late 1830s and early 1840s, priests were placed in Tonga, Fiji, Samoa and New Zealand where they could compete with the Protestants. In the mid-1840s, the Catholics took on challenges which had less of the spirit of enmity and established missions in New Caledonia and the Solomon islands. Both were heroically fruitless for some years; the New Caledonian mission persisted and was saved in the end by French annexation of that group; the Solomons mission was forced to withdraw in 1847 and did not return until 1896.

Most schools were mission schools; the Sabbath was marked both by popular church attendance and the suspension of all labour, and most of the people heard their prayers and sermons from clergy who were not European missionaries, but were Pacific islanders themselves. Nevertheless, the old vanquished religions were not forgotten; continuing in the minds and gestures of many with surreptitious forms of expression, they exercised a latent power, albeit fading with each generation.

One major change which had occurred by the end of the century was the quality of relations between the newcomers to the Pacific and the original inhabitants, as the balance of power passed from one to the other. The early contact period has sometimes been characterized as a time of 'noble savage' sentimentality, the Europeans ostensibly perceiving the Pacific islanders through a romantic haze of idealism which represented them as being naturally virtuous and free from the ethical, physical and political malaise of decadent civilization. Such ideas were current in the eighteenth century, but not among those who travelled the world. In contrast, the typical European who came to the Pacific displayed wariness of the unknown, fear of 'savages', contempt for 'barbaric' ways of life, loathing for ritual murder and cannibalism, and a conviction of the innate inequality of the human races. The islanders, for their part, were seldom overawed by the newcomers, notwithstanding their unearthly appearance and unimaginable goods (metal, glass, cloth, firearms and books), and formed their own stereotypes which were quite as unflattering to the Europeans.

Despite the unfavourable preconceptions on both sides, and the acts of theft, violence and bad faith, relations of a generally amicable kind developed fairly readily, especially in Polynesia. The key element in this relationship was mutual need, in the context of freedom on both sides to withdraw from the relationship if it was not sufficiently productive. This mutual need generated tolerance where prejudice and discrimination might otherwise have been expected, and it was therefore possible for respect and affection to develop between islanders and foreigners; accordingly, the Pacific islands acquired a reputation as one place in the world where relations between people of different races could be good.

Race relations quickly developed other features when the circumstances of contact changed. This change was especially likely to occur where island labour was employed on plantations away from home; or where settlers could own land and establish self-sufficient communities; or where political change put power into the hands of members of only one race. Where one or more of these things happened, as it did especially in Fiji, Hawai'i, New Zealand and Samoa during the middle of the nineteenth century, and in parts of Melanesia towards the very end of the century, the dominant race began to exhibit the familiar symptoms of racism in both word and conduct.

As the century wore on, it became increasingly possible for thoughtful and sympathetic Europeans to accept the theory of racial inequality which purported to account for the visible cultural decay and depopulation. The Pacific turned out to be no exception to the apparently universal law that in the interaction of cultures and the contact of races, one race was bound to prevail and the other to die out. Impending extinction of 'native races' seemed to be as obviously part of natural law as was the law of gravity. At the same time, this theory, in the guise of social evolutionism (sometimes called 'social Darwinism') was becoming popular, with its supercilious overtone of the greater fitness of the survivors serving to justify the ruthlessness of the more aggressive racists. For the paternalistic sympathisers of native races, such theories explained why there was a need to 'soften the dying pillow' (in a phrase commonly used at the time) of those peoples who seemed destined for extinction.

To the subscribers of this theory, the disastrous effects of European contact seemed manifest. Social structures were crumbling; chiefs abused their authority and legitimate authority was undermined; men abandoned their families; houses lapsed into decay and gardens were neglected; the people became visibly indolent or decrepit; the cheerful buoyancy of spirits was superseded by listless demoralization. The natives, it was said, lost the will to live when their cultures came into contact with whites.

In this picture, so frequently drawn, there was both exaggeration and error (it generally took several decades for the natives to realize that they were supposed to be demoralized and dispirited), but there was also truth. The various effects of European contact were uneven not only in their geographical distribution, but also in their nature and depth. All of the evils mentioned above resulted from the unequal contest with microbes and materialism which effectively shifted the balance of power to the foreigners.

The depopulation, at least, was real enough. It was the fundamental problem faced by the earliest colonial administrators, and in most places they reported a dreadful decline. Their concern was both practical and humanitarian, and they consulted physicians and anthropologists in hopeful succession over a period of several decades to try to explain and rectify the problem.

Almost as soon as Europeans came into contact with the island populations which had been isolated from continental influences for thousands of years, the causes of depopulation were introduced, and principal among these was disease. In 1767, venereal diseases were introduced by either French or English to Tahiti; thereafter, over the next few years, and over the next century, deadly diseases were introduced to most island groups, influenza and measles being the most common. The precise effects of these diseases are, in a sense, impossible to assess because of the imprecision of contemporary population estimates, a fact which has led modern historians to conclude that the depopulation during the early contact decades was not severe; and yet contemporary observers in many island groups wrote during particular epidemics of hundreds or thousands dying, and of tracts of land, formerly densely settled, being left all but desolate.

Initial population estimates were a matter of calculated guesswork, but the guesses of different visitors were often remarkably similar. What is most striking is the consistent pattern of decline shown over time. In Hawai'i the population of native Hawai'ians which was estimated at 142,000 in 1823 was down to 130,000 by 1830, to 100,000 in 1839, to 84,000 at the 1850 census, and continued to show a decline at successive censuses, reaching its lowest point at 39,000 in 1896. In the Marquesas, a population estimated at 100,000 (a figure which is almost certainly a gross over-estimate) in 1773, was estimated in 1804 at only 50,000, and was further reduced almost immediately by a great famine which is known to have cost thousands of lives. The population declined throughout the nineteenth century; from 20,000 in 1838, it reached 12,500 in 1856, fell to 4,279 by 1897, and continued to diminish even after that.

The population of Tahiti, estimated at perhaps 50,000 or 60,000 by the explorers, was down to about 8,000 by 1800, a figure which has caused various authorities to call the earlier estimates into question; yet even the most cautious of historical demographers allows a population in pre-European times of perhaps 35,000. A third of a century between discovery and evangelization had seen unprecedented depopulation by war, infanticide and such a regular succession of epidemics that Tahitians recalled the visits of ships by the diseases which followed them. A careful estimate by Captain Wilson in 1797 gave a figure of 16,000; a few years later the missionaries estimated it at perhaps half that, about 7,000. During the first decade of the nineteenth century, the resident missionaries reported a high mortality, much of it from imported diseases; but no doubt much of it was also caused by the more destructive methods of warfare which had become a feature of the age. After about 1810, however, Tahitian population estimates are remarkably uniform, the population showing no major variation from around 7,000 to 8,000 for almost a century.

Further to the west the Cook archipelago showed that the isolation of islands could give them different histories: on some islands in the Cook group the population numbers apparently changed little, although the group as a whole suffered a decline of perhaps one third during the nineteenth century. Rarotonga, in particular, suffered a severe decline in the 1820s and for some decades thereafter, the consequence of introduced diseases being compounded by hurricanes and war. Worse, these early losses distorted the age-distribution of the population so that recovery by a natural excess of births over deaths did not take place for many decades.

The Tonga group, less frequented than other groups, is thought to have suffered little change, with a population apparently of about 20,000 for most of the nineteenth century. There had, however, been heavy losses from epidemics towards the end of the eighteenth century, and the civil wars between 1799 and the 1820s possibly reduced the population by perhaps a quarter. Samoa, its population estimated early in the century at perhaps 60,000 (probably another over-estimate) certainly had only about 30,000 at mid-century, and over the next few decades probably experienced some further fluctuations before beginning an early recovery in the 1890s. In Fiji, the estimates varied enormously, most being between 150,000 and 200,000 for the late eighteenth century; it is impossible to assess the extent to which the protracted warfare of the 1830s and 1840s reduced the population, although it is known that some communities suffered severe losses. In addition, Fiji suffered several disastrous epidemics: those of 1791-2 and 1802-3 were said to have been as costly of human life as the great measles epidemic of 1875 which took between a fifth and a quarter of the population of the group. After the 1875 epidemic, there were perhaps 100,000 Fijians, and the number continued to decline for almost another forty years.

Further west in Melanesia, numerical estimates are unreliable and few, but numerous impressionistic, verbal assessments claim that severe depopulation took place. During the second half of the nineteenth century, Eromanga, Aneityum and Efate in the New Hebrides all had their populations reduced to about one-tenth, according to the estimates of resident missionaries. In the Solomons, the coastal populations were reduced by the heavy recruiting by labour traders, and of those going to Queensland, one third (about 20,000) never returned; other destinations claimed an even higher mortality. Reports late in the century refer to villages being practically childless, with introduced diseases, for once, being one of the lesser causes.

The extent of population loss in Micronesia has been referred to in chapter nine: up to 90 percent on some islands, practically no change on others. Throughout the Pacific, however, there was a general trend towards population decline, contemporary with and usually caused in one way or another by European contact. Sometimes the relationship between cause and effect was indirect, but the coincidence remained for the social-Darwinists to observe and to support their gloomy doctrines.

A theory which was a gloomy doctrine for one race, of course, was a song of triumph for the other. It sprang from, and justified and reinforced their own sense of superiority; it seemed to guarantee success in all their enterprises, and to demonstrate that destiny was with them. As European traders and settlers became more numerous from the middle of the century onwards, they became more outspoken about the desirability—necessity, they called it—for political intervention by their home governments. What they commonly had in mind was government by themselves as the progressive race, under the aegis of a European power.

Until late in the century, European governments were generally not sympathetic to such ambitions: the Pacific islands were not thought to be of strategic value; moreover, their populations and resources were small, and had little to attract the imperialist or the investor. Such European interests as there were in the Pacific were due to an accumulation of chance factors, sometimes merely the overflow of more deliberate activity elsewhere, rather than due to the inherent desirability of the islands themselves. The presence of fur seals on the north-west coast of America and the shortage of marketable commodities for the China trade drew Europeans to Hawai'i and showed them Micronesia. The establishment by Britain of a convict colony on the east coast of Australia brought the first whale ships into the Pacific Ocean; in the same way, it initiated sustained contact with New Zealand for flax, timber and seal skins which were not sufficiently valuable to have brought people from around the world. Similarly, it was the need to feed the convicts which initiated trade with Tahiti.

The subsequent accumulation of capital in New South Wales and the need for commercial development at a time when expansion inland was closed off, encouraged the development of the early trade in sandalwood. *Bêche-de-mer*, like whaling, was to be dominated by American vessels, but both industries were extractive and therefore short-lived. The missionaries came to the Pacific as part of their world-wide activity; they came early to the Pacific mainly because of the European sentimentality propagated about Tahiti. The presence of so many foreigners so variously employed did not imply any expansionist ambitions by the nations which spawned them: these people were the fringe-dwellers of the age of expansion. Nevertheless, powerful governments eventually acted on their behalf.

The absorption of the Pacific islands into the European overseas empires made little immediate change to the daily lives and opportunities of the indigenous inhabitants. In subsequent decades, the extent of such change was to depend on a number of variables: the attractiveness of the land to foreign settlers; the presence of resources which were worth exploiting; the potential use of the native inhabitants as labourers; and finally, the way in which the colonial power defined its responsibilities to dependent peoples.

Chapter Twelve

PRIORITIES IN COLONIAL POLICIES

Despite the aphorism that colonies do not have a political life but only administration, the Pacific islanders under colonial regimes continued the process of jockeying for influence within their own societies and in their relationships with their colonial overlords. Politics were thus not abolished, but they were transformed; power was in new hands and was exercised in a variety of ways ranging from the extremes of exploitation to the extremes of benevolent paternalism. Broadly speaking, colonial policy was a continuation of pre-colonial policy: the objectives which had been pursued before annexation did not suddenly disappear, and so colonial administration reflects the circumstances and intentions manifest in preceding events. Thus France, which acquired part of its empire in indifference, governed it the same way; Germany, which was frankly concerned with exploiting and developing resources, got on with the job expeditiously; Britain, having lacked a positive policy previously, continued to be guided by *ad hoc* principles; the United States of America created an environment for business; and Dutch neglect of western New Guinea was almost total.

New Zealand, the first European colony in the Pacific, was the only one to become a British colony of settlement. Indeed, the major reason for annexation had been that settlement was already going ahead and could not be stopped. Government of New Zealand as a colony should at least control the process, and prevent the inevitable racial conflict and dispossession of the Maoris. Unfortunately, settlement was ultimately to mean dispossession, whether or not the British government approved of it. Despite the Treaty of Waitangi with its unfortunately ambiguous promise of legal equality and preservation of traditional rights, the government had no clear idea of what its 'native policy' should be.

The humanitarian sympathies of government and governor alike were submerged by the clamour of the settlers for protection and for land, and by the need for the government to raise revenue by selling to the settlers land which it bought from the Maoris. Maori society, although ostensibly protected from the worst evils of culture contact by the interposition of government between it and the settlers, continued to be under threat, and the government had neither the power nor the ideas for any alternative. One thing, however, was not on the agenda: there were never any plans to reduce the Maori population by force of law to a semi-servile labouring class, nor to subject them to discriminatory laws of any kind. It was assumed that the end result of contact would be assimilation and miscegenation, and that this would occur by the natural processes of social interaction assisted by formal, legal equality.

The Maoris themselves continued to be as divided as they had been before annexation, but few among the most influential chiefs hoped to eject the Europeans altogether. The old warrior Te Rauparaha, who had been such a scourge of the southern tribes in the 1820s and 1830s, was the man whom the settlers regarded with the greatest dread, but his hostility to the new order was exaggerated, and he had made no overt move against the colony when Governor Grey unjustly captured him in 1846. Even Hone Heke who resorted to arms in 1845 in the far north of the country, was demonstrating his rejection of European authority rather than attempting to eliminate the white population, and since he was supported only by his immediate tribe, was soon subdued. Other communities simply got on with their lives as best they could, giving little thought to the plight of their race and culture until the government land purchase agent made them aware of the threat. Even then, there were many Maoris who were willing to sell their land, sometimes merely for the sake of settling old scores.

The granting of self-government to New Zealand in 1852 marked a new phase in the history of the Maoris. Although land policy and Maori affairs were still reserved to the crown, legislative power had passed into the hands of those whose interests were antagonistic to those of the original inhabitants. Feeling increasingly under threat, the Maoris became more resistant to the sale of land and the loss of social cohesion which was its consequence. In 1857, several North Island tribes combined to elect a king so that they might more effectively oppose the loss of control over their affairs.

Eventually, amid increasing Maori despair and increasing settler belligerence, war broke out in 1860, but with unresolved Maori disunity, the result was never in much doubt; although armed resistance continued throughout the decade, British troops were withdrawn in 1866. Despite the provision in 1867 of four seats in parliament for Maori members, the war had not achieved anything for the Maori people; on the contrary, it provided the government with the opportunity for large scale land confiscations. In addition, most remaining Maori land was converted to individual ownership, with the result that much of it passed by one means or another into European hands.

On a small scale, many Maoris continued to reject European authority in principle, but not European ideas nor their technology and economy. The adherents of the King movement withdrew into less accessible country in the centre of the North Island, insisting on their autonomy but adapting their way of life by the adoption of European customs and techniques. This response, although not lacking in creativity or intelligence, was conservative and hopeless. As the 1880s and 1890s unfolded, other Maori responses developed, aimed at salvaging as much as might be extracted from a European New Zealand. Various tactics were employed: invoking the Treaty of Waitangi, undertaking campaigns of civil disobedience, submitting petitions, and organizing an alternative, Maori parliament. Maori newspapers were begun in the 1890s and flourished for a time, and eventually there came the formation of a political party, the Young Maori Party, led by men of European education, but who nevertheless retained a strong sense of cultural identity and faith in a multi-cultural New Zealand. The alliance of the Young Maori Party with the Liberal Party achieved some major reforms and did much to restore Maori prestige among the white majority.

The Maoris suffered the usual fate of a colonized race, but with the important difference that they had always possessed legal equality. This was not matched by social and economic equality, nor equality of political influence; but it meant that there were no legal disabilities to be overcome when a new generation of Maori leaders was prepared to work within the European structure of the new New Zealand in the interests of all Maoris. On that foundation rested the very considerable progress of the early years of the twentieth century.

The Maori experience was important in another way. The injustices of the nineteenth century were plain for impartial observers to see, and the betrayal of mid-century humanitarianism was scandalously obvious. The nature and legacy of the racial wars in New Zealand needed no explaining; the facts were plain, presenting an awful example of insecurity and brutality which, in the decades following, British governors of Pacific islanders were anxious should not be duplicated elsewhere.

Sir Arthur Gordon was mindful of the New Zealand experience when he arrived in Fiji in 1875 to assume the post of first governor of the new British colony. He was among the first colonial civil servants to make a career out of governing colonies, and the situation facing him in Fiji was one for which he considered himself to be peculiarly suited. Strongly influenced by the humanitarian interest in 'native' peoples as subject races, he considered it his duty to safeguard their interests. In his opinion, this was to be done not by allowing white settlers generous access to Fijian land and labour (the reasons for which they had supported annexation) which would be as fatal to the Fijians as it was proving fatal to the Maoris and to subject races everywhere; rather, he intended to create a protected environment in which the Fijians would progress along the scale of social evolution from their present barbarous condition to the state of civilization represented by contemporary Europe. In his view, the colonial mission was a civilizing mission, and civilization was the result of deliberate, constructive policy, not of *laissez-faire* exploitation.

The objective was high-minded. Was it practicable? To develop the Fijians in a sheltered environment required money, yet the Colonial Office required that Fiji be self-supporting, and therefore Gordon could rely on no subsidies. His only recourse was to encourage further white settlement and the development of commercial agriculture, which required land and labour, which would in turn require the exploitation of the Fijians rather than their protection. This was the eternal dilemma of colonies of trusteeship, and was solved by Gordon in a brilliantly original manner. First, he created an administration which used Fijian chiefs as his regional, district and village officers, inventing positions which served the needs of government as well as bearing some resemblance to traditional Fijian notions of political hierarchy. (This was the basis of the system of 'indirect rule' later used extensively in Britain's Pacific and African colonies, and was made possible in Fiji by the work of the Wesleyan mission over the previous forty years in creating a literate population.) In this way, Gordon was able to provide close government control without the expense of a large European staff, and without depriving the Fijians of political and administrative participation.

The second step was to provide a tax-base by finding gainful employment for the Fijians; at the same time this had to meet the social objective of giving the Fijians experience in economic development without alienating them from their land or labour, and also without harming traditional social organization. Gordon's system of native taxation provided that production be organized on a communal basis through the neo-traditional authority structure which he had created; the produce was to be sold by government tender before it was delivered, and the tax for which the production unit (the village) was liable was deducted from the proceeds of the sales. The cash surplus was then returned to the village, giving the people some awareness of their economic potential.

This native taxation system was not popular with the European settlers, for the native produce competed with their own, and the system freed the Fijians from the necessity of paid labour on European plantations. Wage labour for the Fijians was no part of Gordon's plan; but the settlers had to prosper for the colony to be viable, and since labour had to be found, Gordon chose Indians. Indian emigration to tropical territories with a labour shortage was already a well established practice, and Gordon had had experience of it in Mauritius where he had served previously as governor. Indian labourers were duly recruited, and the first shipment arrived in 1879 despite the lack of enthusiasm for them by the settlers who much preferred the Melanesians whom they had been able to import before cession.

The final component of Gordon's system concerned the land question. Large areas of land had been sold by the Fijians during the 1860s, and in his deal with the Polynesia Company, Cakobau had made over 200,000 acres in exchange for the payment of the American debt. Although consuls since Pritchard's time had registered land sales, there were many disputed claims to land, arising from imprecise boundaries, absenteeism, or disputed rights to sell. The settlers had expected of a colonial government that their land claims would be upheld and that more land would be made available to them. Again Gordon disappointed them. Relying on his own ideas of social evolution, fortified by theories of Lewis Henry Morgan and Sir Edward Tylor (the great anthropological systematisers of the day), and encouraged by the missionary Lorimer Fison who was thought to be the leading authority on Fijian society, Gordon declared that Fijian land was and always had been inalienable. Each tribe and sub-tribe had its own precisely known territory, the possession of which was a precondition of social and personal health, and there was no land which did not have native owners. Land which had purportedly been sold before Cession would be the subject of inquiry, and to this purpose, a Land Claims Commission was established in 1879; those lands which could be shown to have been fairly sold were confirmed as freehold, those judged to have been unfairly sold reverted to traditional ownership. Land sales ceased, but any unused Fijian land could be leased to European planters.

By the end of Gordon's governorship in 1881, he had established an administration which had broken new ground in British colonial history. He had, moreover, in the name of tradition, reconstructed

Fijian society in a manner which the Fijians themselves did not always recognise, but which quickly became a new orthodoxy. That orthodoxy was in time to become fossilized and contentious, but Gordon's original intention had been that it should be merely a means to an end, a framework which would carry the Fijians to the next stage in social evolution. Later governors tried to force progression to that next stage—the most determined, Sir Everard im Thurn (1904-1911), attacked the land system, and sold about 100,000 acres—but they were all defeated, and the *status quo* was maintained.

Until the First World War, there was comparatively little for Gordon's successors to do but administer his system. He had laid the basis for the prosperity of both Fijian and European economies, established an administration and mechanisms of consultation with both the Fijian and the European populations, made provision for the technical education of Fijians for their future improvement, and established a health service which included a training scheme for Fijian medical practitioners. The problems of Fiji and its people had by no means been solved when his governorship ended, but his achievement was remarkable, despite the major defect of the inadequate protection afforded the Indian labourers during and after their periods of indenture.

Gordon's influence was to become widespread through the men whom he recruited and trained in colonial administration. His medical officer, William MacGregor, was to become the second governor of British New Guinea where Gordon's principles were adapted for the changed circumstances. If establishing a government in Fiji had required imagination and force of character, then the other British possessions in Melanesia were to require that and more, for New Guinea and the Solomons lacked the hierarchical authority structure of Fiji. Moreover, Europeans and their ways were less well known in those places, and the customs of violence and suspicion had been rarely modified; the British government was even more reluctant to spend money on these colonies, but it nevertheless expected them to be pacified and to have a system of law and authority established. The early administrators therefore had to rely very much on their own resourcefulness.

General Sir Peter Scratchley was the first governor (technically Special Commissioner) of British New Guinea, and he energetically set about making the new regime's presence known to those Papuan communities which were in reach of the sea. In the absence of any other practicable methods, demonstrations of force conveyed the idea that acts of war between villages, and between black and white were to cease. Before Scratchley's administration could prove itself, the general fell ill and died. An interim administration followed, after which the protectorate was formerly annexed in 1888, and William MacGregor was appointed Lieutenant-Governor. Like Scratchley, he travelled widely, got to know the people and the country, and imposed his own forceful personality on all. In ten years of vigorous work with a tiny staff, he established peace in those areas which he could reach, stamped out petty crime, imposed regulations for the protection of the native people, and gave British rule a real presence in the territory. In this work he established a harmonious and productive relationship with the various missions (Anglican, Catholic, Wesleyan and London Missionary Society), and used this partnership to further the work of pacification and social change.

MacGregor rightly saw that the first job in such a possession as New Guinea was to establish peace, only after which a broadening of native experience and geographical horizons would be possible; further in the distance lay the goals of education, improved health and housing, and economic development. MacGregor was nobody's lackey, neither capitalist's nor missionary's, and he would never have questioned the rightness of either his aims or his methods; on the contrary, his duty as he saw it was the humanitarian obligation to leave the world a better place than he found it.

In 1906, British New Guinea was transferred to the new Australian federation. The years since MacGregor's departure had been a time first of consolidation and then of uncertainty and stagnation, until another Lieutenant-Governor of stature comparable to MacGregor took over in 1907. This was Hubert Murray who was to govern Papua (as the territory was now called) until 1940 in a style which was both paternalistic and high minded, the theme of his administration summed up in a remark made in 1913 that 'any white community left with absolute power over natives would resort to slavery within three generations.'

In developing this humanitarian tradition of colonial government, the British were often bitterly criticised by their own subjects as being hostile to economic development and completely wrong-headed about what was best for 'primitive' peoples, leading to tension between a governor and the settler population. This strain was reproduced in the German colonies, although there were significant differences between the philosophical positions of men like Gordon, MacGregor and Murray, and their German counterparts.

The government of Germany, having claimed sovereignty in 1884 over the Marshall Islands and part of New Guinea in order to protect the interests of its traders and to satisfy the colonial lobby, was not eager to shoulder the burden of colonial government. Instead, it gave a charter to two companies to administer and develop the territories: for New Guinea, the New Guinea Company was formed by a financier called Adolf von Hansemann in 1884; for the Marshalls, D.H.P.G. and Robertson and Hernsheim formed the Jaluit Company in 1887.

This expedient, while in the main unsatisfactory, worked better in the Marshalls where the Jaluit Company enjoyed all the benefits of monopoly and paid the costs of government, but where an Imperial commissioner conducted the administration. The company continued to be concerned with trade rather than with settlement, and thus the worst hazards of a conflict of interest were avoided. That was not the case in New Guinea where a company of colonization was given full legislative and police powers. The plan to colonize meant that a conflict of interest was inevitable, and the execution of those plans was in the hands of men who could not prevent that conflict leading to a heavy loss of life.

New Guinea (both the mainland and the islands) was intended to make its land and population available for the use of colonists who would establish plantations using the local people as labourers. It was naively assumed that a subordinate role in a plantation society would be to the improvement of the native inhabitants, but at the same time it was believed that there could be no serious alternative to a form of warfare between the two races. The company's attempts to buy land and recruit labour were clumsy and marked by bad faith, and its attempts to manage race relations amounted to regulations to organize labour and to punish the unco-operative. Such inept policies resulted inevitably in native resistance to which the standard response was the punitive raid.

The company representatives could hardly have behaved otherwise: they were aiming at large-scale plantation agriculture using a subordinate, coloured work-force; their appetite for land and labour was bound to be resisted once its magnitude was realized, whatever their methods. Moreover, conflicts of personality and authority, combined with the illnesses of that disease-ridden coast, quickly stripped the settlers of any sympathy or tolerance they might have had for those whose interests stood in the way of their own. Over-riding everything, of course, were the company's priorities: it wanted land and labour, not a model government of native peoples. Its utter failure to deal successfully with the local people led it to import labour from elsewhere in Melanesia and from Asia, and these people were subject to such appalling living and working conditions and such severe punishments that by the time the company period ended, up to half of these imported labourers had died.

The situation was less disastrous on the nearby islands where traders and missionaries were already well established; yet even this part of Melanesia was by no means 'pacified'. Killings and raiding were not uncommon, power and property continued to be contested by force, and the company's representatives became another faction in the complexities of inter-communal Melanesian life. By 1893, it was clear that reprisal and counter-reprisal were no substitute for government, and accordingly, the islands were taken over by the Imperial government in 1895.

This step was of the first importance for the turnaround in the fortunes of the German colonies in the western Pacific. It also introduced into German colonial government one of two remarkable men whose names have become synonymous with German colonialism: Albert Hahl. When he became the administrator of the Bismarck archipelago and its adjacent islands in 1896, Hahl brought a completely new approach. He pursued the interests of the colony by working through the existing characteristics of native society, instead of through imagined or hoped-for ones, with the result that roads were built, disputes over land ended, trade between black and white encouraged and peace established. By the study of local languages and customs, by his own fastidious insistence on his own procedures (sometimes severe, but never senseless), and by sheer administrative genius, Hahl secured the respect of both races. He developed his own system of indirect rule by appointing his own chiefs in the various native communities (the *luluais*) and recruited a force of native police which he led personally.

The Imperial government had taken over the whole of the territories of the New Guinea Company by 1899, and Hahl was appointed governor in 1902. In the context of German colonialism, Hahl was a liberal humanitarian, but he was still a servant of colonialism. Free of both denigratory and sentimental prejudices about 'savages', he had an intelligent appreciation of the nature of the human beings with whom he had to deal, and acted towards them with generosity, fairness or severity as the situation seemed to require. He recognized not only that the indigenous people had to have an acceptable place in the new society, but that they also had to be treated in non-antagonistic ways. They had rights as human beings; more importantly, they were a resource which the colony should neither reject nor squander if a plantation economy was to be created.

The second remarkable figure of German colonial history was Wilhelm Solf, governor of Samoa from 1900 to 1911. Less liberal than Hahl, he nevertheless resisted with vigour the belief of settlers that they had a natural right to the land and labour of the original inhabitants of the country. While he believed that the country's destiny was as part of the German empire and was to be developed by German enterprise, it nevertheless belonged to the Samoans who were to share fully in whatever economic and cultural benefits Germans could convey.

This philosophy of colonial rule brought Solf into conflict with both the Samoans and the settlers and his only ally in Samoa was the powerful D.H.P.G. The Samoans preferred self-government, and Solf, lacking sufficient coercive means, could defeat them only by practising the same political shrewdness and guile as the Samoans themselves, dealing with them in accordance with Samoan concepts of power, pride and prestige rather than with German ones. The settlers were more easily handled: land sales were closely restricted, imported labour was denied them, and the competition of the D.H.P.G. kept them impoverished. After Solf left Samoa on leave at the end of 1910, his deputy and successor continued his policies and methods until the first world war when German rule came to an end.

German colonial rule, largely in the hands of these two men, was intelligent and efficient. It served the goals of the German Empire without either sentimentality or needless brutality, and given the inevitability of colonialism, the Pacific islanders in the German empire were fortunate to have Hahl and Solf standing between them and the settlers. Despite the chaos of Samoan politics and the anarchy of Melanesia the regimes of both men brought order and a measure of humanity; but the colonies had been intended to promote imperial prosperity, and on that criterion they were failures.

France's record as an imperial power showed less consistency and is therefore more easily criticized for its numerous failings. In both Tahiti and the Marquesas, there had been resistance to the establishment of French authority, the more serious challenge coming from Tahiti where the warfare persisted until 1847. As a protectorate, Tahiti was to retain a good measure of native government, with the maintenance of existing laws which included a prohibition on the sale of land to foreigners. Native participation in government, however, declined with the increasing evidence of the autocratic temper of the French authorities. The influence of the English missionaries of the L.M.S. over the Tahitians also declined, and after they were replaced in 1852 by French Protestants, the Tahitians were left without even that small defence. After having shown such determination to retain the group, the French showed very little interest in governing it. Although the land laws were changed, the Tahitians retained possession of their lands; few settlers came; economic development remained minimal, and in the hands mainly of a few small traders in pearl-shell and coconut oil. Meanwhile, the education of the Tahitians in the ways of Europe, and the provision of health and other services was left entirely to the missions. France, in short, seemed to have no colonial policy for Tahiti, and in the Marquesas where depopulation was a major problem, the government concerned itself only with pacification. Imperial glory was a sardonic joke.

Tahiti was annexed in 1881, three years after the death of Queen Pomare. This made little change in the lives of most Tahitians, for Tahiti, as beautiful but as economically unattractive as ever, was no Mecca for colonists. Attempts by the administration to facilitate the sale of land by requiring Tahitians to register individual land titles were defeated simply by the Tahitians failing to do so. The politics of the colony were merely squabbles between the officials of the government and the few settlers with greater pretensions to dignities than this somnolent and impoverished territory could support. In the thirty-two years between 1882 and 1914, Tahiti had twenty-four governors, the rapid turn-over indicating the frivolous approach of the French government to the needs of its dependency. The only major development was the exploitation of the phosphate deposits of Makatea, an atoll north of Tahiti in the Tuamotu group. This resource attracted investment, but it was an investment which had no 'down-stream' ramifications: the ore was exported unprocessed, and the labour was imported from the Cook Islands. For all practical purposes, the Tahitians continued to be governed by their missionaries and by those among them in the villages who could by traditional or semi-traditional values command sufficient respect.

In France's other Pacific territory, the native people would have been glad of such neglect. In New Caledonia, misgovernment was a positive evil, for here there were greater incentives to exploitation and more determined resistance by the native inhabitants. Both invited a more vigorous policy by the administration, but one which had no justifying gloss of enlightenment.

New Caledonia was intended to be a colony of settlement, and when potential free settlers did not appear in sufficient numbers, convicts were sent. New Caledonia was designated as a penal colony in 1860 (the only one in the Pacific area since the settlement of New South Wales), although the first convicts did not arrive until 1864, by which time gold had been discovered. Land was taken away from the Melanesians in stages from the 1860s to make room for French settlers, and to force the Melanesians to become tax-paying wage-labourers. Relations between colonists and Melanesians quickly became inflamed as the latter resisted the single-minded domination by the French, and their resolute resistance grew into major revolts in 1878, 1887 and during the First World War, making a strong French military presence a permanent necessity.

In attempts to render the people more malleable, efforts were made to destroy the foundations of their independence: chiefs were obliged to become instruments of French authority (the same device with more benign intention might have been called 'indirect rule'); later, chiefs were stripped of their rank and exiled, and tribes were dissolved and moved off their lands; reserves were created to which the Melanesians were to be confined, but were far too small for the populations involved. In the absence of a masterly governor like Gordon or Hahl who could at once pacify and manipulate the indigenous population, commercial agriculture was bound to fail.

The unresolved strain between the Melanesians and the government, combined with the penal role of the colony, continued to make New Caledonia unattractive to large-scale immigration. The discovery of nickel deposits in 1873, however, touched off a boom which did increase the white population, and introduced immigrant, indentured labour from elsewhere in Melanesia and from south-east Asia. The presence of settlers and capital was the touchstone for demands for settler representation in a government from which the Melanesians would inevitably be excluded and their interests disregarded. Political life was confined to trivial disputes between different classes of Frenchmen.

In 1914, with the Melanesians in a desperate state, the governor of New Caledonia, Governor Brunet, summed up sixty years of French government by admitting that 'the government has no native policy'. Believed by this time to be on the brink of extinction, the natives attracted no sympathy or help except from the missionaries who took upon themselves the work of education and community organization which ameliorated their demoralization and distress.

Of the five colonial powers in the Pacific up to the time of the First World War, the Americans were distinguished by their un-selfconscious style. Unhampered either by scruples of humanitarianism, or by an obsession with imperialist imagery, the Americans adopted a pragmatic approach. American Samoa was under a naval administration which interfered little in Samoan life directly; Hawai'i was technically not a colony but a territory, which implied an interim condition pending statehood. Under American law, Hawai'i was a part of the metropolitan power in a sense which was quite different from the status of the British, German or French colonies. It was quite unashamedly a colony of settlement, and indeed, American settlement was well advanced long before annexation in 1898. Moreover, the Hawai'ians, seriously depleted in numbers by now, were well acculturated and miscegenation had been extensive; although their condition was not enviable, comparatively few of them were in a condition which would have justified the application of a special set of laws to be dignified by the label 'native policy'. It was indicative of the social development of Hawai'i that the Bishop Museum, which was to become a major scientific institution, had been established before annexation, and that the University of Hawai'i was founded in 1907. Outside New Zealand, no other Pacific islands would have universities until the 1960s.

Hawai'i, however, did have its peculiar institutions. It had developed a white-settler planter society with elaborate notions of social gradations which were reinforced by inflexible practices of racial inequality. The racial prejudices of Hawai'i were as effective as any labour laws could have been in keeping the various races of Hawai'i in a state of economic and social subordination to a caste of wealthy, Caucasian plantation-owners and to a commercial élite. Except for the representatives of a few aristocratic families which had generally become blended with wealthy Caucasian families during the nineteenth century, the Hawai'ians occupied the lowest social and economic position in this hierarchy. The Asians of various nationalities were accorded slightly higher esteem, to be placed in their turn below the Caucasian labouring classes. Seldom has there been such a neatly-defined correlation between class and race, with its carefully rationed privileges and obligations. This was the system which, along with the situation in New Zealand, was presented to the world as a model of racial harmony. Harmonious it might have been; equal and happy it was not, and the system's cohesion was provided by the dominance of five large firms, known as the Big Five, whose political influence and economic stranglehold was unchallengeable until after the Second World War.

By 1914, the patterns of colonial dominance had been established in the forms which were to survive with some modification for another half century. Throughout the Pacific Europeans had for a variety of reasons, but without any question about their right to do so, assumed the government of distant territories and peoples. In doing so, they also took upon themselves the right to make decisions about social development and cultural forms which were modified to suit their own needs and values. It is idle to argue about whether they had any right to do so; what matters is how they exercised their power, and whether the circumstances of time and place made their intervention desirable, necessary or gratuitous.

While colonial powers were establishing their regimes during this period, the social changes which had begun in a previous era continued, but were spread more systematically under the organizing hand of a central authority. Economic changes intended to produce a cash surplus for the expenses of the expanding role of government were introduced. Above all, it was the era of the 'Great Man', when imagination and resolution were called for from men who were given greater power than others had exercised in the islands before them, and greater power than they could have exercised elsewhere with so little to restrain them. It was only the First World War which brought this era to an end.

Chapter Thirteen

COLONIAL CONSOLIDATION

The period between the two world wars saw two major changes in colonial administration in the Pacific. The era of pacification was over and attention could now be given to the deliberate change of indigenous societies in accordance with the prevailing philosophies of government. Second, there was an acceptance in principle that the ultimate purpose of those changes was the eventual restoration of independence.

The First World War brought little drama to the Pacific islands. The German colonies were promptly occupied by the armed forces of Australia, New Zealand and Japan, and were governed under military regimes which preserved the *status quo* as far as that was possible for the duration of the war. Direct involvement by Pacific islanders was limited to the service in Europe of a Maori battalion and of a Fijian labour unit, the latter restricted to non-combatant duties.

Of far greater importance was the doctrine among the victor nations at the peace negotiations that the principle of national self-determination should prevail in future international politics. In other words, imperialist domination of subject nations was to cease, and Germany and Turkey were to lose their imperial possessions. It was recognised, however, that not all of these possessions at that time were able to stand alone as independent nations; so it was decided that they should be entrusted to an independent, international body which would supervise their future development. In this way, the Permanent Mandates Commission of the new League of Nations was established, and those imperial remnants outside Europe were given over to various nations to be administered on its behalf. In the Pacific, German Samoa was allocated to New Zealand; Nauru and New Guinea were allocated to Australia; and the Micronesian groups north of the equator were allocated to Japan.

Each of these territories was designated a 'C-class' mandate, which meant that in the present state of social and economic development, independence was not to be expected in the foreseeable future. In the meantime, the territories were to be developed in the interests of the native inhabitants; they were not to be militarized in any way; and an annual report was to be made to the Permanent Mandates Commission where searching questions might be asked of the administering power. In its conception this was a bold and generous-minded innovation, with implications for the future of all colonial possessions, although few gave the matter serious thought. In fact, colonial administrative policy for the mandates and for the other territories was to be dominated by three issues: government penury in an age of international economic recession, the continuing expectation that colonies should be self-supporting, and events in the islands to which governments were compelled to react.

Native welfare and economic development were the two things which were uppermost in the minds of colonial administrators. Increasingly they were to find that these things were both mutually dependent and mutually antagonistic, and it would be rare henceforth for officials to suggest that simply working for white employers was in itself a sufficient and desirable means of native improvement—however much settlers and investors themselves remained attached to that belief. Consequently, the attitudes of the various colonial regimes to economic development and to settlers and investors were ambivalent; as a result, the colonial regimes were usually attacked by humanitarian interests for neglecting the interests of the natives, and attacked by settlers for being hostile to progress.

In the event, the achievements of the various colonial regimes during this era were uneven. The greatest obstacles to progress were in Melanesia where the old problem of difficult terrain and social and linguistic fragmentation impeded the work of government and developer alike. In Papua, the sympathetic paternalism of Sir Hubert Murray saw to the gradual extension of European control, so that by 1940, almost all communities in the territory were receiving occasional visits from a patrol officer. Except in the areas of easiest access, however, this influence was necessarily confined to basic law and order issues, suppressing those practices in native life most objectionable to European sentiments of the time. Punishment—the only way of suppressing undesirable practices—was adjusted according to the degree of acculturation of the community involved. The device of imprisoning offenders at Port Moresby provided an opportunity of instructing a 'criminal' in the new order before returning him to his home, where the supposed benefit of his experiences might be spread around his community.

Murray lacked the resources to do much more in the areas of health, education and improvements to native agriculture than subsidize the work of the missions. Murray, in any case, did not believe that cultural change of the kind which seemed called for in Papua could be hurried, for that could cause great harm, as well as creating invidious inequalities between communities recently contacted and those which had had long experience of white contact. Instead, he concentrated on those things which could be accomplished cheaply and which caused minimum disruption to traditional life: he ensured that sorcery and warfare were suppressed; that village settlements were reconstructed with an emphasis on European notions of hygiene and cleanliness; and that games, mainly rugby and cricket, were introduced to compensate for the emptiness which followed the suppression of other things.

Murray, generally suspicious of outsiders who claimed special expertise, was usually his own expert on almost everything, but in 1922, he took the step of appointing to his staff an anthropologist, F.E.Williams. Murray had come to the conclusion that 'native administration' was merely applied anthropology, in the sense that one needed to understand a society and its people if one was to govern it successfully and intelligently. It was Williams who advocated the introduction of team sports to the Papuan villagers; 'less Christ, more cricket', he is alleged to have said, was the way to save these people.

Anthropology at the time was in its infancy and was specifically the study of 'primitive peoples', the ones whose cultures and existence were under threat. It was therefore sympathetic to the colonized races, and many anthropologists saw themselves as the champions of native interests against the destructive influences of trader, settler, missionary and government. Many, indeed, refused to co-operate with Murray, but Williams, perhaps from an appreciation that change was inevitable and that it was better to manage it intelligently than to let it proceed blindly, was able to work with him. During their long and fruitful relationship, both men had the Papuans' interests at heart; for this reason, incentives, not just punishments, were offered to encourage modest changes in Papuan life. Other changes were deliberately retarded inasmuch as the demands of settlers for compulsory labour were refused, the indenture of women was prohibited and the creation of landless Papuan communities was avoided. Partly for reasons of cost, and partly on principle, Papuans were gradually taken into the administration and acquired experience in law and government. For similarly mixed reasons of economy and principle, Papuans were recruited as medical assistants, and between 1932 and 1936, forty Papuans received basic medical training at the University of Sydney; but this experiment was discontinued amid controversy fired by prejudices of racial superiority and anxiety about the preservation of white status.

Murray was a controversial figure during his lifetime, largely for being 'pro-native'. Subsequently, he has been attacked for having done too little for them, for having retarded development and maintained white supremacy, and for accepting that tribal peoples were still in the childhood of humanity from which condition they had to be raised at a natural pace (as with the growth of a child) by white benevolence. Murray's policy, right or wrong, was at least intelligent and consistent, and made indigenous interests the principle on which all matters should be judged. He would perhaps have been bolder had economic depression and a penurious and unsympathetic Australian government not kept his budget pathetically small.

In the adjacent territory of New Guinea, the former German possession which had come under Australian control, a very different style of administration developed. Different traditions of native policy and development policy had been inherited from the German regime, but more important was the absence of a single directing, autocratic mind. New Guinea between the wars was governed by a succession of military officers whose own limitations were compounded rather than off-set by Australia's failure to establish a stable, professional public service for the territory. In these circumstances, settlers' interests received a more sympathetic hearing, and land and labour for plantation development were more readily available. This greater liberality was not enough to guarantee agricultural prosperity, for the same difficulties faced planters in New Guinea as in Papua: remoteness from markets, low prices, and pests and diseases. It may be suggested also that indentured labour, like slavery, was inherently inefficient. An indicator of the planters' inability to overcome these economic disadvantages is that the numbers of New Guineans employed for wages remained fairly stable from the early 1920s until the late '30s.

The growth area for European enterprise in New Guinea was gold mining, and this was the economic salvation of the government, as well as the source of many of its difficulties. Gold was found in the rivers of New Guinea in large quantities but low concentrations, and the resulting revenue enabled the government to pay higher salaries to its employees and spend more on education and health. On the other hand, prospectors would take themselves wherever the hope of a gold find would lead them, which was frequently ahead of the government's ability with limited staff to explore territory, to make contact with the inhabitants and assert the most elementary control over them. The miners thus had to establish their own arrangements with the New Guineans according to their own circumstances and resources (including weaponry), and became comparatively large employers of native labour, often beyond the reach of official regulation. These prospecting activities were sometimes major exploring expeditions, the most notable being those of the Leahy brothers in the 1930s, which disclosed the hitherto unsuspected presence of vast highland valleys, the home of hundreds of thousands of people.

The New Guinea administration, much criticized at the time and since for what it did not achieve, and castigated for its allegedly severe attitudes and methods in its management of the indigenous people, can nevertheless be defended. A tropical, mountainous, heavily populated country with few exploitable resources of any value presents formidable difficulties of administration at any time. This was still an age when government functions were more restricted than they became in later years, and prevailing economic conditions did not allow for much boldness. The limitations of the government's achievements are readily understandable considering that they took place in an era when roads and bridges still had to be constructed by men without machines, when radio technology was still so rudimentary that it could be easily defeated by the hostility of terrain and climate, and when the absence of domestic refrigeration, antibiotics, sulpha drugs and modern pest-control made every foreign resident a pioneer. Nevertheless, progress was made: new peoples were contacted and brought under an administration which made life more secure, elementary medical services were provided, and steps were taken to create a public service with relevant professional training. If the administration seemed harsh, it nevertheless compares favourably with many contemporary colonial regimes.

One such colony with which the Australian administration of New Guinea compares favourably was the adjacent British possession of the Solomon Islands. Here the difficulties were fundamentally the same, but the achievement was substantially less owing to the fewer opportunities for economic development. It was not until 1940 that the whole group could be said to be under administrative supervision, and on the larger islands that supervision was very tenuous. The native population continued to decline, and foreign rule was both resented and resisted from time to time. The problem was not any lack of goodwill on the part of the colonial officials, nor any shortage of advice from missionaries and anthropologists, but a pathetic want of resources. The government could not govern without income, and few people at the time considered that the interests of the Solomon islanders would be best served by the absence of government.

Unlike every other major group in the Pacific, colonial government in the Solomons was not preceded by the establishment of a foreign settler community. Woodford, the first resident commissioner, had to try to create an economy, and offered generous concessions to would-be planters and in particular to the Pacific Islands Company which acquired 200,000 acres of land on a ninety-nine year lease in 1901. Within a few years, this had been transferred to Lever Brothers, the soap manufacturers, on extremely generous terms in the hope that the resulting investment would underpin the development of the group. By the 1920s therefore, Lever Brothers was the giant of the Solomons, with about half of the total planted area in the group; but even this amounted to an asset of only 20,000 acres, which employed perhaps a thousand men, and this enterprise was profitable only because its production was bought at favourable prices by another Lever company. In other words, without heavy government expenditure, progress in the Solomons was impossible, and before the Second World War the British government was not prepared to make that expenditure. The tiny administrative staff in the Solomons struggled on, accomplishing little more than the exercise of judicial functions, leaving the rest to the missions with their various approaches, policies and divergent attitudes to native culture and native development.

The British tradition of colonial government (there seems no particular reason to classify the Australian administrations as anything but British at this time) thus showed common conditions and circumstances, but not uniformity. Fiji, as in the earlier period, remained the show-case, with its orderliness, the subsistence prosperity of the native population, the schools and health services, the land policy, and the overall impression of a cultivated, husbanded landscape. The Fijians were involved in the administration in ways which changed with a succession of constitutional developments during the 1920s and '30s, and there was a strong bond of mutual respect between the administration and the Fijian chiefs. In a speech in 1938, Ratu Sukuna, the Oxford-educated, Fijian aristocrat and senior public servant, lampooned the English and the other varieties of white people, but concluded by congratulating the British on their achievement in Fiji, and finished with the words, 'To you . . . Fijians say—"Carry on." '

But all was not well in Fiji. Despite the abundant evidence of Fijian loyalty to the colonial regime, there was not only an undercurrent of Fijian disquiet which was occasionally evident, but also the more conspicuous, unhappy situation of the Indian population. Between 1878 and 1916, about 60,000 immigrants had come to Fiji as indentured labourers for five-year terms, and since a free passage back to India was conditional on staying in the colony for a further five years as free labourers, most never returned to India. In 1920, when all indentures were cancelled and the system brought to an end, there were about 60,000 Indians in Fiji.

Free mixing between the races had never been government policy, and indeed there had been deliberate efforts to keep the races apart since the 1880s, a policy which promoted short-term peace, but was not the best way to ensure future racial harmony in Fiji. Nor did the government seem to be deeply concerned with the fact that its policies, deliberately or otherwise, were creating a new community in Fiji, and consequently, the needs of this population were neglected. Services which later came to be accepted as government responsibilities were initially supplied only by the Christian missions, and they too were slow to extend their work to the Indians. When eventually the government took responsibility for schooling from the missions, it found the Fijian population amply provided for, but few schools for Indians, a situation which was not rectified. In 1926, most of the 19,000 Fijian children of school age were at school, but of 14,000 Indians of the same age, only about 2,500 were at school, and only about 300 of these were girls. By 1930, the Indian community, which supplied the bulk of the labour for the monetary economy of Fiji for half a century, had had none of its members rise by education to professional levels.

What seemed to the Indians to be an even greater grievance, however, was their exclusion from the political and civil rights enjoyed by the small European population, and they continually pressed for reforms after the Legislative Council was enlarged in 1929 to include three Indian elected members. Associated with the Indian demand for political and civil rights was their continuing grievance over exclusion from land ownership. Land which was held on native tenure was inalienable; so the only land which Indians could aspire to buy was land already owned by Europeans, and there was never likely to be much of that available. Native land could be leased, originally for only ten years, later for twenty-one, and the Indians were galled at seeing land which they had leased and cultivated being returned to its native owners only to revert to bush. For the most part, their farming was restricted to cane-growing on land which they leased or sub-leased from the Colonial Sugar Refining Company. In the late 1930s, a more generous policy for leasing Fijian land was adopted which ameliorated Indian hardship, though it did little to diminish their sense of grievance at apparently having no real rights in a country to which they had been invited and which they had made their home. Thus in Fiji, native interests were protected by the involuntary sacrifices of the Indian settlers.

In New Zealand, recognition was growing that the original inhabitants were the victims of injustice, and in the 1920s and 1930s, the New Zealand government set up a number of agencies and projects; their purpose was to improve Maori education by making specific provision for it, and to enable the Maoris to make better use of the lands still remaining under native tenure. Those few Maoris who at this time had achieved national prominence had had the advantages of at least a partial Pakeha upbringing and a privileged education; the majority, still living apart from the Pakeha (that is, European) communities, had access only to rudimentary education and lived in such conditions that their death rates were far above those of the white population. Indeed the death rate from tuberculosis among the Maoris in the 1930s was one of the highest in the world; the Pakeha death rate from the same disease was among the lowest. Discrimination in employment and less access to all forms of training required positive government action, of which an increasing amount was taken after 1935. This affirmative action, of course, remained insufficient to achieve social and economic equality between the two races, but at least it was based on the premise that equality was a possible and desirable goal, while at the same time recognizing that the preservation of certain things which were distinctive about Maori life (mainly arts and the communal identity) was also desirable. These were goals not shared in the tropical Pacific.

Alone among the English-speaking territories of the Pacific, Tonga seemed uncomplicated. It continued to be governed by its own constitutional monarchy, although under the supervision of the British consul who possessed virtual veto rights over all important matters of government. Problems concerning development and the reconciliation of conflicting rights of different classes of people were absent, because the strong, centralized government, rooted in Tongan traditions and history, maintained an absolute prohibition on the private ownership of land, thereby ensuring the absence of any significant number of European settlers. Copra production, practically the sole source of foreign earnings, was almost totally in Tongan hands, and the government was free of debt. The Cook Islands to the east might have been similarly placed, but for the absence of strong, central government, and the uncertainties of a diffident and largely uninterested New Zealand administration.

Samoa was a troubled territory, but the historical accidents of the recent past had given it some great advantages. Colonial government had supplied the political unity previously lacking; the

Solf regime had discouraged foreign settlement, and the confiscation of German estates after the First World War placed large tracts of well-developed, productive land under the direct control of the government, and gave it an economic base independent of overseas investors. As in Tonga, most of Samoa's production was in native hands, and was of a volume which offered encouragement. The 'Samoa for the Samoans' policy of successive administrators, if not always tactfully pursued, at least saved Samoa from the more awkward anomalies of colonialism.

To the north-west, the British colony of the Gilbert and Ellice Islands was under firm, paternalistic rule, free of exploitation if only because there was nothing there to exploit. That colony, indeed, lived off the exploitation of the Banabans, the people of Ocean Island, whose island of phosphate was being steadily destroyed by mining operations in exchange for only nominal compensation. This callous treatment of the Banabans in the 1920s and 1930s, like that of the Nauruans on a similar island 250 kilometres to the west, is a demonstration of the self-interest of colonial governments when there was a sufficiently valuable resource worth exploiting.

The French colonies, as in the earlier period, continued to demonstrate two extremes: neglect in French Polynesia, and exploitation in New Caledonia. In the former, a dictatorial regime continued to provide only basic administrative functions and to collect taxes, and regarded its relationship with the tiny settler population which was demanding political rights as its only serious problem. No serious economic planning occurred until the eve of the Second World War.

In New Caledonia, the First World War had less impact than in the English and German possessions. A high turnover of officials continued until the arrival in 1925 of a new governor, Guyon, who during his seven years of service initiated a 'native policy', by which he tried to make some provision for improving the health and education of the Melanesian population, and strove for less one-sided labour laws. His comparative liberalism was funded by the revenues from the high metal prices of the 1920s, but the end of his regime and its policies came with the worst year of the Great Depression. Development in the 1920s, and the need to encourage further development after the depression in the 1930s, simply put more pressure on the little amount of native land which remained. Concessions in the legal status of the New Caledonians, or Kanaks, were made towards the end of the 1930s, but the social disabilities of the Kanaks made these gestures valueless at that time.

What principally distinguished the French colonies from the British during these decades was the focus of policy: the British did not always succeed, and were not always faithful to their principles, but they retained a strong sentiment that the indigenous people had an over-riding claim to just treatment and the enjoyment of the benefits of such resources of nature as they possessed. The French lacked even this amount of idealism; French interests were to prevail over all others, and if, as in Polynesia, there was no French interest to be served, then there was no need for official vigour at all.

No colonial regime, however, questioned the rightness of its dominance, or the rightness of its policies. Despite its goals, colonial government assumed a European cultural superiority, usually shored up by a belief in European racial superiority. The resulting forms of discrimination were not simply expressions of racism: governments typically believe that they know what is best for the populations which they govern, whether or not differences of race or culture are involved. Moreover, there was much in the Pacific which by any standard of humanity needed changing. It was equally obvious that the total absence of regulations to control dealings between peoples of different cultures was bound to give rise to abuses of various kinds; after all, it was the existence of such abuses which had made colonial rule necessary in the first place. Given the absence of common values, experience, wealth and circumstance (especially in Melanesia), it seemed sound policy to discriminate by legislation between peoples whose differences at that time were identified in terms of race. Equally, the eventual elimination of such discrimination and its justification ought to have been the ultimate goal of all governments. In much of the Pacific, and in Melanesia in particular, the attainment of this goal seemed such a distant prospect that it was frequently lost to sight.

Although discriminatory legislation might not have been inspired by racist doctrines, racism was a basic assumption of most of the settlers, who behaved as if they were a species apart from the surrounding population. An enormous social gulf was maintained between the races, often bolstered by bizarre European fantasies about sexual attitudes and behaviour, contradictory beliefs about the childishness and natural submissiveness of natives, and their perverse savagery and innate aggressiveness. Any native assertiveness was anxiously suppressed, as settlers and governments alike feared for their privileges and safety. Apart from occasional individual acts of defiance, or acts which were merely mundane crimes, there were several developments which caused concern for fear of what they might lead to. These included strike action by labourers, independent economic activity which attempted to bypass white merchants, and the so-called cargo cults with their overtones of religious messianism and incipient nationalism.

Strike action was rare, but not unknown. In 1929, however, a major withdrawal of labour occurred in Rabaul, the administrative centre of New Guinea. The strike was neither spontaneous nor over a petty grievance; it was a carefully organized protest, led by Sumsuma, a man who enjoyed unique privileges among New Guineans and who seems therefore to have been concerned with basic questions of the relationship between black and white, rather than with specific industrial relations questions such as wages and conditions of work. Although the movement was not an uprising it did aim at redefining the roles of the two races in New Guinea, and as such was remarkable in attempting to find a common identity between New Guineans of different clans and tribes, many of them traditional enemies. To the white population of Rabaul, the unthinkable had happened, and their reaction was both hysterical and brutal, going beyond the particular issues to a general tightening of controls over native labour and native police; the leaders of the strike received harsh sentences of imprisonment with hard labour.

In Fiji, a similar motivation—that is, the quest for racial equality—probably lay behind the formation shortly before the First World War of a bold enterprise which became known as the Viti Company. It was founded by a young man called Apolosi Nawai, whose own experience with the cash economy suggested to him things that might be achieved if Fijians pooled their meagre resources, and did the commercial things which white men did. Capital might be raised, transport businesses established, profits invested, and white men, instead of being served, might be employed at the meagre wage levels which they offered to Fijians. A sense of a common Fijian identity was being promoted, and the rhetoric of the movement certainly had overtones of nationalism and anti-European sentiment. Nawai's methods and his growing influence was a cause for concern to the colonial government, and it is scarcely possible to distinguish between concern for continued commercial dominance and anxiety about the political implications. Eventually, in 1917, Nawai laid himself open to a charge of sedition, was convicted and exiled to Rotuma, having not only unsettled the government and settlers, but having become a folk hero to the Fijians as well. The affair of the Viti Company had religious, even messianic, overtones, which had been a factor in its spread. How much this owed to Christian influence in Fiji, or to traditional Fijian concepts is unclear, but it was something which it had in common with protest movements elsewhere in Melanesia.

More overtly anti-European but at the same time less constructive was the John Frum movement in Tanna, in the New Hebrides. Like other religious movements in Melanesia in the 1930s and later, it was labelled as nativistic; that is, it seemed to be rejecting European culture and aimed at reviving a lost and dimly known traditional culture. In fact, the movement showed elements of both. The John Frum movement was a continuation of earlier expressions of discontent on Tanna, but emerged into a more vigorous and popular form in 1940. There was talk of destroying all present forms of wealth, of overturning by supernatural means the existing relationship between Europeans and Tannese, and of the appearance of a prophetic leader. The movement had a dream-like quality in that it frequently changed its form, content and manifestations, sometimes being put down by a puzzled government agent, but recurring again and again over the coming decades.

The most serious challenge to European dominance between the wars came not from such movements as these, but from a culturally unified people with a long and sophisticated political tradition. This was in Western Samoa, where in 1921 the New Zealand administration began to apply itself seriously to the problems of government after seven years of military rule. A busy programme of development was undertaken, providing roads and drainage, constructing village water supplies, extending hospital services and supplementing the mission schools. Samoan contributions of cash and labour were encouraged for practical reasons and also to foster Samoan interest and sympathy with the activity being undertaken. During the 1920s, the administration under General Richardson vigorously pursued a programme of practical reforms, and Richardson himself took a sympathetic interest in the Samoans and learnt their language.

There was nevertheless discontent both with New Zealand as the administering power, and with Richardson as the administrator. The ill-feeling came to a head over the issue of the representation of Samoan interests in government. Richardson refused to accept a part-Samoan trader, O.F.Nelson, as a spokesman for the native Samoans, believing that he was too much a European in outlook to represent honestly Samoan interests. Other issues became involved, and an opposition movement began, called the Mau. An influential grass-roots organization was set up, powerful enough to counter any government undertakings; soon it had its own police force and taxes, European businesses were boycotted and picketed, and by 1928, the Mau was virtually the real government of the Samoans. Mass demonstrations and civil disobedience made the colonial regime powerless, despite arrests of leaders and the deportation of Nelson. Finally in December 1929, a demonstration turned into an armed clash in which ten Samoans (including the high chief, Tupua Tamasese) and one European policeman were killed; repressive measures followed and the key people in the movement had to take to the bush. A petition of almost eight thousand signatures (out of a total population of perhaps fifty thousand) was sent to the League of Nations requesting that Western Samoa be transferred to another power, but without effect. A stalemate developed which could not be broken until 1935, when the Labour Party came to power in New Zealand promising eventual Samoan self-government; cordiality, however, was not restored until after the Second World War.

The New Zealand regime in Western Samoa had been wrecked by its own well-intentioned paternalism. This indeed, was the dilemma of colonialism in the Pacific. It was difficult to know what was right, harder still to be able to do it, and practically impossible to do it as a foreign regime without alienating a people which felt itself to be perfectly capable of managing its own affairs. Since the achievement never lived up to the expectations of the Permanent Mandates Commission, the League of Nations was critical of both Australia and New Zealand in their administration of their mandates. The third mandate power, Japan, was less concerned with what the League of Nations might think and was less forth-coming with data about its territory. Withdrawing from the League of Nations altogether in 1934, it showed its contempt for the toothlessness of that body by retaining its possession of Micronesia.

During the first half of its thirty-year administration of Micronesia (that is, to about 1930), Japan differed from the other mandate powers in pursuing a more active development policy. Initially, land could be alienated only through the government which seems to have made it easily available, but after 1931, land could be bought directly from the native owners with official approval. Christian missions were allowed to continue, but government schools soon overshadowed their influence, and pursued a policy of Japanization which in essence probably differed little from the schooling received in other Pacific possessions. Health facilities were provided, but not homogeneously for Micronesia's scattered population. Taxation was graded according to the scale of development. Community organization was not much interfered with and native chiefs were appointed to implement the government's wishes as in other colonies.

What did distinguish Japan's rule was the amount of land that was alienated, and the large numbers of Japanese settlers who arrived in the islands, most of them during the 1930s; by 1937 the immigrants equalled the Micronesians in number, and the latter possessed only about a quarter of Micronesian land, the rest having been appropriated mainly for sugar plantations. At the same time, economic opportunities for the Micronesians declined, and taxation rose steeply: Micronesia was rapidly being transformed into a colony of exploitation as Japanese ambitions began to take a more visibly sinister form; there was no pretence of this development being ultimately for the good of the native inhabitants. Finally, fortifications were begun to fit Micronesia into the needs of Japan's expansionist plans.

Those plans, suspected and feared during the late 1930s and during the first two years of the Second World War, became clear to everyone after the bombing of the American fleet in Pearl Harbour, Hawai'i, on 7 December 1941. Simultaneous attacks were launched in the Philippines and French Indo-China, and a rapid advance through south-east Asia followed. Japanese plans, however, had not been to invade Hawai'i, and the intentions towards other Pacific island groups are uncertain; their prime objective was south-east Asia, but that inevitably meant war with the United States, Australia and New Zealand. In practice, it proved impossible to draw a line on the map to say where the war should stop; and the importance of trans-Pacific communications to Japan's enemies seemed to dictate the invasion of the island groups of the western Pacific. The northern Gilberts, beginning with Tarawa, were invaded on 10 December 1941; Ocean Island and Nauru were taken immediately afterwards; in January 1942, the invasion of New Guinea and the Solomon Islands took place; and Rabaul, the administrative centre of the Territory of New Guinea, was taken on 23 January.

The American response was as startling as the rapidity of the Japanese advance. Within three months of the attack on Pearl Harbour, American garrisons were taking up positions in New Caledonia, the New Hebrides, the southern Solomons, Fiji, Samoa, and the other groups to the east. Construction units were building bases which were small cities capable of undertaking major ship repairs, and air-strips were built with heavy machinery in a matter of days. The machinery being used, the numbers of men involved, the frenetic activity, the changes being made visibly to the landscape, the tremendous noise generated, the lighting of the night, all were beyond the previous experience and imaginations of islanders and settlers alike.

The great aircraft-carrier battles of the Coral Sea and Midway in May and June 1942 crippled the mobility of Japan's forces, and over the next few months, the advance in New Guinea was turned back by Australian soldiers on the Kokoda track and by American and Australian soldiers at Milne Bay. In December 1942 and January 1943, the Japanese beach-heads at Buna and Gona were retaken by combined allied forces and from then on the Japanese were on the defensive; the ultimate outcome of the war could be no longer in doubt, but nevertheless the fighting was to be long and bitter.

The length, bitterness and costliness of the Pacific campaigns are matters of continuing controversy. The allied commander in the south-west Pacific, the American general Douglas MacArthur, demanded the systematic reduction of Japanese strongholds all the way back to Japan. Other strategists, including the American admiral, Chester Nimitz, argued for containment of the Japanese, by-passing most of their island possessions, to strike directly at Japan itself. Nimitz's strategy would have been less costly, but MacArthur's was more likely to produce the early victories which would raise allied morale. MacArthur had his way, although substantial garrisons of Japanese were left alone until the war ended. For the whole of 1943, a savage war was waged in the Solomons, and towards the end of the year, on 20 November, the re-taking of the Gilbert Islands and the invasion of the Marshalls were begun. By April 1944, the New Guinea campaign was over, and the islands of Micronesia and the Philippines were invaded. There were still pockets of resistance—large pockets in some cases, including Rabaul—when the war ended in August 1945.

Pacific islanders had experienced the war in different ways. Some had fought in the allied armies: in the end there were five battalions of Papuan and New Guinean soldiers with a formidable reputation as jungle fighters, remorseless and efficient, never failing to exact a heavy toll of enemy lives for negligible losses of their own; the same was true of the Fijian battalion in the Solomons. Those islanders whose lands had been overrun by war witnessed the total destruction of jungle, gardens and villages. In New Guinea and parts of the Solomons, many of them lived under Japanese occupation for up to two years, some for even longer; to some of those under Japanese rule the occupation troops were courteous and fair; more often, and especially as the Japanese became hard-pressed, the treatment was brutal. Native opinion ranged from fatalistic acceptance of yet another change of masters, through willing and unwilling collaboration, to a very dangerous loyalty to the Australians for which the penalties of discovery were terrifying. Tens of thousands of Papuans and New Guineans were employed as labourers by the Australian army, and experienced an entirely new relationship with white men who were egalitarian and friendly comrades rather than arrogant, white 'mastas'.

For the island groups to the south and east of the Solomons, the war was a time of stimulus and excitement without danger. Samoa and Fiji, besides being garrisoned, were forward staging-areas for American troops destined for the western battlefields. Because these troops were well paid and well supplied, with the generosity of those who had no material needs and no future worth thinking about, there was an economic boom: prices soared and so did wages; employment opportunities exceeded all previous limits, and there came a widespread interest in learning the English language for its economic value. The same was true on a smaller scale of the other groups which had smaller garrisons and were of less strategic interest: Tonga, the Cooks and French Polynesia.

In Fiji, the native warrior tradition combined with strong pro-British sentiments produced a ground-swell of support, attested by the ten percent of the Fijian population which enlisted in combat or labour units; generous cash contributions paid for a warship (HMS *Fiji*) and helped the 'Sponsor a Spitfire' programme. The Indian population, realistic and embittered, withheld its support and used the opportunity presented by the war to draw attention to its permanent disabilities. Indian labourers went on strike in 1943, and Indian entrepreneurs made the most of the commercial opportunies which the war gave them. This difference in response between support for the war, and exploitation of the war's opportunities, drove the wedge of antipathy between Indians and Fijians a little deeper.

All wars end in anti-climax, as the people who were involved try to return to their ideas of normal life, and a period of restlessness is bound to follow. In the Pacific islands, the war boom finished as suddenly as it began, leaving behind disappointment and nostalgia, and the memory of squandered wealth. Devastating as the war was in places, its greatest impact was on the distant policy-makers of the colonial regimes; even before the war ended, new plans were being made by Europeans for a new world and a new age for the peoples of the Pacific.

Chapter Fourteen

PLANNING A NEW WORLD

World War Two was fought in the name of freedom and justice, and in the idealism with which men contemplated the end of the war, there was hope that the ills of the past could be cleared away. The need for reconstruction in the war-devastated areas was obvious, and discussions about ends and means were initiated before the war ended. But reconstruction was not taken to mean merely a return to the pre-war arrangements; that would have been easy enough, for although the destruction was total in some areas, the nature of pre-war development was not such that a great deal of time or money would be needed to make good the damage. The worst aspect of the economic damage for the islanders was the loss of coconut trees on native and commercial plantations which after replanting would not bear for seven years, and would not be in full production for some time after that.

The real issue was that governments of the time, probably more than ordinary men and women, wanted the post-war world to be different from the old; such wishes for reform were not new, proposals having been discussed well before the war had begun. The idea of trusteeship was not new even when it became incorporated in the mandate agreements at the end of the First World War, and informed discussions before the war had explored proposals and possibilities for colonial development. As far back as 1926, an international conference had been convened on Pacific islands' health issues, and during the 1930s, there had been a growing recognition of the need to co-ordinate activity and share information on many things, including administration, production, marketing and welfare policies. In 1940, when the future of the world was far from certain, Britain had passed a Colonial Development and Welfare Act, increasing expenditure on research and development in its colonies.

In 1944, with the war not yet over, the government of Fiji appointed a committee to plan future development. At the same time, Australia and New Zealand were discussing future policy directions and proposed the creation of an international consultative and advisory body for the South Pacific. As a result, the South Pacific Commission was formed in 1947, its membership including all those nations which administered dependent peoples in the Pacific. Its role was to conduct and disseminate the results of research into every imaginable subject from anthropology to zoology, to co-ordinate common action and to provide a forum which would encourage better government of the Pacific islanders. Proposals for a variety of pan-Pacific agencies were made towards the war's end, embracing education, health, agriculture, information and library services, and even a literature board; none of these proposals was formally adopted, but most of them were taken up later by the South Pacific Commission.

One thing was clear to everyone involved in this forward planning: not enough was known about the people and resources of the Pacific. Formulating objectives was one thing, but specific policies had to be based on reliable information about current circumstances and realistic possibilities. While some data had been obtainable from anthropologists and natural scientists before the war, their work had been specific and unco-ordinated rather than comprehensive, and was not usually addressed to the particular matters upon which government policies might be based. The first serious attempt to make good this shortcoming in expert knowledge was undertaken by the Australian army in its capacity as the government of Papua and New Guinea from 1942 to 1945.

The army had established a Directorate of Research and Civil Affairs under the enigmatic Colonel Alf Conlon. Before the war, Conlon had been a perpetual student at the University of Sydney, meandering his way through degrees in Arts, Law and Medicine, and becoming an expert practitioner in student politics. The war provided both a challenge and a focus for his unusual talents, and his career was both dramatic and controversial. Creative and devious, he was a generator of schemes, and chance had pitched him into circumstances in which he had real power and which required imagination and boldness. Conlon's research unit, a heterogeneous collection of eccentric talent, produced ideas which were not always practicable, but his staff adhered to the notion that new directions were necessary, and they exercised a powerful and long-lasting influence through a School of Civil Affairs which provided training in the administration of Australia's colony. After the war, this school became the Australian School of Pacific Administration, which was intended to be the means of creating a professional public service to supersede the erratic staffing procedures of the past. A further result of this activity by Conlon's unit was the post-war publication of a series of books addressing the problems of the south-west Pacific, the research for which was undertaken or published under the auspices of the Institute of Pacific Research and the Institute of International Affairs.

Conlon also had an influence in the decision of the Australian government to establish a new university (the Australian National University) as a research institute, within which a school would be devoted specifically to social science research in the Pacific, leading to practical results for the development of policy and the improvement of administration. Similarly inspired, but on a much more modest scale, Auckland University College appointed a Professor of Anthropology, expecting some direct results in terms of improved administration of the Maoris, Cook Islanders and Samoans under New Zealand rule.

The new order did not, perhaps, justify the hopes held by and of these experts. The idealism of the 1940s failed to overcome mundane habits and constraints, but nevertheless the policies of the immediate post-war years showed that politicians were taking some of their promises seriously. Foremost was the belief of the Australian government that it owed a debt to the people of Papua and New Guinea, a belief which was compounded by the conviction that pre-war trusteeship had been inadequate. The policy henceforth was to be that native interests were paramount (not a new thing, for that had been the principle which guided MacGregor and Murray), made real by much higher levels of Australian government funding. Nor was there to be any delay: if a wrong needed righting, it would be done, and therein lay the root of great difficulties. Wrongs that needed righting included the labour system: because thousands of labourers had been kept working during the war beyond the expiry of their indentures, labour contracts were abruptly cancelled in October 1945; because labourers had wages owing to them, they were paid comparatively large cash sums without banks and without goods to buy; when compensation was due for the loss of lives, pigs and homes, it was paid, and often with more enthusiasm than fairness. The immediate result was an acute labour shortage, and because of the undeveloped nature of the territory's economy, this munificence brought no benefits to the people it was intended to help.

The government of Papua and New Guinea (a single government administered both territories after the army took over in 1942) depended almost entirely on expatriate staffing for its enlarged functions, and although more money was available for government activity than ever before, it could only be spent if the staff was available to administer it. In the early post-war years, the administration was acutely understaffed, and trained, experienced personnel were needed. There were few with training, and many of those with experience (the 'befores', those who had been in the territory before the war) simply wanted to get back to an ordinary life as planters or merchants, while others wanted to return to Australia to make a more normal life. Australia itself was suffering a labour shortage which made recruitment for work in New Guinea difficult. Shortages of manufactured goods of all kinds continued for some years in an ironic contrast to the profligacy of war, and for all the idealism of the Australian government, the needs of Papua and New Guinea were not its highest priority; the government was stretched even to meet domestic needs.

Thus the achievements of the post-war regime in New Guinea were disappointing, and accordingly the government was bitterly attacked both by the liberal idealists and by the conservatives. Two things were worth noticing, however: the administrative union of the two territories of Papua and New Guinea which would avoid perpetuating some of the anomalies of the past, and the formation of co-operative societies. The co-operative societies were attempts to combine economic development and economic democracy, and thus to enable native participation in the money economy in a more responsible role than merely being labourers for foreign interests. Co-operatives, it was claimed, would build on the supposed communal ethics of Melanesian society and give the native people control over their own economic future, and provide the foundation stone of a future independent country. The history of the co-operative societies was to be disappointing but by 1950, when they had scarcely begun, there was reason for optimism.

The administrative union of the two territories, formalized in 1949, was a sign of the difference between the new United Nations and the old League of Nations. Whereas the League of Nations mandates were subject to a standard formula which required that they be maintained as distinct territories and not be militarized, the United Nations did not impose a standard formula for the trusteeships which were to replace the old mandates. Moreover, the trusts were voluntary as there was nothing except political expediency to prevent any of the territories in question being annexed by their conquerors. Indeed, the United States threatened to annex Micronesia by right of conquest unless it had its way on the terms of the trusteeship agreement.

Under the United Nations, the old distinction of A-class, B-class and C-class mandates was abandoned, and a separate agreement was made for each territory with its trustee. Colonial powers were invited to place other territories under trust, but none did so; in the Australian case, this resulted in the anomaly of one half of Papua-New Guinea after the administrative union being subject to United Nations scrutiny but not the other half. The trustees collectively were to make guarantees concerning human rights and to promote progress, but generally they had the right to govern the territories as if they were integral parts of the governing nation. This, of course, allowed the governing nation to claim privileges of trade and investment. An active role in defence was also required, in contrast to the former 'demilitarized' condition, and in the case of Micronesia, a separate category of 'strategic trust' was created, allowing the United States the right to close all or part of the territory to other nations for security reasons, as well as granting the right to fortify it. World War Two had taught the Americans that their own security was bound up with the destiny of Micronesia, a position which it has not modified in the succeeding four decades. In the allocation of territories, Micronesia was the only one which changed hands after the war; Australia retained Nauru as well as New Guinea, and New Zealand retained possession of Western Samoa.

The trusteeship agreement for Western Samoa had scarcely been concluded at the end of 1946, when a petition was received at the United Nations requesting self-government under the protection and guidance of New Zealand, referring specifically to the model provided by the protectorate relationship between Tonga and Great Britain. The United Nations Trusteeship Council, to its credit, took the petition seriously, immediately sending a mission of inquiry to Samoa. The mission reported promptly, pointing out serious obstacles, but also drawing attention to the aspirations of the Samoans, and concluding with perhaps as much caution as optimism that 'the risks of trouble . . . are greater if much is withheld than if much is given.'

It was fortunate that this view accorded closely with the opinion of the New Zealand government; having already made its own inquiries, it was formulating plans to re-organize the Samoan government and give increasing responsibilities to Samoans, involving them more in decision-making. Experience of government cooled the Samoan ardour for progress, and they had misgivings about some of the social and economic changes which Europeans considered necessary for independence. These preconditions of independence threatened great changes in Samoan life, which the often conservative Samoan nationalists seemed reluctant to accept. It was, however, good for the relationship between Samoa and New Zealand that the latter was able to keep a step ahead of Samoan aspirations. In economic affairs, the Reparation Estates (the former

German properties) were used to promote agricultural diversification, and more Samoans went into commerce; village co-operatives were organized to bring greater rationality to production and transport; at the same time, the subsidised administration was able to spend heavily on the infrastructures of electricity, transport and water supply. The constitution was modified every few years to transfer responsibility gradually, with Samoans being progressively incorporated into the public service as more of them gained higher educational qualifications, and in 1952, the New Zealand administrator, Guy Powles, set a timetable aiming at independence in 1960; full internal self-government came in 1959, and complete independence on 1 January 1962.

A short span of time—fifteen years—had seen enormous changes in Samoa, and the war unquestionably hastened the process. Once independence was on the way, however, the most striking feature of the whole process was Samoan caution in political experimentation. It was not part of the thinking of Samoan leaders that independence should make their country a political replica of the western democracies, and the United Nations Trusteeship Council had misgivings about the Samoan proposal for a restricted franchise. Much of the success of Samoan decolonization, however, was due to the willingness of the New Zealand government to encourage the Samoans to be the architects of their own country. The result, if not satisfactory to the aspirations of the most progressive thinkers, endowed Western Samoa with stability and cultural integrity.

The goals for Western Samoa had been much more easily set and pursued than was to prove possible for New Zealand's Maori population. The welfare and land development programmes of the late 1930s were continued during the war, although at a slower pace. The government's plan after the war was simply to get back 'on track' with the policies which it had initiated ten years before, for which purpose the Maori Social and Economic Advancement Act was passed in 1945. The policy was one of 'positive discrimination': special programmes aimed at a particular section of the population (in this case defined by race) were inaugurated to counteract specific disabilities, the underlying assumption being that establishing equality was not just a good thing in itself, it would lead eventually to New Zealanders becoming one people. Attaining this goal of assimilation would ultimately make discriminatory laws of all kinds unnecessary; accordingly in 1948, Maoris were given the same access to alcohol as Pakeha (white) New Zealanders, and were required to conform to the same marriage laws in 1951.

During the 1950s, a subtle shift took place from the pursuit of social and economic equality to legal (or perhaps legalistic) equality.

The Maori Affairs Act rationalized the mass of legislation relating to Maoris, and simplified their administration, but was still aimed ultimately at assimilation. The problem of devising fair and effective policies was, however, becoming more difficult, rather than less so: the Maori population was increasing rapidly and becoming urbanized at an even greater rate (16 percent more Maoris were living in cities each year, on average). In 1960, an inquiry into the Department of Maori Affairs was published which argued forcefully for a return to policies of positive discrimination in order to counteract the deteriorating position accompanying urbanization. In addition, it was recommended that the goal of Maori policy should no longer be assimilation but integration, whereby Maori cultural differences might be preserved while facilitating the attainment by the Maori population of a socio-economic distribution similar to that of the Pakeha. Since then, the Maoris themselves have become more assertive about the development of their cultural differences, and more inclined to condemn and reject white paternalism, reflecting the resurgence elsewhere of subordinated peoples.

In the post-war period, the relative position of the Maori has improved, but not to the same degree that colonized peoples elsewhere have experienced improvement. Whereas most of the latter have gained control of their affairs, the Maoris have not, because they are part of a larger society and no longer a separate community. Thus, the success which New Zealand could claim in Western Samoa has not embraced its own Polynesian population.

Western Samoa, besides being different from New Zealand, was also a quite different case from the Melanesian dependencies. It had a national language, a homogeneous culture, a homogeneous degree of acculturation, and a universally recognized, indigenous élite whose status was rooted in the traditional culture. None of the Melanesian territories had any of those characteristics, and this absence was at the heart of the debate which developed in the 1950s about the nature and rate of national development. No-one could seriously deny that the Samoan people were potentially a single nation (the exclusion of American Samoa is an historical anomaly, which has often been ignored by the Samoans); but in Melanesia, the task was one of nation building by fostering a national consciousness, by trying to make rational and acceptable decisions about national boundaries, a national language, and a political system where the facts of human society defied rationalization. Why should one language be preferred to another? Why should a tribe be divided by a line on a map? Why could not cultural and linguistic groups be kept together? Why should different communities be grouped together? Was federation a feasible option, and if so, how large could it be made? What about a federation of all Melanesia? What distinctions should be made in law or policy between populations which had long experience of European culture like the Motu or the Tolai, and those like some highlanders of New Guinea who were contacted only in the 1950s? Should the recently-contacted groups be put at a permanent disadvantage by handing them over to an élite composed entirely of alien tribes? Was it fair to those people long contacted to retard their aspirations and progress until the others could catch up?

These questions were debated mainly by the few Australians who took an interest in New Guinea affairs. There was a radical group which favoured accelerated progress, and a conservative opinion which held that development, and therefore independence, would be a work of generations. The Australian Minister for Territories from 1951 to 1963, Paul Hasluck, held the middle ground. Hasluck was for faster rather than slower development, but believed that the fastest possible development would simply favour expatriate interests, especially in economic matters. He also urged uniform development so that 'internal colonialism' by one native community at the expense of others might not develop: Papua-New Guinea should not have a university, for example, while most of the population did not have access even to a primary school. This was a policy bound to exasperate the new élite which was already emerging.

Development could hardly proceed without creating inequality, and so the Melanesian response to their circumstances of the post-war years showed a corresponding diversity. The response which caused the administration most concern and which received the greatest publicity was the kind which became known as the 'cargo cult'. Cult movements occurred throughout Melanesia, but only rarely in parts of Polynesia, and although they had been observed and reported in the nineteenth century and in the earlier decades of the twentieth, the time of their greatest proliferation was the era after the Second World War.

The cargo cults were quickly recognized as having much in common with millenarian movements around the world. Such movements had been reported in other colonial areas where profound social and political change had caused dislocation, and were also known to have flourished from time to time in European history, generally in times of deep social distress. Wars, plagues and depressions typically drive the helpless and oppressed to religious extremism: at such times, when no pragmatic solution to distress can be found, a prophet is most likely to find a sympathetic audience which then evolves into a following, adopting ritual practices and doctrines which promise either a new order of justice or restitution in a new world. The new world typically is to be ushered in by some cataclysmic event in which the old with all its evils and wrongs is destroyed.

All these elements were common in the Melanesian cults: prophet, doctrine, ritual, and inevitably, disappointment; and many theories were developed to account for them. To some, they were simply an irrational response to change; others saw them as a form of collective hysteria or madness; to others, they seemed to be the beginnings of a revolutionary movement because of their overtones of rejection of European authority and apparently military forms of organization. There were perhaps elements of all these things in the hundreds of outbreaks which took place. Many of them did seem to reject all things European, and to try to reassert native values and ways of life, but many of them openly preached native assertiveness and the end of European dominance; others seemed to want increased acculturation but with native superiority; yet others seemed to imply racial and cultural equality. It was not uncommon for the cult rituals to ape European things: flag-poles might be raised, airstrips built, the men might drill like soldiers, and even mundane changes could occur, such as adopting the use of tables and chairs. Traditional wealth might be destroyed as an act of faith to trigger the new order, but which instead often left the people starving.

The most detailed study of a cargo cult, by the anthropologist Peter Lawrence, traced the cyclical rise, fall and reappearance of cult movements among a single population over a period of about sixty years. The form and content of the cult was traced to the changing circumstances of culture contact, and reflected the dominant experiences of particular times: variously foreign trade, Christian missions, war, and post-war reconstruction. The enduring characteristic which linked the different forms of this cult was the traditional Melanesian world-view with its inseparable compound of supernatural power, ritual and material circumstances; although modified by foreign influences, this world-view persisted throughout the decades of contact with Europeans.

The cargo cult fundamentally was the application of traditional Melanesian thinking to changed circumstances. Traditional belief intertwined the secular and the supernatural: ghosts and spirits involved themselves in human affairs, and the natural order also reflected their influence. If crops grew, if storms came, if disease struck, if women became pregnant, then the interest or hostility of spirits was almost certain to be involved. It followed that any great misfortune was made, or at least enabled, by supernatural forces, and that the correct way to put things right was by using supernatural means to lend efficacy to human efforts. The way to achieve this was by ritual: that is, some prescribed action which was not usually effective in secular terms but which constrained spirits to act in a predetermined way. The ritual actions usually bore some resemblance to the intended result: for example, if one wanted yams to grow to a certain size and quality, it was wise to plant among them a large stone which might resemble a good yam, as well as to choose the proper season, soil and seed for planting.

In the context of European contact all kinds of disasters happened, and there were new and unattainable wants. It was thus entirely consistent with traditional thinking that experimentation should occur with new rituals or modified old ones, sanctioned by new or old myths to try to bring about the desired transformations in the natural and social order. This is what led to the apparent chaos in Melanesian society, and the enormous variety of forms taken by the cargo cults.

But why the name 'cargo'? The overwhelming difference between Melanesian society and European society which the Melanesians sought to explain and to eliminate was the European mastery of physical nature. Europeans had wealth, they had property—tools, machines, clothes, weapons and ornaments in variety and quantity. The Melanesians, no less materialistic than any other race, wanted the same, and wanted to know why they could not have it. Early in the contact history of Melanesia, the great wealth of the Europeans was evident, and Melanesian covetousness could be satisfied by trade and labour recruitment. Later, missionaries came who seemed to have the secret, and seemed willing to share this secret of European wealth. Christianity would make all men the same, would it not? It was worth a try, but the results were disappointing; the whites continued to have more than Melanesians, and there always seemed to be more arcane knowledge which the missionaries had not previously divulged. Then came the Second World War in which Melanesians were exposed to greater material wealth than ever before: hitherto they had seen only a fraction of European material culture, and even that seemed poor and shabby once the American armed forces arrived in strength. This increased exposure, and the association with it of a new kind of white man (some of whom were black, like the Melanesians themselves), suggested new possibilities to fertile native minds about their own future and possible material wealth. Then the war ended, and with it the riches and Melanesian access to them disappeared.

After the war, the returned European administrations of Melanesia spoke of economic development for the islands and their people, but the social equality and the wealth seemed as far away as it had been before the Americans had come. The people were prepared to try development programmes; they were prepared to form co-operatives and amass money, to borrow, to attend classes and conferences, and to listen to visiting experts on how to do this or that which was supposed to raise productivity and bring in a cash income; but the results were slow in coming, sometimes never came, and a lot of time and effort was wasted. In disillusionment and frustration, other means were tried to make the cargo appear; since the people were still trying to explain wealth in traditional ways, they turned again to traditional methods of production with their emphasis on myth and ritual.

Hence, the cults, while appearing bizarre to the outside observer, were perfectly rational within the framework of Melanesian society, and their proliferation at this particular time was logical. Although it was not well understood at the time by Europeans, the cults demonstrated that there was a strong, unsatisfied, native demand for economic change, and that the Melanesians wanted to participate in it fully. They also demonstrated of course, that there were two great gulfs of understanding: Europeans understood little of how Melanesians were thinking, and the Melanesians understood little of European intentions and even less the reasons for the European mastery of the physical world.

It was hoped that the first gulf could be bridged by anthropological research and its transmission to officials through professional training; bridging the second was what the development debate was all about, and it came down to this: would Melanesians adapt better to the modern world by being simply exposed to European-led development and the creating of demand for native labour, or should there be ambitious educational programmes in the islands and elsewhere? In other words, should progress come as the result of training or as the result of performing menial work? It was very like the debate conducted in missionary circles one hundred and fifty years before as to whether 'civilization' should come before new ideology, or whether it should be the other way round. In both cases, talking and planning could continue endlessly, but in the meantime the world did not stand still, and events seemed to have a logic and momentum of their own.

Chapter Fifteen

ATTAINING INDEPENDENCE

During the 1970s, the phrase 'the Pacific way' became a popular slogan, and was meant to identify a way of making decisions and resolving disagreements without leaving any party feeling defeated. Decisions were made by consensus, not by a majority outvoting a minority; rancour could thus be avoided and everybody could be a winner. The art of 'the Pacific way' was not merely one of compromise but of finding a solution which could meet the aspirations of all. This was the style, it was said, of traditional Pacific politics.

Consensus methods certainly had their place in traditional society, but so did less gentle means of resolving conflict: force and domination are as much represented in the histories of the Pacific islanders as of other people. But in the era of decolonization there was reason for faith in 'the Pacific way': sweet reasonableness prevailed, and the wars fought elsewhere in the name of freedom and national self-determination did not need to be acted out in the Pacific.

This impression of decolonization is, however, no more than half true; decolonization has been almost entirely free of violence, but the principal reason has been that the major colonial powers in the Pacific decided for their own purposes to end their colonial role. Where that has not happened, little progress towards decolonization has been made: France remains as strongly entrenched as ever, and the United States has circumvented the aspirations for independence of the peoples under its rule. From the end of the Second World War, the independence of the British, Australian and New Zealand colonies in the Pacific was really only a matter of time, although contemporaries did not always perceive it, nor was policy always consistent.

The story of Samoa's progress to independence has already been told: it was the culmination of the persistence of the Samoans throughout their colonial period, and the wisdom of a sympathetic

New Zealand government which, recognizing the inevitable, set a pace which allowed time for adequate preparation while making the Samoans conscious that progress was being hastened. New Zealand's other territories, Niue, Tokelau and the Cook Islands had never been trusteeship territories, nor had they a history of such determined protest as the Samoans. Soon after the war, however, a trade union movement began in the Cook Islands which evolved, under the leadership of Albert Henry, first into a progress association and ultimately into a political party; this was the Cook Islands Party, the main policy objective of which was self-government. The New Zealand government was understandably less sympathetic to this movement than it had been to Samoan ambitions because of the practical problems. Composed of fifteen islands or atolls spread over a wide stretch of ocean, the group had a population of just under 17,000 in 1956, possessed no natural resources to speak of, and depended for its income on the export of bananas and citrus fruit to New Zealand. Its size and poverty did not offer much hope for its future as an independent nation. The Cook Islands leaders could themselves see this and negotiations proceeded on the basis of self-government rather than full independence. Under the formula finally accepted, the Cook Islands were to become entirely self-governing in 1965, with New Zealand undertaking responsibility for foreign affairs and defence. In addition, Cook Islanders were to continue to have free access to New Zealand and to enjoy the rights of New Zealand citizenship, and the Cook Islands government was to continue to receive aid from New Zealand. This was an extremely generous formula: it gave the Cook Islanders the self esteem of nationhood without having to accept all the hazards of independence and also left open to them the unilateral option of declaring full independence whenever they wished. In the 1970s, a similar arrangement was made for Niue which was even more vulnerable than the Cook Islands. New Zealand's other dependency, the Tokelau group, was still in the 1990s preferring to remain a New Zealand dependency, although enjoying a large measure of local control.

In the case of the Cook Islands, New Zealand had tried to circumvent doubts about the viability of small states as independent nations. Such doubts were indeed the only serious obstacle in the way of independence for several Pacific island states. The first territory to build on the precedent created by the Cook Islands was Nauru, the tiny phosphate island under Australian administration. Anticipating the eventual exhaustion of Nauru's phosphate deposits, the Australian government had made a number of proposals for the resettlement of the people, since the mining operations rendered the land useless and uninhabitable. At the beginning of the Second World War, the Nauruans' neighbours, the Banabans (or Ocean Islanders), had been resettled on the Fijian island of Rabi for that reason. A quarter of a century later, however, the Nauruans were unwilling to accept that sort of solution, and after some years of hard bargaining, became independent in 1968, winning at the same time complete control over their phosphate ore on which previously they had been receiving small royalties.

By the late 'sixties, independent Pacific island states were still a novelty; decolonization was still experimental, but within the next few years the 'experimental' stage came to an end as Tonga, Fiji and Papua New Guinea became independent. Tonga, technically, had never lost its independence, but after 1905, the British consul had had extensive powers of supervision with rights to intervene in the government of Tonga. Nevertheless, the Tongan monarch and parliament continued to govern, and the public service was staffed mostly by Tongans. Key senior positions requiring training which no Tongan possessed were filled by Europeans, but by the 1960s, it was possible to fill most of these positions with Tongans who had been educated overseas. In 1970, Tonga 're-entered the comity of nations', as the Tongan government preferred to put it, when the attenuated powers of the British representative were given up, and Tonga became an independent monarchy within the Commonwealth of Nations. Apart from the ceremonies which marked the event, the change was imperceptible.

The coming to independence of Fiji was an altogether different affair. Whereas the Tongans had a strong sense of nationhood, and had held that common identity since pre-European times, the creation of a sense of common identity for the native peoples of Fiji was one of the tasks of the colonial regime. One factor which helped that to emerge was the presence of the population of Indians, which had outnumbered the indigenous Fijians since just before the Second World War. The presence of the Indians, their numerical strength, and the absence of a common identity—the inevitable result of three generations of segregation—restrained any urge towards political change on the part of Fijian nationalists. The Indians, however, were not so self-effacing, a fact which caused the Fijians some concern.

The colonial regime, however, had never been sympathetic to Indian claims for proportional representation in government, and the Fijians themselves made no push for independence. It came as a surprise to most people therefore, when in 1961, less than a year before Samoa was to become fully independent, the governor of Fiji foreshadowed modest reforms which suggested a gradual transfer of power. Fijians and Europeans alike voiced misgivings, but the government pressed on over the next few years, enlarging the legislature and giving executive authority to elected members. In 1964, a committee was established to work out plans for future constitutional developments.

The real issue at stake in these negotiations concerned the terms on which Britain was willing to modify its plans for Fiji's independence; in discussing these terms, the representatives of the three major races in Fiji (the tiny European population being the third) brought their own sectional interests to the conference table. The Fijians wanted preservation of their lands and special interests, meaning that Westminster-style democracy was not wanted. The Europeans also had special privileges which they wanted to preserve, and therefore claimed equal representation with the other races; so they were not interested in democracy either. The Indians were democratic, probably less from conviction than from the awareness of their numerical superiority, and the opportunity democracy would give to correct the discrimination against which they had protested for so long and without effect.

This debate continued without much change during the constitutional evolutions of the 1960s and into the negotiations for a constitution for an independent Fiji. By the time Fiji became independent in October 1970 (on the 94th anniversary of the cession of the islands to Britain), the 'Pacific way' had produced a formula which all parties accepted as workable, but which in the long term did not resolve the basic issues between the races. The losers were the Indians who, having pressed for a democratic system with a common electoral role, secured only a complicated communal role which had the merit of avoiding a clean cleavage in politics between the races. Under the new electoral system, every voter would have four votes and was required to vote separately for members of each community, and to cast one vote for a common-role candidate. This system of cross-voting gave an incentive to politicians of every race to court electors of the other races, a plan which was hoped to minimise the sinister and dangerous consequences of racial politics. An expected consequence was that in the formation of political parties—the British typically expected party systems of politics to develop in their colonies after independence—other interests would be found to over-ride the divisions of race, and multi-racial parties would form.

In 1970, there was reason for optimism about this issue, for a multi-racial party, the Alliance, had already emerged. It was organized as a federation of communal political associations, and succeeded in winning the support of most politically-active Fijians and a sufficient number of Indians and Europeans to give it a solid appearance of multi-racialism. Whether it would succeed in keeping Fijian politics non-racial or not would depend on its meeting Indian expectations of a fair deal.

The constitutional compromise in Fiji was achieved partly by Fijian leaders winning the support of some Indians, and it allowed the Fijians to emerge clear winners in terms of the protection of their special interests: their land rights were entrenched in the constitution, and the constitution could not be changed without a 75 percent vote in both the House of Representatives and the Senate. The senate was to be appointed: eight by the prime minister, seven by the leader of the opposition, and a further eight by the Great Council of Chiefs. This last body was composed of certain high chiefs and senior public servants, and although they might not all be Fijians, the effect of this provision was to give the native Fijians an additional political weighting. The success of the Fijian constitution was therefore going to depend heavily on the continued operation of that nebulous 'Pacific way' which up till that time had demanded more of the Indians than of the other races.

The progress of Fiji towards independence had been closely paralleled by events in Papua New Guinea, where conditions were very different. After the enthusiasm for planning in the late 1940s, the 1950s had been a period of slow progress under a government which no longer felt any urgency and under an expatriate public service which, like the settler community, assumed that the 'backward' Melanesians needed several more decades of tutelage. In 1961, the Australian government realized with some shock that world opinion would not allow it the luxury of gradual development, that plans had to be made and programmes put immediately in place for accelerated change. In the following year, that realization was bluntly reinforced by the report of the United Nations Visiting Mission to the Trust Territory of New Guinea which had asked more searching questions than its predecessors, and was extremely critical of the assumptions that Australia had plenty of time to do its work in New Guinea.

Notwithstanding the research and the idealism of the 1940s, and the continued activity of scholars in the 1950s, the basic questions about New Guinea's future were no closer to being answered. It was as if the administration had purchased a decade but had spent it daydreaming instead of thinking. Now the thinking had to be done under pressure, and the provision of the essential national infrastructure had to be provided in haste. This was a task the difficulty and gravity of which should not be under-estimated, and every step the government made over the next decade was to be criticised in strong terms by one interest group or another.

Three measures were set in train almost immediately: the World Bank was commissioned to make an economic survey of the territory and recommend on future policy; a university was to be established (there were at that time no Papua-New Guinean university graduates) to create an educational élite appropriate to the needs of the new nation; and a House of Representatives was to be elected to replace the existing legislative council which still included nominated and nominal native and settler representatives. Furthermore, legislative discrimination, such as in liquor laws, was to be done away with. The House of Representatives was elected in 1964, the World Bank report was presented in the same year, and the university opened in 1966. Meanwhile, Australia's budgetary allocations to Papua New Guinea increased substantially, and high salaries with taxation concessions were offered to attract an enlarged public service.

Popular attitudes, however, changed more slowly than the policies. The expatriate population continued to believe in racial inequality, or at least in the need for protracted paternalism; and it was also unwilling to surrender its economic and social privileges. At the same time, it was difficult for the Melanesian population to become aware of the changed climate, to break the habits of subordination and to claim the new opportunities which were being offered. In this respect, the creation of a fully-fledged House of Representatives was of great importance, for although its powers were limited, and although expatriate public servants were apt to lecture the parliamentarians, it gave the country a political life which eventually forced some moderation on the more stubborn expatriates.

The creation of a political life forced the consolidation of various interest groups into political parties which all had ambitions of their own for the future of the country. These parties were mostly naive groupings with little real political sense, or were imitations of Australian political parties in name and ideology. One group alone, formed in 1967 towards the end of the life of the first parliament, showed both zeal and political acumen. Like the first indigenous political parties in Africa, its programme was built around one goal, early self-government leading to independence. The asset which distinguished it from the other parties was leadership, in particular that of Michael Somare, a young man from the Sepik River who had worked as a journalist and who had already achieved some public recognition over his objection to legal discrimination in public service salaries and working conditions. The party took the name Pangu—an acronym for Papua New Guinea Unity—thus addressing not only the peculiar political status of the territory (half of it an

Australian possession, the other half a United Nations trusteeship territory) but also the diversity and jealousies of the indigenous population, and the potential divisions between native and expatriate.

The formation of the Pangu Pati (or party) had an immediate effect in that it put new life into the more conservative interests: parties were formed specifically to oppose Pangu with its radical plans. In the 1968 elections, Pangu was by far the most successful party, but most members of the new house were independent. Somare and his associates took advantage of every opportunity which public office gave them, except that of exercising power. It was part of the administration's political education programme, modelled on the pattern in Fiji and in Britain's African colonies, to give the most successful politicians a form of limited ministerial experience. It was, in fact, not a bad way of devolving power, but it would work best where there was no real contest for political prizes.

Somare had the perception to see that to accept such office would be to align himself with the policies of the government at a time when his political career and the attainment of his goals depended on his maintaining a distance from it. He therefore kept his party aloof, and gained his political experience by vigorous opposition, a tactic which kept him in the headlines, and taught him more about parliamentary procedure and political debate than he could have learned as a ministerial apprentice. By the time of the next elections in 1972, Somare had a widespread party organization, a core of experienced politicians, and a name for himself and his party which was known throughout the country. He also had the advantage of a simple and easily communicated policy: independence now. In the ten years since the famous United Nations mission in 1962, Papua New Guinea had become a scene of contentious and ubiquitous change.

The election of 1972 could not have been imagined ten years earlier except by the most sanguine or the most naive. An electorate had been educated and re-educated, the first graduates of the University of Papua New Guinea were already going into schools, into government service, and were themselves teaching at the university. The co-operative societies had increased in number and represented an impressive volume of activity, and a class of indigenous entrepreneurs was emerging. Not all of these enterprises, collective or individual, would succeed, but the native experience of the world was changing and broadening. Visiting experts were advising on crops to be grown for export, and highlanders who could still remember the first contact of their people with Europeans were planting their own coffee or cocoa plantations and using trucks and tractors. Not all of this development was wise or successful, but the day of an all-powerful official who could make a decision for an entire territory, and then by sheer force of personality make it work, was gone. The development schemes of this decade in Papua New Guinea were aimed mainly at one goal: creating an infrastructure which would ensure Papua New Guinea a reliable and sufficient income of foreign currency which was the one essential condition for a stable, independent future. Despite the debates at the time, and notwithstanding the sometimes acrid criticisms of academics, concerns about justice, social equity and what was called 'appropriate technology' (that is, technology which was labour intensive rather than capital intensive, and which did not commit the country to continued reliance on foreign experts and suppliers) had become irrelevant. Those concerns had lost the debate when the decision had been taken to accelerate towards independence. It was ironical that some of those who were most critical of the administration's programme, and who were most vocal about equity, justice and appropriateness, were also the advocates of acceleration.

At the 1972 elections, the Pangu Pati did well, but Papua New Guinea society was so fragmented that no party could win a majority. Somare hastily negotiated a coalition with other nationalist groups, and having thus seized the initiative, insisted on being appointed chief minister, to the astonishment and dismay of the conservative, predominantly European parties. Towards the end of the same year, a general election in Australia was won by the Labour Party which had a policy of early independence for Papua New Guinea with the result that self-government was achieved in 1973, with full independence two years later.

Unlike Western Samoa and Fiji where the colonial government had kept ahead of indigenous demands, the impression had been given in Papua New Guinea that Australia was trying to stave off independence. The presence of a fairly large settler interest with the accompanying institutionalized racial inequality, and the condescending attitudes which went with it, provoked a sense of confrontation that was happily absent from the other territories. One of the worrying things about the emerging politics of Papua New Guinea was the disunity of the nationalist movement; it was nationalistic in the sense of wanting indigenous control, but there was not a sense of common nation-hood. Many of these 'nationalists' tended to be regional in their thinking, to the extent that some of them advocated secession from the rest of the territory. In this way, the highlanders felt aggrieved at having been left behind in development; people of Papua asserted that New Guineans were different (a legacy from pre-war differences); there was suspicion of the numerical strength of the highlanders; the people of

Bougainville, geographically part of the Solomons, claimed to be ethnically different from the rest, and having suffered the dislocation of the gigantic Bougainville copper mine, did not want to be subsidizing the rest. In the Bismarck Archipelago, there were also perceptions of different interests arising from the longer experience of its people with commercial agriculture, and an adherence to perceived ethnic distinctions. Moreover, some of these nationalistic groups were socialist in their thinking, while others had more conservative leanings. In the apparent absence of unity, it is not surprising that the Australian government up till the 1972 election wanted to move cautiously, and it was particularly concerned, given Papua New Guinea's strategic importance to Australia, that instability or any suggestion of animosity be avoided.

It was Somare's achievement that he was able to bring the various nationalist groups to a workable consensus, and to provide in his own person, a nationalist, indigenous leader who could present to the Australian government the face of unity and progressive moderation. The Whitlam government in Australia, although ideologically committed to early independence, seized the opportunity to hand over power before the situation in Papua New Guinea deteriorated. Despite the mutterings which had been occurring, Australia and Papua New Guinea parted company on cordial terms but with mutual relief. Many observers had expected much worse.

It was in the French colonies, however, that the independence issue has proven difficult. The root of the problem has been that France has not considered its Pacific possessions to be colonies: rather, they are overseas territories, and so while there might be a case for reforms of various kinds, independence has not been negotiable. During the Second World War, the settler populations of both New Caledonia and French Polynesia aligned themselves with the Free French government of Charles de Gaulle rather than with the Vichy regime. This choice perhaps had some influence on the liberalization of French policy immediately after the war, when both territories were granted representative assemblies, French citizenship was extended to the indigenous people, and both territories gained representation in the French parliament. These concessions gave political rights to Pacific islanders far in excess of anything existing in the English-language colonies of the Pacific at the same time, but it was a concession which meant continued French domination, and implied no real sensitivity to indigenous aspirations.

In both territories, indigenous political activity had developed during the war; in New Caledonia, political parties representing a variety of opinion had formed in 1944, whereas agitation by Pouvanaa a Oopa in Tahiti did not mature into a political party until 1950. Political change in both territories was retarded by the difference in objectives between settlers and natives; both groups wanted greater freedom from central control, but each wanted power to be transferred to itself, not shared with the other race. Until 1958, local agitation for more power-sharing was interspersed with piecemeal reforms which were intended to quell opposition rather than to facilitate political justice. In that year, after the coup which ushered in the Fifth Republic, President De Gaulle acknowledged the trend in world opinion and held an empire-wide referendum on the future of France's colonies, and both New Caledonia and French Polynesia voted for continued association with France by comfortable majorities. In French Polynesia, the autonomist leader, Pouvanaa a Oopa, was discredited before the election on a charge of arson for which he subsequently served eight years in prison, probably unjustly; in New Caledonia, the leader of the pro-Melanesian party (a Frenchman, Maurice Lenormand) did not advocate independence.

Having voted in favour of continued membership of the French community, it was now much more difficult for an independence movement in either territory to survive. In Tahiti, the victory was consolidated by the imprisonment and exile of Pouvanaa in 1959. Future leaders of the autonomist movement in the 1960s, John Teariki and Francis Sanford, could not compete either with the dominance over the media enjoyed by the government or with the prosperity brought to Tahiti after 1962 by the construction and operation of the Centre d'Expérimentation du Pacifique which was the facility for developing and testing nuclear weapons. Since the mid-1970s, further discontent has been headed off by reforms in 1977 and 1984, allowing greater local control of policy and budget, but without any suggestion that France ever intends to surrender its eastern Pacific outposts.

In New Caledonia, the activity of reformists also brought a reaction, and in the 1960s many of the political concessions of the previous decade were withdrawn. The issue in New Caledonia had never been independence; it had been social justice and racial equality. But with the abrogation of reforms, and with increased immigration and further development of mining and agriculture, the bi-racial politics which had been achieved by Lenormand broke down. By the late 1960s, autonomy had become an issue and the racial division in politics had again become important. During the 1970s, the Melanesians in New Caledonia lost their numerical superiority, and having previously lost over 90 percent of the land without at the same time gaining any compensating political power or representation in secondary or tertiary industry, they became increasingly anxious about their future, noticing the emergence of independent Melanesian nations among their neighbours.

During the 1980s, while Melanesian opinion became more unified and coherent, and thus more forcefully expressed, French policy wavered and wandered, sometimes being liberal and offering political reforms and social progress, at other times reversing direction, depending on the swings of French domestic political fortunes. There was a short-lived experiment in 1985 with regional councils, but when three of the four of them were dominated by Kanak autonomists, the French government reduced their powers. At the time of the 1988 French presidential election, New Caledonian issues achieved a new prominence with the kidnapping of French hostages by Kanak nationalists. The French government, determined to make a show of strength for electoral purposes, responded in force, and the militants were massacred. After the elections which gave President Mitterand a government of his own party, a new agreement was worked out between the settler interests and the Kanaks, dividing the territory into provinces, and providing for an independence referendum after ten years. This is the first substantial indication that France might have recognized that its old colonial role might be obsolete; hitherto, the only consistent theme in French policy has been that New Caledonia should continue to be a French possession. Throughout the 1970s and '80s, France maintained French numerical superiority so that it could rely on democratic principles to preserve its dominance.

Britain, by the 1970s, was increasingly anxious to relinquish its Pacific responsibilities, and proceeded hastily with constitutional developments which progressively introduced elected legislatures and ministerial responsibility to its remaining territories: the Solomon Islands Protectorate and the Gilbert and Ellice Islands Colony. The latter presented a dilemma; the decision to grant independence was taken belatedly, inhibited both by the absence of any indigenous demand for independence (much as the islanders wanted more responsibility in managing their affairs) and the absence of any resource base with which to sustain an independent state, since Ocean Island, which had been attached to the Gilberts since 1901, was nearing the end of its phosphate reserves.

There was a further complication: once independence was seen to be a possibility the Polynesian Ellice Islanders emphatically declared that they would prefer not to be joined with the Micronesian Gilbert Islanders. The sentiment was reciprocated because in addition to the cultural differences, the Gilbertese outnumbered the

Ellice Islanders by about six to one (there were less than 8,000 Ellice Islanders, but almost 48,000 Gilbertese) and in proportion to their numbers, the Ellice Islanders were over-represented in public service positions. The Gilbertese, moreover, resented the phosphate wealth of Ocean Island being used to subsidise the resource-deficient Ellice Islanders. Therefore, since both races were discontented with their political union, the colony was partitioned in January 1976. The Ellice Islands, renamed Tuvalu, became independent in October 1978 and the Gilberts, renamed Kiribati, followed in July 1979. The whole affair was watched with amazement by the United Nations Committee on Decolonization, for both new nations made quite clear their regret at being cast off by an imperial power which they regarded as benevolent and just.

The Solomon Islands also became independent in 1978 after a remarkably uncontroversial programme which saw the development of political parties, but without the great differences which had characterized Papua New Guinea's political development. The political climate locally and internationally had changed remarkably in about eight years: whereas developments in Papua New Guinea had been experimental and harried by strongly felt disagreements, in the Solomons the inevitability of the process was accepted, and people no longer feared that independence for Pacific islanders would mean a reversion to barbarism or the harassment of foreign investments and residents. A mere three years separated the independence of Papua New Guinea and the Solomons.

Controversy, however, did surround the independence of the Solomons' southern neighbour, the New Hebrides. The condominium government, never satisfactory because of the division of authority between Britain and France, and the absence of unified policy, approached decolonization the same way as it had approached everything else since 1906. The British wanted to withdraw, but the French did not. Apart from any other consideration the French were worried about the contagion of independence: a withdrawal from the New Hebrides would encourage dissidents in New Caledonia who would find help, refuge and a bridge-head with their independent neighbours.

The absence of unified policy meant the absence of development. The advantages to the administration of this neglect were strictly short-term, for neglect meant that in any change which might occur the initiative would be seized by the New Hebrideans, rather than being controlled by the administration as was the case in Fiji and the Solomons. The beginning of this indigenous assertiveness came in the late 1960s, when the New Hebrideans realized how much of their land had been alienated—about 36 percent and not uniformly distributed. A nationalist movement, Nagriamel, was formed on the land issue, but failed to achieve widespread support, unlike a new nationalist movement which emerged in 1971, under the leadership of an Anglican priest, Walter Lini. The situation which developed over the next few years closely resembled the experience of Papua New Guinea; the nationalist party, the Vanuaaku Pati, was modelled on the Pangu Pati, and similarly, rival 'moderate' parties were formed, both for expatriates and for Melanesians.

Amid growing tension and fears for the future, the administration tried to seize the initiative in 1975 by creating an assembly which, since it did not meet the nationalists' demands, was boycotted by them. In 1978, exasperated with French intransigence, and what was perceived as British prevarication, Lini formed a People's Provisional Government—in fact a rebel government—but continued to negotiate. Knowing that he had the sympathy of the United Nations and the support of the independent Pacific islands nations, Lini refused to compromise. In 1979, a constitution was agreed on, foreign claimants to rural land were dispossessed (with compensation from their respective governments) and elections held in which Lini's Vanuaaku Pati won 62 percent of the popular vote. Even at this late stage, French resistance had not ceased, and French government complicity was alleged in two rebellions which occurred (one on Tanna, the other on Espiritu Santo) shortly before independence was due to be proclaimed. Lini, chief minister since 1979, persisted with his plans and the New Hebrides, renamed Vanuatu, became independent on 31 July 1980, after a needlessly acrimonious transition. French unwillingness to yield at strategic moments created much ill-feeling which left a legacy of resentment in Vanuatu, and a bitter suspicion of anything which appears neo-colonialist. Vanuatu alone in the Pacific came to independence with a sense of having had to fight for it, and of having defeated a more powerful adversary.

North of the equator, the Pacific was an American lake. Hawai'i, extensively Americanized even before annexation in 1898, looked forward to statehood rather than independence, and in 1959, became the fiftieth state of the American union, a little ahead of a native revival movement which might have desired otherwise had the timing been different. In the Trust Territory of the Pacific Islands, American policy became controversial; the trusteeship negotiations in 1945 and 1946 had shown that American interest in Micronesia was largely self-serving, and the relative inaction over the next fifteen years confirmed that stance. During the late 1940s and 1950s, the United States used several atolls in the Marshall group as test sites for nuclear weapons, having first relocated the inhabitants by compulsion. Policies for the next thirty years lacked coherence and positive direction, but continued to be expressions of the same assumptions of the priority of American interests.

In keeping with world-wide trends, an informal process of consultation with Micronesian leaders was begun in the late '50s, and this had evolved by 1965 into a representative body, the Congress of Micronesia. The Americans, meanwhile, had begun to take more visible action in the territory, but although they were spending large sums on the development of health, education and communications services, no initiative was taken towards political change until the Congress of Micronesia itself set up a commission to advise on constitutional development. Negotiations on this matter were not begun until 1969, and continued for over fifteen years while the terms of the debate changed; differences developed between the various Micronesian groups, and new issues were introduced. The unavoidable inference was that the United States wished to give the impression of political devolution without actually doing anything to advance the process.

The status which the Micronesians had preferred when the negotiations began was that of free association, similar to the relationship between the Cook Islands and New Zealand, but by 1973, each island group in Micronesia was negotiating separately with the United States. Thus, in 1976, the Mariana Islands became a 'commonwealth', which meant an integral part of the United States. While negotiations on the relationship with the United States continued, the rest of the territory formally split into three parts, each with a republican constitution and internal self government: the Republic of the Marshall Islands, the Federated States of Micronesia (formerly the Caroline Islands, comprising Yap, Truk, Pohnpei and Kosrae) and the Republic of Belau (formerly Palau).

During the early 1980s, a formula for free association was worked out and was approved by popular votes by the Federated States and by the Marshalls. Implementation of the agreement was then delayed by the U.S. congress and did not finally come into force until 1987. The conditions of free association contained conditions which gave the United States extensive extra-territorial authority which related mainly to defense and foreign affairs, but also derived from the access of Micronesians to various U.S. government agencies. In return, the islanders would receive lavish subsidies (estimated at perhaps US$2.5 billion for the Marshalls and Federated States, and $1 billion for Belau) and trade concessions for the fifteen-year term of the compact. The defense provisions, however, were in conflict with the constitution of Belau which provided for a ban on nuclear materials of all kinds, and while a majority of Belauans supported the compact of free association in several plebiscites conducted between 1979 and 1986, the majority was never sufficient to effect the necessary constitutional change. For a new plebiscite in 1987, the constitutional change was declared unnecessary so that the way could be cleared for the compact to proceed. After the plebiscite, in which a majority voted in favour of the compact, the validity of the declaration ignoring the constitutional requirements was successfully challenged in court, so that the political status of Belau remains unresolved.

The process of the decolonization of the Trust Territory of Micronesia with its protracted negotiations, has therefore defeated any hopes of true independence: the American style of administration of the territory simply committed the peoples of Micronesia to levels of government expenditure which could not be sustained without a continuing relationship with the United States and this has left Belau in a very vulnerable position without its Compact of Free Association. American strategic interests ensured that the U.S. government would not negotiate frankly on the basis of seeking the best outcome for its trust.

The last colonial territory, West Irian, appears to have no realistic hope of independence. The Netherlands, after embarking on a rapid development scheme after the war, reluctantly handed the territory over to a militant Indonesia in 1962. In the following years, the Indonesians have established a regime which is comparable in brutality and inhumanity with the worst of the seventeenth-century Spanish or nineteenth-century French regimes, and unlike the other colonial powers, is equally indifferent to local protest and international opinion.

In the late 1980s, the decolonization of the Pacific remains incomplete, and 'the Pacific way' has proven viable only in cases where all parties were in substantial agreement from the beginning. Examining the history of any one island group can give the impression that the islanders themselves shared a large measure of responsibility for reclaiming their independence. In fact, in this as in the beginning of colonial rule, their fate was determined largely by events beyond their control. The history of decolonization has simply shown that the great powers serve their own interests first, and allow the island communities only as much as is compatible with those wider interests.

Chapter Sixteen

SINCE INDEPENDENCE

The attainment of independence was viewed with ambivalence by both expatriates and islanders, for there was much about which to be nervous. The new order would bring both continuity and change.

In many areas of government, there were procedures which had acquired some momentum of their own and could be continued. These related mainly to matters of domestic policy; but in trade and foreign policy new initiatives were required, and although preparations had been made, the future was bound to contain uncertainties. None of the new states had a full complement of indigenous public servants or of skilled people to meet all the needs of secondary and tertiary industry, and thus dependence on expatriate personnel was continued. The 'localization' of such positions necessitated the appointment of people of limited experience and often extreme youth, and in whom there was probably more hope than confidence. Finally, the last years before the handing over of power were often years of heavy government expenditure, especially on construction, education and agriculture. This expenditure was invariably in excess of the local productive capacity and its continuation was another uncertainty. Spending could not stop abruptly on independence, and therefore some arrangement for budgetary support was necessary. Such economic development as had occurred during the colonial period was overwhelmingly foreign-owned and reassurances of security or arrangements for expropriation had to be made.

Independence in the modern world was thus rather different from the pre-colonial independence of the nineteenth century and earlier. By investment, by production, and by habits of consumption, all the island territories were now locked into a world system. The problem now was essentially the same as that confronting the colonial governors: how to match aspirations with a slender resource base, or in other words, how to stay locked in to the international network of trade and communications. Two approaches were developed accordingly: the pursuit of further economic development, and the development of regional organizations.

Throughout the colonial era, most Pacific territories having similar environments and resources were producing similar products for a limited world market. Copra, the marketable product of the extraordinary coconut palm, was the economic staple of the whole Pacific. Fiji produced sugar in large quantities, most of it owned and exported by an Australian company, the Colonial Sugar Refining Company. The Cook Islands produced citrus fruit for export. Timber was developed after the war in the Solomons and Papua New Guinea, and coffee and cocoa were also being grown for export in Papua New Guinea. Mineral exploitation showed promise in the Solomons and in Papua New Guinea, which by the time of independence had the world's largest copper mine; Nauru and Kiribati had phosphate. Generally speaking, the various island nations were competitors in the same markets.

Foreign economists from the International Monetary Fund, the World Bank and the Asian Development Bank were called to consult, and advocated diversification. They often recommended tourism to take advantage of indigenous cultural assets and the beauty and tranquillity of island settings. Despite its reliance on indigenous culture, tourism required extensive capital development in roads, hotels, airports and electrification, and money for this could come only from foreign investment. Inducements were offered in the form of tax concessions and government subsidies, as well as low wage levels for indigenous employees and low land prices. These policies succeeded to the extent that they increased economic activity in the islands, and brought in foreign exchange, but much of it had to be used to import foreign food for the tourists, the means to transport them and manufactured articles for them to buy as souvenirs or 'duty-free' bargains. On top of that, the assets built up by foreign investment remained the property of the investors, leaving the host nation vulnerable to adverse capital movements in the future.

Foreign investment, island governments found, commits a government to social and economic policies which will protect those investments. Such policies may be contrary to the other aspirations of a government, creating regional disparities in development, social inequalities of wealth and opportunity, and the erosion of traditional values or practices which a nationalistic government might want to preserve. This was especially the case in Papua New Guinea, where the Somare government at the time of independence adopted an eight-point plan with vaguely socialist sentiments of equality and fairness, and which was ostensibly rooted in traditional Melanesian values. Emphasis was placed on sharing, on mutual concern for individual and communal well-being and on consensus methods of decision making. Included also was a leadership code stressing honesty, reciprocal obligations, and the minimizing of differences in status and wealth between those who had power and those who did not. But within a decade of independence this government (unique among the first generation of new Pacific nations for its ideals of political and economic democracy) was to be accused of corruption, extravagance, injustice, of being dictatorial, of increasing the discrepancies between rich and poor, and of allowing crime rates to soar. Foreign investors found Papua New Guinea a better place than did the Papua New Guineans—essentially the same criticism that was made of colonial regimes. The cause was much the same in both instances: the necessity to conform to the requirements of a blind, impersonal economic system.

The goal of all governments was primarily to be independent economically as well as constitutionally; but by the early 1980s, none of the independent island nations had achieved even a favourable balance of trade. Papua New Guinea, the giant of the Pacific, received for its exports only about two thirds of the value of its imports; the Solomons almost achieved a balance temporarily; Western Samoa's imports were worth about four times the value of its exports; Vanuatu's imports were worth about two and a half times its exports; Tonga's imports were worth about five times its exports. In no cases were the profits from tourism or remittances from citizens overseas sufficient to make up the balance. In most Pacific island nations, at least one third of the budget was foreign aid; in half of them, two-thirds of the budget was foreign aid. In the mid-1980s, even Papua New Guinea relied on foreign aid for one-third of its spending; Western Samoa, more than twenty years after independence, depended on foreign aid for one fifth of its budget. Nauru alone received no foreign aid, having a substantial income from the investment on its phosphate profits, as well as from continued mining. Aid to Fiji was only about 3 percent of its budget, making Fiji by far the least dependent of Pacific nations. Fiji's apparent prosperity however, was underpinned by trade conventions which allowed it to sell its sugar at well above the prevailing world prices.

Far from decreasing with the passing of time, the need for assistance to Pacific island economies increased. At the same time as the island nations were becoming more dependent on foreign assistance, their subsistence economies became less efficient. Wage labour, cash cropping and a growing sense of individualism have all weakened the traditional, mutual supports of village life, while urbanization has placed many outside it altogether. Subsistence agriculture became less efficient with the decreasing availability of land and the consequent depletion of soil fertility. The range of crops grown by subsistence farmers declined, and the traditional practices of irrigation and food storage in many places disappeared. Internal migration and emigration distorted the age and sex structure of the population in the villages so that despite increasing populations, labour shortages contributed to the troubles of subsistence agriculture.

Population growth was also a problem of the early decades of independence, with annual growth rates occasionally as high as 4 percent. Family planning programmes during the 1970s reduced these to the order of 2 and 3 percent, but overall the crude natural rate of increase in the island groups most beset by overcrowding was offset by emigration. During the 1970s the population of the Pacific islands increased by about 23 percent in a decade; yet the populations of Niue and the Cook Islands actually declined, while Tonga and both Samoas registered only a very small increase. The destination of most emigrating islanders was New Zealand, followed by Australia, with Hawai'i and the continental United States receiving people from the American possessions. By the 1980s, there were more Cook Islanders and Niueans living in New Zealand than in their homelands.

The grave economic and social problems of the Pacific islanders during the post-colonial years called for imaginative responses. Since increasing foreign aid was not always palatable to new nations proud of their independence, regionalism became the concept which it was hoped would lead to less dependence on the old colonial powers. Mutual dependence had the attraction of resembling traditional social arrangements, as well as making practical good sense.

There had been some move towards regional co-operation before the Second World War, and the war itself had further stimulated thinking along those lines. In 1947 the South Pacific Commission was established to offer advice, to co-ordinate development projects and to conduct research into various aspects of administration and development. The Commission was joined by several of the new nations, and all territories in the Pacific eventually joined the South Pacific Conference which reviews the work of the Commission. The old colonial powers remain members of the Commission and still provide almost all of its funds.

Useful though this body was, it was of value to governments rather than a meeting place for governments, and a different sort of organization was required to co-ordinate common political interests. The first of these was The Pacific Islanders Producers' Association, an initiative in the 1960s of the governments of Fiji, Tonga and Western Samoa to facilitate the marketing of their exports. In 1971, the association was reconstituted as the South Pacific Forum which, throughout the 1970s and into the 1980s, provided a means for the heads of Pacific governments (Australia and New Zealand were included as members) to meet and arrange matters of common interest.

In 1972, the Forum established a structure for continuing economic consultation, calling it the South Pacific Bureau of Economic Co-operation (SPEC) which soon became the secretariat for the Forum. SPEC later also managed an Energy Unit to co-ordinate and research the uses of alternative sources of energy to expensive, imported petroleum fuels. The Forum, like the South Pacific Commission, has grown with the list of independent nations, and in 1991, its members were the Cook Islands, Fiji, Nauru, Niue, Papua New Guinea, Kiribati, the Solomon Islands, Tonga, Tuvalu, the Federated States of Micronesia, the Marshall Islands, Vanuatu and Western Samoa, as well as Australia and New Zealand. Much of the Forum's work has been to tackle the vulnerability of the islands caused by distance. It established a shipping line to reduce dependence on extra-regional enterprise, a Civil Aviation Agency, a Regional Shipping Council, the South Pacific Maritime Development Programme, and the Forum Fisheries Agency for the better management of the Pacific's resources of fish. These resources were considerable, with most Pacific states claiming fishing rights over a two hundred mile exclusive economic zone; by the early 1970s large-scale operations by Japanese, Korean, Taiwanese and American ships were taking vast catches, and the Fisheries Agency aimed at negotiating licensing arrangements so that the island states could not only benefit from the catch but also apply controls to conserve the resource. Small states like Kiribati placed heavy reliance on fishery licensing, and by negotiating licenses with the Soviet Union in 1976 attempted to provoke greater interest from the United States. The Forum also established a South Pacific Trade Commission in Australia to represent the island nations collectively in promoting exports to that country. That objective was further pursued with the negotiation of the South Pacific Regional Trade and Economic Co-operation Agreement (SPARTECA), which gave member countries less restricted access for their produce to Australia and New Zealand.

In 1968, before most of the nations concerned had become independent, a regional university was established, entitled the University of the South Pacific. The new university was located in Fiji, but paid for, and its facilities shared by, most of the territories of the South Pacific region. Associated with the university has been the development of satellite communications which have given scattered populations access to university courses and extension programmes.

All this regional activity, however, has perhaps done more for the self-esteem of island nationalists than for their economies; these programmes coincided with the growing economic dependence of the Pacific nations on the outside world, and the regional bodies themselves continue to be funded largely by foreign governments. By the early 1980s, trade within the region amounted to only about 1 percent of the total trade conducted by Pacific nations, and the South Pacific Commission estimated that it could grow only as high as 5 percent. This intra-regional trade was, however, just as grossly unbalanced as the extra-regional trade, the large states of Papua New Guinea, the Solomons, and Fiji being mainly exporters (and re-exporters), and the smaller nations importers. True reciprocity and mutual support were as distant as ever.

The economies of the Pacific, therefore, either remained fragile or became worse. Increasing populations and declining agriculture, combined with the distorted development required by foreign investment, prevented Pacific governments providing as much for the needs and wants of their populations from their own resources as was hoped; there have been communities where standards of living have declined since the end of the colonial era, and symptoms of underdevelopment have become more apparent.

The Forum has also from time to time tried to give a common voice to diplomatic issues, the first of which was the testing of nuclear weapons by the French at Mururoa in the Tuamotu group. This programme had begun in 1966 and the detonations were conducted in the atmosphere; the south-east trade winds carried fallout in the direction of all the inhabited territories of the south Pacific. Pressure from the Forum, combined with agitation by the Greenpeace movement and diplomatic activity by Australia and New Zealand, induced the French to change the programme to underground testing in 1975.

Several Pacific territories adopted anti-nuclear stances on becoming independent. Fiji, for example, was explicitly anti-nuclear from 1970, and banned visits by nuclear armed or powered vessels in 1982. The ban was lifted in 1985, but its re-imposition was under consideration by the government elected in April 1987. Vanuatu declared itself nuclear free in 1982. The collective concern of the Pacific nations about the strategic and environmental implications of nuclear technology had been expressed in Forum resolutions in 1975 and 1983. In 1985, the Forum sponsored a

South Pacific Nuclear Free Zone Treaty which banned the manufacture, testing and stationing of nuclear weapons in the south Pacific, and which France, Britain and the United States declined to sign. The USSR and China signed, and of the Forum countries all signed except Vanuatu, whose government argued that the treaty was too weak, and Tonga, whose government was out of sympathy with it. A subsequent convention, the South Pacific Regional Environment Protection Convention, has banned the disposal of nuclear wastes in the ocean.

In foreign policy generally, the Pacific nations have followed the leads of their colonial predecessors and aligned themselves with the west. In the mid-1980s there was concern about increasing Soviet influence in the Pacific, with several nations willing to make diplomatic and commercial arrangements. Libya aroused concern among the white nations bordering the Pacific with its alleged plan to establish diplomatic missions in 1987, and its disquieting sympathy with the advocates of radical politican change. Vanuatu, the nation least sympathetic to the west and its policies, was portrayed as Libya's bridgehead in the Pacific. Apart from that minor disturbance, the Pacific nations showed little interest in cold-war issues, and their orientation was unquestioned.

New Pacific nations were eager to join extra-regional organizations. Fiji, the Solomons, Papua New Guinea, Vanuatu, Western Samoa, the Federated States of Micronesia and the Marshall Islands joined the United Nations; all those eligible to do so joined the Commonwealth, including Papua New Guinea, the Solomons, Vanuatu, Fiji, Tonga, Western Samoa, Nauru, Kiribati and Tuvalu; all the South Pacific states except Nauru and including the French territories became associated with the European Community through the Lomé Convention; the Cook Islands, Fiji, Kiribati, Papua New Guinea, the Solomons, Tonga, Vanuatu and Western Samoa became members of the Asian Development Bank; and Fiji, Papua New Guinea, Solomons, Vanuatu, Tonga and Western Samoa joined the World Bank (the International Bank for Reconstruction and Development) and the International Monetary Fund.

Elsewhere in the post-colonial world, the strains of underdevelopment have been manifested in political turbulence or repression but the Pacific nations have generally escaped that colonial sequel; indeed, orderliness has characterized post-independence politics in the Pacific. The most serious tensions have arisen from allegations of corruption which have been, all too often, well founded. Nepotism in particular is a serious problem: loyalties in traditional Pacific societies were to individuals and to kinship groupings, not to abstractions or institutions, and this has been one of the values least modified by a century or so of colonial government. Moreover, in a small society—and most of the nations of the Pacific number their populations only in thousands or tens of thousands—the claims of kin and friends are less easily avoided, and the holders of high office, because they are so few, cannot distance themselves from the comparative intimacy of island society which makes personal claims so pressing, often at the expense of abstract principles. The resulting conflict of interest is additional to the usual temptations of power, to which Pacific islanders are as susceptible as others.

Notwithstanding the tensions arising from corruption, the Pacific is distinguished in the former colonial world for the longevity of its political institutions and for the smoothness, even graciousness, of constitutional changes of government. The real test of a political system is not its survival during placid times, but whether a government will accept its defeat at a democratic election. Seven of the new Pacific nations have undergone that test since independence: Western Samoa, the Cook Islands, Tuvalu, Fiji, Nauru, the Solomons and Papua New Guinea.

Western Samoa for the first twenty years after independence had no political parties; instead, election campaigns were waged by individuals on the basis of personal or local issues. The prime minister was elected by the parliament, and he chose his cabinet from among all the elected members; lobbying occurred and deals were made without fixed allegiances or alignments. This political style has proven stable: the first prime minister, Fiame Mata'afa held office from 1959 to 1970, when he was defeated by Tupua Tamasese Lealofi; only two prime ministers served during the 1970s and early '80s. In 1982, for the first time, a political party contested an election—the Human Rights Protection Party. The new prime minister lost his seat almost immediately when an inquiry found irregularities in his election. The previous prime minister was then re-elected, but he was defeated in parliament in December, 1982. In the late 1980s, political parties were still unimportant in Western Samoa, and on the twenty-fifth anniversary of independence, the original constitution was still operating.

The Cook Islands also had a long-serving, first prime minister in Albert Henry, leader of the Cook Islands Party, one-time labour organiser and a leading figure in the negotiations for self-government. After twelve years in power, Henry had become increasingly autocratic, and his family was heavily represented in senior positions; misgivings about Henry's political style culminated in 1979 when the general election of that year was declared invalid because of vote-buying by Henry's party. Henry was disgraced and a new election was held in 1980; his successor, Dr Thomas Davis, a distinguished medical scientist who had spent most of his working life abroad, was in his turn dismissed after losing the confidence of the house in 1987. Davis, like Henry, had become autocratic in old age.

Politics in Nauru were dominated for two decades after independence in 1968 by the man who was mostly responsible for achieving independence, High Chief Hammer De Roburt. De Roburt was president until 1976 when he was defeated, but was re-elected two years later, after his two successors had been defeated in parliament. On two subsequent occasions De Roburt has been in and out of office, in each case by constitutional means.

Papua New Guinea was the state for which the greatest fears were held before independence. There were predictions in the early 1970s of secessions, of a racial blood-bath and of the possibility of a military coup; yet after more than a decade of independence, none of these things had happened. The secession movements were headed off by creating regional governments, and the army adhered to its role as the servant of the government with an important role to play in national development. At the election in 1977, the first after independence, Michael Somare and his Pangu-led coalition were returned to power, but Somare was replaced as prime minister in 1980 by his former coalition colleague, Julius Chan, after losing a vote of no-confidence. Somare became prime minister again after the 1982 election, but again lost office by a vote of no-confidence in 1985. At the 1987 election the man who displaced him, Paias Wingti, retained office, only to lose it in 1988 through a vote of no-confidence. Political parties have been much more influential in politics in Papua New Guinea than in any other Pacific state except Fiji, but their membership has been fluid and their discipline weak. All governments of that country have been fragile coalitions involving several parties, a situation which might have invited radical methods.

Extra-constitutional politics came to the Pacific in a country where it was least expected, where the party system was well-developed and where respect for law seemed strongest: Fiji. The military coup of 1987 is the only event of its kind to have happened in the modern Pacific. There were, however, hints which might have foreshadowed this event, rooted in the racial antagonisms of Fiji's plural society. The anxieties of both Fijians and Indians had been clearly and loudly expressed in the negotiations leading to independence; cultural and racial differences were further compounded by conflicting economic interests and a history of segregation and differential opportunities. The first prime minister, Ratu Kamisese Mara, preached in his early career a doctrine of moderation, compromise and racial harmony, and founded a multi-racial political party called the Alliance. Indians and Fijians were thus represented in his early cabinets, and a sufficient number of Indian votes kept his party in power at the 1972 election.

The slight Indian numerical superiority was vitiated by internal divisions in the Indian community, which Mara was able to exploit. But at the 1977 election, the Fijian vote became divided when an extremist group, the Fijian Nationalist Party, cost the Alliance its majority. The National Federation Party (representing mainly Indians) found itself rather unexpectedly the largest party after the election, though with only half the total number of seats. After inviting the leader of the National Federation Party (NFP) to form a government, the governor-general, Sir George Cakobau, subsequently changed his mind, and re-appointed as prime minister his kinsman, Mara. At the first meeting of parliament, the outraged NFP moved and carried a motion of no-confidence, whereupon the governor-general opted to dissolve parliament and call fresh elections, rather than appoint an Indian prime minister.

These events re-united the Fijian electorate, and further divided the Indian, with the result that the Alliance won a comfortable victory at the second election of 1977. The impression was left, both in Fiji and abroad, that the democratic process had been thwarted, and that the governor-general had not observed due constitutional propriety in not allowing the majority party to attempt to govern. At the next elections, in 1982, tensions again ran high; Indian representation in the Alliance had dwindled significantly over the previous decade, and the Fijian Nationalists, explicitly anti-Indian, became vociferous again. Politics were thus becoming much more racial in complexion. The Alliance was again returned to power, but during the life of this government a new element was introduced into Fijian politics by the formation of a new party which was based not on race, but on class. This was the Labour Party, primarily speaking for the new urban working classes composed of both Indians and Fijians whose interests had not been well served by either of the major parties in the past.

By 1987, the Fijian Labour Party had become a significant factor, although nobody could say what its role might be. Led by a medical practitioner and public servant of Fijian race, Timoci Bavadra, the party attracted support not only from the urban poor, but also from the educated, professional class of Fijians. In an attempt to break the power held by the Alliance, which was by now little more than an oligarchy of Fijian aristocratic interests based in eastern Fiji, the National Federation Party of the Indian community and the Fijian Labour Party entered into a coalition for the 1987 election.

The election was a victory for this coalition, and Bavadra became prime minister.

The election result was condemned by the extremist Fijian Nationalist Party, and explicitly anti-Indian demonstrations of protest were organized around the country, alleging that Bavadra was merely a puppet of the Indians. On 14 May 1987, after the coalition had been in office for only a few weeks, parliament was invaded by a party of hooded soldiers led by Lieutenant Colonel Rabuka. After the prime minister and cabinet were arrested and escorted from the chamber, Rabuka announced that the government had been overthrown in the interests of national security, alleging that popular unrest would be prevented from worse excesses in no other way. The action was also taken in the name of protecting Fijian land rights and other special interests of the true natives of the country.

Subsequently, an interim government was appointed under the leadership of the governor-general, Ratu Sir Penaia Ganilau, and filled mainly by members of the former Alliance government, pending the formulation of a new constitution which would guarantee indigenous Fijian control of the country. But in September, following a compromise for power-sharing between Mara and Bavadra, Rabuka executed a second coup, this time declaring Fiji a republic, and withdrew from the Commonwealth. The governor-general's position was now abolished. Rabuka next appointed an interim government with Mara as prime minister and Ganilau as president, pending the drafting of a new constitution, which was to be more consistent with his thinking than the Mara-Bavadra compromise.

The crisis of 1987 in Fiji had unique causes. It was the result of the peculiar combination of elements which had been part of Fijian society for a century or more. These included the roughly equal division of the nation into two distinct racial groups which wanted to preserve their cultural differences and which were distinguished by economic conditions; the anxiety of the chiefly oligarchy of eastern Fiji which saw its power being challenged from four different directions (Indian, commoner, western and extremist Fijian) to a degree which not even the colonial regime had challenged it; and the rising frustrations of the increasing numbers of urban Fijians whose interests ran counter to old communal Fijian interests which had been entrenched since the time of Governor Sir Arthur Gordon.

Other Pacific nations either expressed their approval of the coup, or cautiously announced that it was an internal Fijian matter—a range of opinion which would not discourage potential emulators elsewhere; but although other potential trouble spots were discernible in the Pacific in the late 1980s, nowhere else was this particular combination of circumstances duplicated. Only Fiji and Papua New Guinea have defence forces of any size among Pacific nations and their forces were of similar size, despite Papua New Guinea having about three times the population, a much larger territory, and a common border with a powerful neighbour. Fiji's disproportionately large army, moreover, was almost entirely Fijian in racial composition—an imbalance which governments in other plural societies try to avoid.

The era of independence has thus for the most part shown a respect for constitutional propriety and the rule of law. No other part of the world formerly ruled by Europe has demonstrated a comparable record, and this in a region which despite its small population is made up of thirteen independent or self-governing states, over a time span of up to twenty-five years. The period has been one of creativity and imagination in constitution-making and in regional organization. That the Pacific islanders have not solved their other problems is due to nature or the world economy allowing them too little room to manoeuvre.

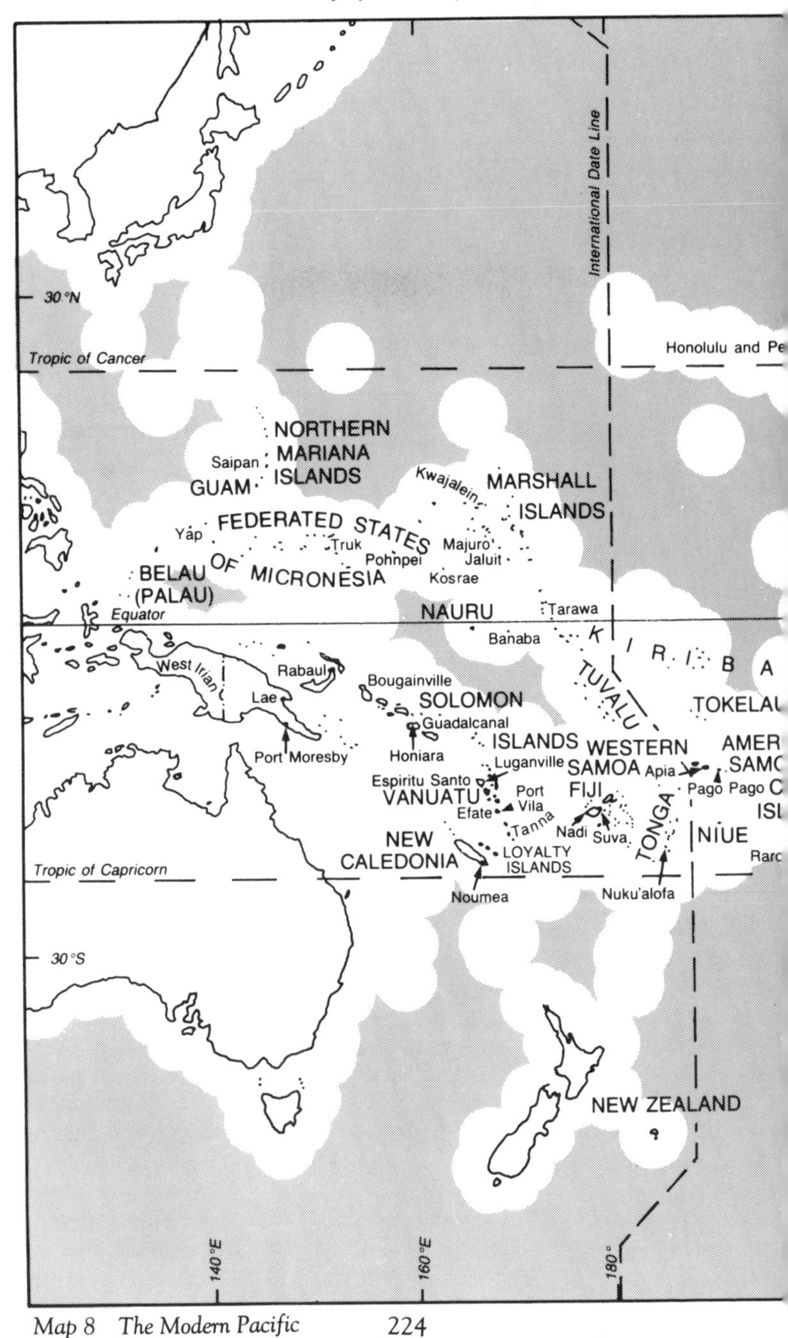

Map 8 The Modern Pacific

The unshaded areas indicate the overlapping 200 mile exclusive economic zones being claimed in Law of the Sea negotiations.

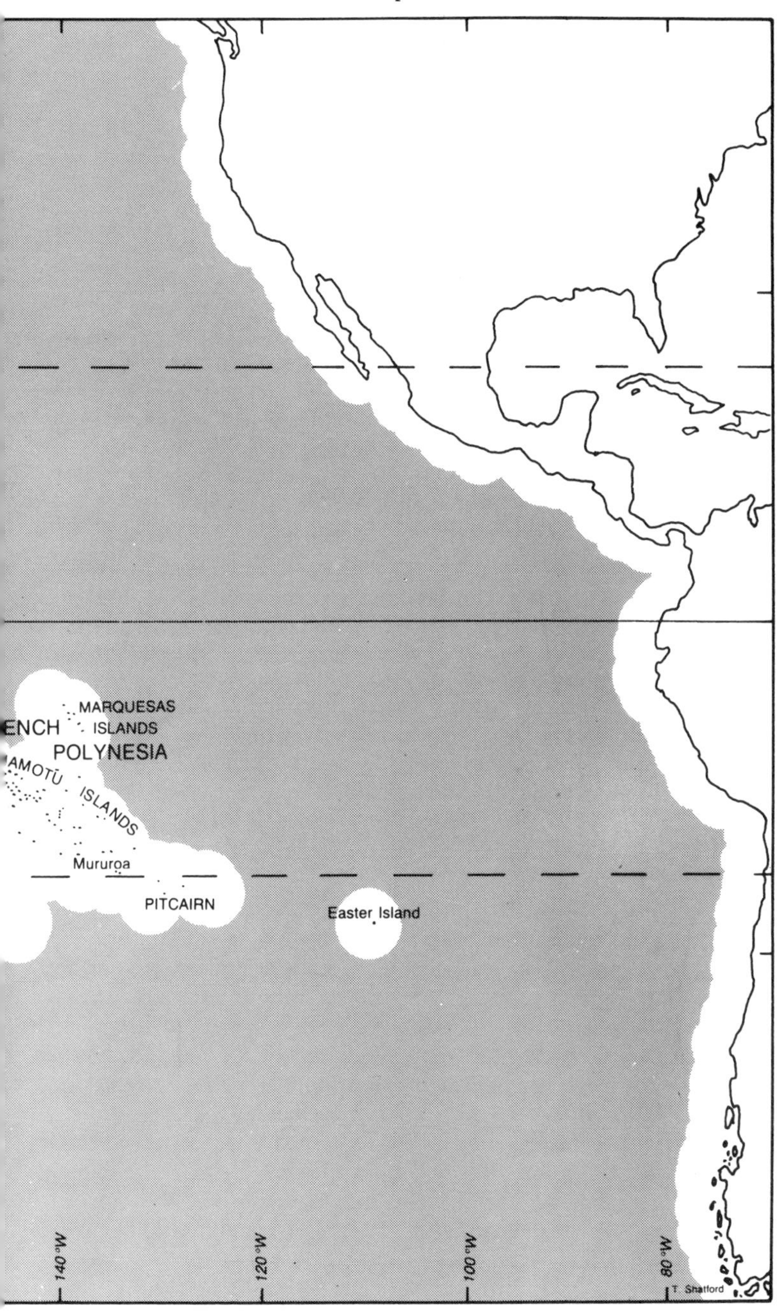
MARQUESAS
ISLANDS
ENCH
POLYNESIA
AMOTU
ISLANDS
Mururoa
PITCAIRN
Easter Island
140°W
120°W
100°W
80°W
T. Shatford

Chapter Seventeen

LOOKING BACK

History reveals both continuity and change in human affairs, and for all the changes that have taken place in the societies of the Pacific since the first European incursions, the transformation has been less than total. The distinctive physical appearance of the people has been modified by miscegenation but not eradicated, and in many cases no modification is obvious. Village settlement patterns, with the distinctive use of local materials in characteristic, traditional styles are still to be seen. The tourist industry has created a demand for traditional crafts which in many cases have no other apparent reason for survival, and these are prominently displayed for the visitor's eye. Music, dance, language and story, games, food and an apparently relaxed tenor of daily life remind the visitor that Pacific cultures have their own identity by which they are set apart from all other parts of the world. In the things that have changed, most of the imports from the west have been 'localized': imported clothing has been adapted to traditional ideas; church services bear a local idiom in song, prayer and sermon; public meetings and social functions frequently begin with prayer.

The cultural change which has taken place over a period of up to two hundred years has been a phenomenon of adaptation rather than a case of loss and replacement. Pacific islanders, having been exposed to western culture (and not always involuntarily), have rejected some aspects and adopted others. Western Samoa, for example, accepted the idea of representative politics, but rejected the idea of universal franchise; Tonga accepted the idea of parliament, but not of cabinet responsibility to parliament. The sentimental regrets about cultural change often expressed by tourists and others with a sympathetic interest in Pacific cultures are not often shared by Pacific islanders, who are themselves critical of the values of the visitors, and of the capitalist, individualistic, mass society from which they come.

In some respects, Pacific islanders want to maintain the differences between themselves and the rest of the world. The 'Pacific way' exercises a powerful pull, but as in the 1760s when Tahitians and Maoris first became acquainted with iron and glass, there is much of the west's material wealth and comfort which Pacific islanders still covet, and for which many of them migrate each year to New Zealand, Australia and the United States.

The sentimental regrets of sympathetic outsiders belong to a long tradition. Visitors as far back as the time of Captain Cook have wondered whether, or have insisted that, the islanders would be better had Europeans never come among them. There was even in the eighteenth century a long European tradition of condemnation of the decadence and emotional costs of being civilized, and a corresponding idealization of societies which because of their differences from Europe, were called uncivilized. As the physical, cultural and social decay of the Pacific islanders proceeded during the early decades of contact, there was considerable justification for this point of view. Arguing, as some historians do, that the islanders had preferences, and made conscious choices, and desired the things of the ship-people, is really beside the point. The islanders did not deliberately and knowingly choose disease, social disruption, the abuse of chiefly power, indebtedness, humiliation or the loss of independence; the visiting Europeans did not deliberately and knowingly introduce these things; they simply happened as the result of contact. At the conscious level, contact was a process of two peoples trying to satisfy their own needs by meeting the demands of the other; but on another level, it contained an implicit agenda of decay.

The same range of sentiments and the same conscious and implicit patterns of contact prevail in the late twentieth century. The sentimental visitor deplores the changes, but would not go there without them, and in going there advances them. He deplores the evils of money, and the love of it, but tips the waitress and the taxi-driver, and then tries to bargain for a better price on the things that he buys. The bringers of the west in former times, whether in the pre-colonial period, during the colonial hey-day, or during the frenetic post-war development period, all carried with them the double helix of change.

Those who condemn the sentimentalists (these are the critics of the 'fatal impact' theory of culture contact) have made history into too rational a process. They have made the historical actors into omnipotent, omniscient beings. There have been no cosmic architects in the history of the Pacific islands, any more than in the history of other parts of the world. People from all cultures acted as they thought best or from motives of personal advantage, as they continue to do today. Their critics forget that people do not at any time in history conduct their affairs knowing their long term effects.

Similarly, there are among Pacific islanders people who are critical of European influences, past and present. They have good reasons, as have all peoples who are discontented with their present circumstances; but most Pacific islanders have accepted acculturation so readily that it is clearly not European things or ideas which are objectionable as such. After all, Pacific societies have experienced greater change since independence than before it. What really troubles them is the loss of control of social processes, whether in the past or in the future. The quest for independence as well as control over the terms of contact are the real issues, as they are world-wide. The complaints of Pacific islanders about acculturation are neither more profound nor less serious than French objections to 'franglais', Basque objections to Spanish domination, or Australian objections to the ascendancy of American television programmes.

This alone is certain in the late twentieth century: the cultural and economic independence of the Pacific islands is at an end as irrevocably as is their isolation. Acculturation, which takes place in all aspects of private and public life, is a morally neutral, natural process which is the inevitable and unavoidable consequence of contact between peoples everywhere. It is also inevitable that both contact and acculturation take place on unequal terms, which are set by the relative strength of the partners in contact. How the Pacific islanders fare in the future, as in the past, will depend very much on the wisdom, benevolence and restraint of others.

GLOSSARY OF TERMS USED

Aliki	Chief in Polynesia. Cognate forms are *ariki, ali'i, 'eiki, haka'iki.*
Bêche-de-mer	The black or brown sea 'slug' which inhabits tropical tidal reefs, and grows up to 30 centimetres in length, of the Holothurian species. Large quantities were gathered in the nineteenth century for export to China where it was used in soups. The *bêche-de-mer* trade was especially important in Fiji between 1828 and 1850.
Camakau	Fijian name for the symmetrical twin-hulled voyaging canoe, probably the type which had been used for Polynesian voyaging for several centuries before the development of the *drua*. In Tonga this canoe was called *tongiaki*, and in Samoa, *va'a tele*.
Copra	The dried flesh of the coconut, used as the raw material for desiccated coconut and coconut oil. It was the staple export for most Pacific islands from the 1860s, and remains important.
Drua	The Fijian name for the great twin-hulled, asymmetrical voyaging canoes which incorporated structural and rigging innovations which had diffused from Micronesia, and which during the eighteenth century was adopted by the Tongans (who called it *kalia*) and the Samoans (*'alia*), and was known further to the east.
Endogamous	An anthropological term describing marriage in which the partner is always chosen from within the community in question.
Exogamous	When the marriage partner is chosen from outside the community.
Lapita	An archaeological culture distinguished by a characteristic form of pottery with impressed designs. Named after Lapita, the site in New Caledonia where it was first found, this pottery is important because it is associated with a seafaring people widely distributed in Melanesia, and perhaps Micronesia, and who were the first colonists of Tonga, Samoa and Fiji. These people were probably the ancestors of the Polynesians.

Malietoa	A senior Samoan title, and the one at the centre of Samoan political change in the late nineteenth century when it was associated by Europeans with kingship.
Mana	A supernatural attribute endowing prestige, authority and efficacy on a person, community or object. Indispensable for anyone aspiring to leadership, its presence is known only by its effects. Both the name and the concept are widespread throughout the three cultural areas of the Pacific.
Matanitu	The largest, traditional, political division in Fiji; a tribal confederation.
Matrilineal	A kinship system which traces descent through the female line. Common in Melanesia, but important also in Micronesia and Polynesia.
Matrilocal	A social system in which a man lives with his wife's people. Common in Melanesia.
Pakeha	New Zealand term for a person of European ancestry.
Patrilineal	A kinship system in which descent is traced through the father; characteristic of Polynesia, where it did not usually exclude matrilineal reckoning.
Patrilocal	A social system in which a woman lives with her husband's people; characteristic of Polynesia.
Ramage	A type of social organization in which the entire community is descended from a common ancestor, with rank graded according to closeness to the senior line of descent. Although sometimes said to be typical of Polynesia and Micronesia, it is best thought of as an indigenous model for chiefly castes rather than as a description of society as a whole. The New Zealand *hapu* was a typical ramage, but was probably unique in Polynesia.
Swidden	A type of agriculture, sometimes called 'slash and burn', in which forest areas are cleared and cultivated, to be abandoned in favour of another area after a few seasons. This shifting agriculture was characteristic of much of Melanesia.
Tafa'ifa	Collectively the four major titles in traditional Samoa, and the ultimate object of political contest. The four titles were Tui Atua, Tui A'ana, Gatoaitele and Tamasoali'i.
Tapa	A fabric made by soaking and beating the inner bark of trees, and commonly used for clothing in traditional Polynesian and Micronesian societies. *Kapa* is a cognate form.
Tapu	*Tapu* is a spiritual quality which sanctifies a person or thing, and removes it from mundane use. In this way it sometimes seems to mean revered, holy, accursed or forbidden.
Tohunga	Maori term for one who possesses arcane knowledge; usually a priest, but in some groups simply a specialist in any craft. Cognate forms include *kahuna, tufunga, tau'a, tahua*.
Tu'i or Tui	King, or high chief in Tonga, Samoa, Fiji, and the groups

closely related to them. The word is usually followed by a place name.

Tu'i Ha'atakalaua — In the traditional polity of Tonga this was one of the three highest titles. Its holder's role is not known for certain. The last holder of the title died in 1797, and the title Tungi was created in 1875 to compensate a potential claimant for the abrogation of the title.

Tu'i Kanokupolu — The third of the three highest traditional titles of Tonga, and the focus of the political turbulence of the eighteenth and early nineteenth centuries. In 1845 it came to be equivalent to King of Tonga.

Tu'i Tonga — Literally 'King of Tonga', the highest of the traditional Tongan titles, the holder of which was so *tapu* that he was remote from day to day government. After the last Tu'i Tonga died in 1862 the title was abolished, and the title Kalaniuvalu created for his heir.

Vasu — A custom which entitled a man to support from his mother's family, and certain privileges tantamount to enjoying higher rank than the children of his mother's brother. *Vasu*, the Fijian word, was also known in Tonga where it was called *fahu*, and in Samoa where it was called *feagaiga*.

FURTHER READING

The popular literature on the Pacific is huge. The earliest travel literature provides some of the best information available to scholars about Pacific islands societies, and the production of such books has continued on a large scale.

Scholarly books written before the second world war were few; since the Second World War a great many books of a detailed nature on Pacific anthropology and history have been published. Many of these are best suited to a professional audience of scholars, and most of them have gone out of print quickly, so that the general reader faces a difficulty in the pursuit of further knowledge. The following list is merely a guide to what might be most readily available.

1. Ancient history.

Peter Bellwood, *Man's Conquest of the Pacific. The Prehistory of Southeast Asia and Oceania*. Auckland, Collins, 1978. This book is a comprehensive survey of the racial, cultural and linguistic prehistory of the Pacific and South East Asia, which includes discussion of the various alternative theories. This is the definitive work.

Thor Heyerdahl, *Aku Aku*. Harmondsworth, Penguin, 1960. This is the most accessible of Heyerdahl's works dealing with the origins of the Polynesians. His views are not generally accepted by modern scholars, but his books remain valuable and interesting.

Jesse Jennings (ed), *The Prehistory of Polynesia*. Cambridge, Massachusetts, Harvard University Press, 1979.

David Lewis, *From Maui to Cook*. Sydney, Doubleday, 1977.

David Lewis, *We, the Navigators*. Wellington, Reed, 1972.

Richard Shutler and Mary Elizabeth Shutler, *Oceanic Prehistory*. Menlo Park, California, Cummings Publishing Company, 1975.

2. Traditional Society.

William H. Alkire, *An Introduction to the Peoples and Cultures of Micronesia* Menlo Park, California, Cummings, 1977.

Peter Bellwood, *The Polynesians*. London, Thames and Hudson, 1978.

Ann Chowning, *An Introduction to the Peoples and Cultures of Melanesia*. Menlo Park, California, 1977.

Peter H. Buck, *Vikings of the Sunrise.* Christchurch, Whitcombe and Tombs, 1954. Although out of date on Polynesian migrations, this book is still valuable and interesting, and has been frequently reprinted.

3. European Exploration.

J.C. Beaglehole, *The Exploration of the Pacific.* London, A.&C. Black, 1966. (Third edition.)

Ernest S. Dodge, *Beyond the Capes. Pacific Exploration from Cook to the "Challenger" (1776-1877).* London, Victor Gollancz, 1971.

David Lewis, *From Maui to Cook.* Sydney, Doubleday, 1977.

4. Early Trade — Polynesia.

Caroline Ralston, *Grass Huts and Warehouses.* Canberra, Australian National University Press, 1978.

5. Early Missions — Polynesia.

John Garrett, *To Live Among the Stars.* Suva, The World Council of Churches and the Institute of Pacific Studies, 1982.

Niel Gunson, *Messengers of Grace.* Melbourne, Oxford University Press, 1978.

Ralph Wiltgen, *The Founding of the Roman Catholic Church in Oceania.* Canberra, Australian National University Press, 1979.

6. Trade and Missions in Melanesia.

Peter Corris, *Passage, Port and Plantation. A History of the Solomon Islands Labour Migration 1870-1914* Carlton, Melbourne University Press, 1973.

E.W. Docker, *The Blackbirders. The Recruiting of South Seas Labour for Queensland, 1863-1907.* Sydney, Angus and Robertson, 1970.

John Garrett, *To Live Among the Stars.* Suva, The World Council of Churches and the Institute of Pacific Studies, 1982.

David Hilliard, *God's Gentlemen.* St.Lucia, University of Queensland Press, 1978.

H.M. Laracy, *Marists and Melanesians: A History of Catholic Missions in the Solomon Islands.* Canberra, Australian National University Press, 1978.

Dorothy Shineberg, *They Came for Sandalwood. A Study of the Sandalwood Trade in the South-West Pacific, 1830-1865.* Carlton, Melbourne University Press, 1967.

7. Micronesian Contact History.

Francis X. Hezel, *The First Taint of Civilization. A History of the Caroline and Marshall Islands in Pre-Colonial Days, 1521-1885.* Honolulu, University of Hawaii Press, 1983.

8. Political Intervention By Europe and America.

W.P. Morrell, *Britain in the Pacific Islands.* Oxford, Oxford University Press, 1960. More comprehensive than the title suggests, this is the most authoritative and wide ranging work on nineteenth Pacific history yet written.

Deryck Scarr, *Fragments of Empire. A History of the Western Pacific High*

Commission 1877-1914. Canberra, Australian National University Press, 1967.

John M. Ward, *British Policy in the South Pacific. 1786-1893*. Sydney, Australasian Publishing Company, 1947.

9. Colonial Government.

Colonial government, as distinct from histories of the colonial period, has not been the subject of separate treatment, but the following are important books:

Carmel Budiardjo and Liem Soei Liong, *West Papua: The Obliteration of a People*. Third edition, Thornton Heath, TAPOL, 1988.

Peter Hempenstall, *Pacific Islanders Under German Rule: A Study in the Meaning of Colonial Resistance*. Canberra, Australian National University Press, 1978.

Peter Hempenstall and Noel Rutherford, *Protest and Dissent in the Colonial Pacific*. Suva, Institute of Pacific Studies of the University of the South Pacific, 1984.

Stephen Henningham, *France and the South Pacific. A Contemporary History*. Sydney, Allen and Unwin, 1992.

Bruce Knapman, *Fiji's Economic History 1874-1939. Studies in Capitalist Colonial Development*. Canberra, National Centre for Development Studies, Australian National University, 1987.

Malama Meleisea, *The Making of Modern Samoa. Traditional Authority and Colonial Administration in the History of Western Samoa*. Suva, Institute of Pacific Studies of the University of the South Pacific, 1987.

Norman Meller, *Constitutionalism in Micronesia*. Honolulu, Institute for Polynesian Studies, 1985.

M. R. Peattie, *Nan'yo. The Rise and Fall of the Japanese in Micronesia 1885-1945*. Honolulu, University of Hawai'i Press, 1987.

Howard van Trease, *The Politics of Land in Vanuatu from Colony to Independence*. Suva, Institute of Pacific Studies of the University of the South Pacific, 1987.

10. Twentieth Century Missions and Religious History.

Lanier Britsch, *Unto the Islands of the Sea. A History of the Latter Day Saints in the Pacific*. Salt Lake City, Deseret Books, 1986.

Charles W. Forman, *Island Churches of the South Pacific: Emergence in the Twentieth Century*. Maryknoll, Orbis Books, 1982.

John Garrett, *Footsteps in the Sea. Christianity in Oceania to World War II*. Suva and Geneva, Institute of Pacific Studies of the University of the South Pacific and the World Council of Churches, 1992.

Garry Trompf, *New Religious Movements in Melanesia*. Suva, Institute of Pacific Studies of the University of the South Pacific and the University of Papua New Guinea, 1985.

11. The Second World War.

There are numerous books about the fighting in the Pacific and its wider historical setting, but no comprehensive studies of the Pacific as a whole during the war years.

12. Decolonization and After.

The decolonization era spawned many books offering contemporary comment on events and future prospects. Studies of contemporary economic development were also numerous. For sweeping reflections on contemporary Pacific societies by a well-informed scholar, see the first of the following:

Ron Crocombe, *The South Pacific: An Introduction*. Fifth edition, Suva, Institute of Pacific Studies at the University of the South Pacific, 1989.

Ron Crocombe and Ahmed Ali (eds), *Foreign Forces in Pacific Politics*. Suva, Institute of Pacific Studies at the University of the South Pacific, 1983.

Antony Hooper and others (eds), *Class and Culture in the South Pacific*. Suva, Institute of Pacific Studies at the University of the South Pacific, 1987.

Uentabo Fakaofo Neemia, *Cooperation and Conflict. Costs, Benefits and National Interests in Pacific Regional Cooperation*. Suva, Institute of Pacific Studies at the University of the South Pacific, 1986.

13. Particular Island Groups — all periods.

J.A. Bennett, *The Wealth of the Solomons. A History of a Pacific Archipelago, 1800-1978*. Honolulu, University of Hawaii Press, 1987.

I.C. Campbell, *Island Kingdom. Tonga Ancient and Modern*. Christchurch, Canterbury University Press, 1992.

J.W. Davidson, *Samoa mo Samoa. The Emergence of the Independent State of Western Samoa*. Melbourne, Oxford University Press, 1967.

Gavan Daws, *Shoal of Time. A History of the Hawaiian Islands*. University Press of Hawaii, 1974.

Greg Dening, *Islands and Beaches. Discourse on a Silent Land, Marquesas 1774-1880*. Melbourne, Melbourne University Press, 1980.

R.P. Gilson, *The Cook Islands, 1820-1950*. Wellington, Victoria University Press, 1980.

R.P. Gilson, *Samoa, 1830-1900. The Politics of a Multi-Cultural Community*. Melbourne, Oxford University Press, 1970.

James Griffin, Hank Nelson, and Stewart Firth, *Papua New Guinea. A Political History*. Richmond, Victoria, Heinemann Educational, 1979.

Martin Lyons, *The Totem and the Tricolour. A Short History of New Caledonia since 1774*. Kensington, University of New South Wales Press, 1986.

Barrie Macdonald, *Cinderellas of the Empire: Towards a History of Kiribati and Tuvalu*. Canberra, Australian National University Press, 1982.

Barrie Macdonald, *In Pursuit of the Sacred Trust: trusteeship and independence in Nauru*. Wellington, New Zealand Institute of International Affairs, 1988.

Malama Meleisea, *Lagaga: A Short History of Western Samoa*. Suva, Institute of Pacific Studies, 1987.

Colin Newbury, *Tahiti Nui. Change and Survival in French Polynesia 1767-1945*. Honolulu, University Press of Hawaii, 1980.

W.H. Oliver (ed), *The Oxford History of New Zealand*. Wellington, Oxford University Press, 1981.

David Routledge, *Matanitu. The Struggle for Power in Early Fiji*. Suva, Institute of Pacific Studies, 1985.

Deryck Scarr, *Fiji, A Short History*. Sydney, George Allen and Unwin, 1984.

14. Biographies.

Biography as a genre has not been developed much by historians of the Pacific. There are a few major biographies, a few volumes of biographical essays, and a comparatively large number of autobiographies, the latter extending back to the beginning of the nineteenth century. Autobiographies are not included in the following list.

J.W. Davidson and Deryck Scarr (eds), *Pacific Islands Portraits*. Canberra, Australian National University Press, 1970.

Gavan Daws, *A Dream of Islands: Voyages of Self Discovery in the South Seas*. Milton, Queensland, The Jacaranda Press, 1980.

James Griffin (ed), *Papua New Guinea Portraits. The Expatriate Experience*. Canberra, Australian National University Press, 1978.

R.B. Joyce, *Sir William MacGregor*. Melbourne, Oxford University Press, 1977.

Diane Langmore, *Tamate — A King. James Chalmers in New Guinea, 1877-1901*. Carlton, Melbourne University Press, 1974.

Diane Langmore, *Missionary Lives: Papua 1874–1914*. Honolulu, University of Hawai'i Press, 1989.

Noel Rutherford, *Shirley Baker and the King of Tonga*. Melbourne, Oxford University Press, 1971.

Deryck Scarr (ed), *More Pacific Islands Portraits*. Canberra, Australian National University Press, 1979.

Deryck Scarr, *Ratu Sukuna: Soldier, Statesman, Man of Two Worlds*. London, MacMillan, 1980.

Francis West, *Hubert Murray. The Australian Pro-Consul*. Melbourne, Oxford University Press, 1968.

INDEX

3329